SETTLEMENT ARCHAEOLOGY

Edited and with an Introduction by

K. C. CHANG

Yale University

National Press Books

Palo Alto, California

Library of Congress Catalog Card Number: 67-20071

Manufactured in the United States of America

Acknowledgments

The idea of editing a book of this sort goes back to the spring of 1961, when I was teaching a seminar at Harvard dealing with the issues of settlement archaeology. At the end of the course I had in my hands a collection of twelve excellent papers submitted by the members of that class. It occurred to me that the time was perhaps ripe for an exploratory volume in this relatively unexplored field of query. Between 1961 and 1965, new contributions were invited, and old papers were withdrawn or laid aside. None of the twelve original papers is now included in the book, and the substance of this volume is entirely different from its 1961 prototype. But in the works of these more experienced spokesmen, the spirit of the original group survives. I am indebted to the twelve members of that class – Philip H. Auerbach, Norman F. Barka, Jorge E. Hardoy, Michael Hoffman, Alice B. Kehoe, Sarah Keller, Douglas MacKinzie, Dolores Newton, William S. Simmons, Augustus J. Sordinas, Ronald Spores, and R. J. Wyatt – for their stimulation, their confidence, and their patience. To them, and to all archaeologists of their generation, I dedicate my part of this book.

In many ways it is more complicated and time-consuming to put a number of original articles by different authors together into a book than to write one. But it has given me great pleasure and satisfaction to work together with the authors of this volume, whose enthusiasm and understanding are forever appreciated. It is, of course, understood that the authors have contributed to the volume to participate in a discussion of settlement archaeology but in no wise to endorse my own theory of it.

To Messrs. Richard W. Bare and Palmer W. Pinney of the National Press, and to Mr. William W. Carver, whose editorial eye scanned the manuscript, we are all thankful for their devotion and cooperation.

K. C. Chang

March 8, 1968
New Haven, Connecticut

Table of Contents

Editor's Introduction

This volume consists of eleven independent papers on various aspects of archaeology and/or settlement study. Each author is responsible for his own contribution, and none but the Editor is to blame—or to praise—for the company he keeps.

On what grounds are these papers being brought together between two covers? In a recent review of the field of anthropology, Eric Wolf sees the emergence of a new archaeology that, "freeing itself from both the collector's madness of obtaining show pieces and from the infantile wish to restore the lost splendor of ruins long covered by earth or jungle, turned to the recovery of entire settlements of past populations. It just began to look beyond the mechanical gathering of isolated bits of material culture to the reconstruction of past communities, attempting to grasp the archaeological equivalent of the ecologists' groups and the social anthropologist's organization-bearing unit" (*Anthropology,* Prentice-Hall, 1964, pp. 68-69). Most of us cannot help feeling that this new face on our old discipline has already exhibited enough charm to begin attracting a whole generation of young archaeologists. Settlement archaeology is in fashion, and many archaeologists are becoming more and more interested in the larger picture of culture and society, less and less in artifacts viewed as entities in themselves and analyzed for their own sake.

Let us suppose that this shifting emphasis is agreed as a matter of principle. How this emphasis is then to be reflected in practice is an entirely different matter. Throughout its existence, archaeology has been a discipline concerned with artifacts. Such concepts as type, style, and attribute have been the basic tools of archaeological research, but "whole communities" and "entire settlements" have not. To be more than a momentary aberration, the new archaeology must offer a conceptual frame of reference that is logically consistent and practically feasible. I believe that such a frame of reference does not yet exist, and that the so-called new archaeology is at this point something of a forced marriage between broad, anthropological concepts and specific, empirical, archaeological methods and techniques. This tentative alliance could lead easily to any or all of the following consequences: the use of clichés that are sufficiently broad and self-evident to fit an anthropological definition of archaeology but are practically useless; a divorce of theory and practice, i.e., the continued use of conventional methods and techniques despite a broad anthropological disguise; the rejection of proved archaeological methods and techniques; or sharp divisions of archaeologists into different theoretical persuasions.

To avoid these undesirable results, and to make the most of the gathering trend toward a revitalized archaeology, it becomes necessary to consider this question: How is an archaeologist to study an entire settlement, when all he has are bits of material culture? An approach of obvious merit is to study these bits in a settlement context. But because this is a new area of archaeological study, we need not, and cannot, produce a new conceptual frame of reference with haste. We must know what the most fundamental problems are, when bits of material culture are being studied in a settlement context.

This book is an exploratory step toward this goal. If a master scheme of archaeology is only implicit, and if a strong coherence of the constituent papers of the book is less than obvious, that is the way it should be. The one inescapable conclusion that has come out of the volume is that a settlement approach to archaeology is one that requires much fresh thinking and careful deliberation before a new frame of reference ever can emerge.

"Toward a Science of Prehistoric Society" was read on December 30th, 1962, at Philadelphia, before the annual meeting of the American Association for the Advancement of Sciences. It outlines some major problem areas of settlement archaeology, and serves as an introduction to the book. The tentative and exploratory nature of this introduction is made very explicit by Rouse's "Prehistory, Typology, and the Study of Society," which follows it in this volume. That there exist basic and wide-ranging disagreements between these two introductory articles indicates very clearly the kinds of problems we face. Is it necessary to adopt a new, "settlement-oriented" approach at all? Does not the old, "artifact-oriented" approach serve just as well—at least on some occasions, and for some purposes? The readers must judge for themselves. In any case, it is clear that the issues involved here are basic. When archaeological remains are regarded primarily as products or by-products of human behavior in social and cultural contexts, they must be looked upon as something more than scientific specimens. Deetz's paper, "Cultural Patterning of Behavior as Reflected by Archaeological Materials," exemplifies the kind of search into cultural anthropological fundamentals that at first glance may seem to bear little or no immediate relevance to settlement archaeology. But settlement archaeology is the archaeology of man in settlements more than it is the archaeology of the settlement in its physical sense. Deetz's article must be viewed as an initial step in the study of man as a cultural and social being whose behavior in cultural and social contexts is our concern. It is in these areas that the settlement archaeologist will become identified with the cultural anthropologist.

Ascher's "Time's Arrow and the Archaeology of a Contemporary Community" steers the discussion from general issues to the specific problems of the archaeologist, elucidating the various phases of change whereby a living community becomes things archaeological. The papers that follow in the book–Trigger's "The Determinants of Settlement Patterns," Cook's and Heizer's "Relationships among Houses, Settlement Areas, and Population in Aboriginal California," Whiting's and Ayres' "Inferences from the Shape of Dwellings," Sears' "The State and Settlement Patterns in the New World," and Vogt's "Some Aspects of Zinacantan Settlement Patterns and Ceremonial Organization"–each discuss one aspect of man's behavior in relation to his settlement and community, as seen from archaeological or archaeologically recoverable evidences. Some of the papers are ethnological in the conventional sense, but no one should fail to see their archaeological relevance. Others deal with specific regions in which the authors have competent knowledge, but we are free to make our own generalizations. These papers together outline not only the kinds of problems an archaeologist must face as he pursues his archaeology on a "settlement" basis, but also the kinds of research he can use to solve or resolve them.

Adams' paper, "Settlement Patterns in Microcosm: The Changing Aspect of a Nubian Village During Twelve Centuries," illustrates how the archaeologist can shed light on a wide range of problems by exploiting the one important advantage he has over his ethnological colleagues in pursuing settlement research, namely, the great, inherent dimension of time.

It is fitting, finally, that Gordon Willey appraise the volume. More than any other single person, he is responsible for what is new in our discipline.

I

K. C. CHANG

Toward a Science of Prehistoric Society[1]

In preparing to reconstruct the history of human groups and the various aspects of their culture, and to formulate the patterns of their social and cultural growth and change, historians and anthropologists customarily gather their data from living informants, from observed behavior, from behavioral products of the present as well as the past, and from written documents. But these opportunities are not afforded the prehistorians and anthropologists seeking to acquire and interpret data from a past, illiterate period. Archaeology is not so much a self-contained discipline as it is a system of specialized techniques and methods for the acquisition and interpretation of such data. The process of archaeological operation must select for its basic theoretical concepts the relevant theoretical premises of the historical and anthropological sciences; there probably cannot be a single conceptual framework of archaeology underlying all of its manifold operations.

It follows that an archaeological operation dealing with one aspect of history and culture does not constitute a precondition to an operation dealing with another aspect; nor is the one necessarily more innately reliable than the other. To presume, for example, that the archaeological interpretation of artifacts is *a priori* more basic and more reliable than the archaeological interpretation of religion is to suggest that as a field of learning the study of technology is both preconditional to and more reliable than theology – certainly a dubious proposition. Studies of artifacts and of religions belong to different fields of inquiry, their frequently overlapping dimensions notwithstanding.

Should we presume, then, that archaeological operations are pursued in two separate and successive stages – the collecting of data, undertaken by the archaeologists in the role of field technicians, and the interpretation of these data in conjunction with nonarchaeological data, carried out by technologists, economists, sociologists, theologists, art historians, and other specialists? For me, the answer is No: in the first place, the archaeological process is one of continuous interpretation, and the gathering of data in the field is conditioned by and dependent upon individual judgment, selection, and shifting emphases quite as

[1]Revised from a paper read at the American Association for the Advancement of Sciences meeting in 1962. The themes of this paper have been more fully treated in a recent book, *Rethinking Archaeology* (New York: Random House, 1967).

much as is the interpretation of data in the laboratory or the library; and in the second place, the interpretation of archaeological data, of whatever kind, is commonly associated with problems of know-how that the specialist, with his particular training and experience, is perhaps not equipped to tackle. An archaeologist, therefore, must assume a double role: he must be both a competent technician, on the one hand, and a historian or anthropologist, on the other. Whether he concerns himself solely with artifacts or solely with religion, he must be both a technician, wise in the ways of amassing and assessing reliable and relevant archaeological data, and a specialist in the study of artifacts or of religion, adequately founded in the theoretical premises of the relevant disciplines; but if he concerns himself with the whole gamut of culture, as we are wont to suppose him to do, he must then be both an all-round technician and a general anthropologist, a role few of us could possibly fulfill.

With these thoughts in mind, we shall set out to construct a methodological framework for archaeology, oriented toward the interpretation of data in terms of social grouping.

Typology

The first step in an archaeological interpretation is usually classification, whereby apparently orderless data are grouped into meaningful categories. Typology, which has been defined as classification for theoretically explicit purposes (Kluckhohn, 1960, p. 134), is thus a procedure for isolating units from our data, as well as a prerequisite to the construction of models in which the various units relate to one another in definable and meaningful ways.

In that they deal with various aspects of history and culture and thus have a variety of theoretically explicit purposes, archaeologists would seem to be justified in employing a variety of typological classifications, with shifting criteria and different points of departure.

The Settlement

Archaeological types may range in dimension from single attributes of artifacts to entire cultural co-traditions, depending on the purpose for which the typology is designed. Similarly, the unitary social group selected for purposes of describing and characterizing a prehistoric people is generally one of a whole range of alternatives of various dimensions and magnitudes. A useful as well as meaningful point of departure for our synthesis of a methodological system is the primary social group called *community* by sociologists. I have two purposes in choosing community, rather than household or tribe, as the primary unit for classification. In the first place, community is universal; it defines the boundary of social activities an individual daily engages in, and it molds or conditions an individual's mode of behavior and his view of life and the world perhaps more effectively than any other primary or secondary social group; therefore, the distinction between community and larger social groups–i.e., between "within" community and "beyond" community–is a meaningful one in terms of behavioral mode. In the second place, the community is the social group that is archaeologically most definable, but its definability is clearly not self-evident, as it generally is for example in social anthropology. In formulating our methodological system, we shall do well to make community our point of departure.

The community, however, can be defined in archaeology only as an abstraction, by means of reconstruction, because of the perishability of its constituent elements–men and their interactions. In practice, therefore, the *settlement*–the local context wherein the community is presumed to have resided and to have gone about its daily business–must substitute for the community.

An archaeological settlement is the physical locale or cluster of locales where the members of a community lived, ensured their subsistence, and pursued their social functions in a delineable time period. In space, then, an archaeological settlement need not lie in one continuous expanse of ground, but it must be occupied and made use of by a single group of people. In time, it must certainly be related to the natural stratigraphy of its cultural remains, but the physical depth and subdivisions of a site are not necessarily relevant to a definition of settlement: if a repetitively occupied site with a great depth of cultural debris can be demonstrated to have been the locus of a single community during one or several occupations in which no significant and meaningful changes in community configuration or structure took place, then we may consider the site to be that of a single archaeological settlement. If, on the other hand, such changes can be shown to have occurred during the continuous deposition of even a thin layer of cultural debris, within even a relatively brief period of time, then we must consider the site to be that of not one but a series of archaeological settlements, each of which must be characterized separately.[2]

Changes are to be considered "significant and meaningful" if the total configuration and structure of the community are affected, producing a significantly new organization. An appreciable immigration into a community or the replacement of one community population by another at the same site would constitute "significant and meaningful" changes. The introduction of new ideas would be significant and meaningful only if a reorganization of the community configuration and structure were effected as so often happens following the introduction of a new technology, a new form of government, or a new religious system.

[2]It may appear that we have defined community in *archaeology* in terms of settlement, while at the same time defining settlement by appealing to the principle of identity of the community in residence, thus creating a circular argument. Actually, the concept of "community" specifies the properties of an archaeological settlement, whereas in archaeological operations we recognize and characterize a prehistoric community within the actual conditions of these properties. Thus, the argument describes not so much a circle as a pair of contiguous semicircles pursued at different levels. See Householder (1959) for a similar problem in linguistics.

The archaeological settlement thus formulated is our operational basis. Thus we distinguish two kinds of archaeological types: those collectively constituting an archaeological settlement, and those comprising archaeological settlements as constituent elements. Before elaborating on this basic dichotomy, we must introduce two other dichotomies: objective vs. relative types, and function vs. style.

Objective and Relative Types

Whether a "type" in archaeology is simply invented and designed by the classifier or is in fact inherent as a category in the artifacts themselves has been a classical problem in American archaeology for many years. The question can be argued *ad nauseam* if we do not emphasize that different kinds of types can and should be categorized for different purposes and according to different criteria (Willey and Phillips, 1958, p. 13; Rouse, 1960, pp. 313-23; Steward, 1954, pp. 54-57).

An archaeological attribute has a wide range of variations, both possible and actual. An *objective type* in archaeology may be defined as consisting of actual variations selected from archaeological assemblages, regardless of origin, and classified into a single category according to objective cross-cultural and cross-social criteria that are, to the best of our knowledge, universally valid and applicable. The color of pottery, for example, may be classified according to a color-scale supplied by physicists, and the floor plans of dwellings according to the measures and geometric forms that exist in all parts of the world. A *relative type*, on the other hand, includes only those variations that cluster around a common modal standard of behavior, in contrast with and relative to other variations clustering around other modal standards, within a single cultural or social system. The cultural or social system in question may range from a family or a household to a nation or a cultural tradition, but in the present context it is the community. Objective and relative types are not mutually exclusive categories, and may in fact totally coincide in many cases. The important distinction here lies in their respective criteria for categorizing (Pike, 1954).

The objective and relative types are formulated in archaeology for different purposes. Objective types are useful (1) in establishing initial categories out of which relative types are to be isolated by a process of elimination, analogy, and combination; (2) for purely physical description; (3) for cross-cultural comparisons in areas where cultural considerations themselves offer little insight, such as the correlation of natural environment and house shape, or the correlation between descent systems and residence rules; and (4) probably in the designing of mechanical devices for documentation and index compilation.

Relative types, on the other hand, are formulated at the community level in order (1) to analyze and assemble structural models of social and cultural behavior within individual communities; and (2) to provide a basis for intercommunity comparisons directed toward the determination of historical relationships.

Analysis and Model Construction It is safe to assume that the social/cultural behavioral structure of a community is composed of a number of substructures or subsystems, and that each substructure or subsystem is composed of a number of sub-substructures or sub-subsystems, and so forth, down to the level of minimal elements of behavior and their tangible manifestations. Further, it is safe to assume that the various subsystems of the structure are mutually conditional, contrasting, and relative. It follows, therefore, that the archaeological types, taken in this context to designate the component parts of the structure, vary in composition, dimension, function, and meaning from one community to the next, even though two types of two different communities may have been abstracted from remains that are objectively similar or even identical. In order to synthesize a social/cultural model for a given archaeological community, then, it is necessary to characterize the archaeological types relatively–to group actual variations within the same system around central tendencies that are inherently in contrast with and relative to other central tendencies within the archaeological assemblage of that particular community.

Comparison In order to determine the historical relationship, at a certain time level and for a certain time depth, between two or more communities, the archaeologist generally must compare their respective remains–or, more accurately, the respective *types* of their remains, inasmuch as the vast number of actual variations usually preclude comparison on a piece-by-piece basis. The purpose of comparing types of different communities is in most cases to determine whether (1) type A of community X derived from type A' of community Y, or vice versa; (2) the two types derived from a common origin; or (3) the two came about independently.

One might well ask: Are the types to be compared for this purpose *objective* types or *relative* types? Because of the vast array of variables to be considered, and the broad disparity in available data from one community to the next, no simple answer can be presumed. But it *can* be presumed, perhaps as a general rule, that when types of different communities are found to be similar, or even identical–in composition, dimension, function, and meaning–the historical relationship suggested can be postulated with greater confidence if the types in question are relative, rather than objective. Relative types, after all, represent central modal tendencies of behavior, as well as their tangible manifestations, whereas objective types reflect only the tangible manifestations. Both tendencies and tangible manifestations vary from one culture to the next, and their degrees of variance are independent of each other. More simply, form can diffuse independently of meaning. But where this occurs, the archaeologist's case for diffusion or common origin is likely to be weak, especially when the forms in question are simple and represent examples drawn from only a narrow range of possible variations. On the other hand, a similarity or identity observed between relative types reflects not only form (tangible manifestations of behavior modes) but also meaning (the behavioral modes themselves), and a more substantial case can be made for diffusion or common origin.[3]

Function and Style

Any archaeological type can be credited with a function or cluster of functions, and a style or cluster of styles. To function we extend here a meaning somewhat beyond that generally accorded it in the anthropological literature, so as to place the type both in its context and in its correlative relations–concomitance, compatibility, congruence, conflict, contrast or codetermination–with the other types in the same structural system. Obviously, then, function must be considered at a static time level, although its character often becomes recognizable only in dynamic juxtaposition, because of its involvement in the relentless process of contextual realignment with time.

To serve a given function, an archaeological type possesses a given form or bundle of forms; but the particular form it exhibits has very likely emerged simply as one out of a number of possible alternatives–all more or less equally suited to the function served. We call the particular form that has actually emerged *style.* By definition, the style of an archaeological type is determined only by the historical experience of the community members over time.

For example, shell temper, in potterymaking, can be an archaeological type of both functional and stylistic significance. That it is functional is evident from its contextual associates: potterymaking; making and use of cooking vessels; availability of mollusk shells in the natural environment; mollusk collecting; etc. That it is also stylistic is evident in the typical example from a minimum of three facts: the local availability of sand, grit, fiber, mica, and other potential tempering materials; the use of shell temper as an archaeological type by a neighboring community at the same time level; the use of shell temper as an archaeological type by one or several communities previous in time.

Microstructure and Macrostructure

Let us now return to the settlement as a methodological point of depar-

[3] Archaeologists may find useful, for their own purposes, the discussions among linguists of form and meaning, as regards their mutual relations and their significance to the determination of historical relationship. See, for example, Greenberg (1953) and Jakobson (1961).

ture. I have suggested that we shall find it useful to distinguish between the "within" and the "beyond" of a community; the distinction is equally as useful in the context of settlement–the tangible evidence of community. The cultural and social structure of a settlement we call its "microstructure." The larger cultural and social systems, on the other hand, composed as they are of individual settlements, become "macrostructures." The microstructure is the model for an archaeological community reconstructed on the evidence from an archaeological settlement, whereas the macrostructure is the model for the larger sphere of social/cultural activities (beyond those relevant simply to the community) in which members of the community participate, as well as the sphere of cultural and social influences the community imparts to the outside world during a certain time span.

At a given point in time, then, a community has a single microstructure, but belongs perhaps to several macrostructures variously formulated; these may lie at the same time level or at different time levels; and their correlative relationships may be characterized functionally or stylistically or both.

Microarticulation and Macroarticulation

If microstructure and macrostructure are typological models of and for archaeological settlements, then the archaeological operation can be said to be a model-building process. The building up of structural models from their constituent units and according to their structual relationships we shall call "articulation." The articulatory process for microstructuring a settlement can be termed "microarticulation," and that for macrostructuring two or more settlements, "macroarticulation." The "structure" is our goal, and the "articulation" the means to achieve this goal; the "structure" inevitably must fall short of the ideal or of the past reality, but the "articulation" can be conceived and pursued as a scientific process and can be improved upon constantly. To assert that our reconstructions are themselves "structures" is possibly presumptuous and misleading; but the process of articulation, on the other hand, can be precisely described, demonstrated, and evaluated.

To effect the microarticulation, we must categorize relative types, but for each type we need consider only its functional aspects. Moreover, it is theoretically sound and practically possible to "fill in" some of the gaps in the reconstructed model. And because pervasive functional regularities and structural principles are known over a wide range of aspects of culture and society, it often becomes possible to confine our missing links to a very limited range of possibilities. The more structural constituents there are available for our consideration, the narrower will be the range of such possibilities. To illustrate: Suppose we have found, for our archaeological settlement, that because type A of aspect 1, B of aspect 2, and C of aspect 3 are well established in our structure, the relevant regularities and environmental constants have, in theory, limited the typological variations of aspect 11 to five in number. Should the established types of aspects later increase, to include, say, type D of aspect 4 and type E of aspect 5, then the typological variations of aspect 11 that are theoretically possible might decrease to two. And so on.

Macroarticulation is considerably more complex than microarticulation, but we may at least distinguish among macroarticulations: (1) of settlements from a single time level, according to the functional aspects of their respective constituent types; (2) of settlements from different time levels, according to the functional aspects of their respective constituent types; (3) of settlements from a single time level, according to the stylistic aspects of their respective constituent types; and (4) of settlements from different time levels, according to the stylistic aspects of their respective constituent types. Whether objective or relative types are to be used for macroarticulation depends of course upon the immediate field of inquiry and the specific types concerned, as has already been discussed.

SUMMARY AND COMMENT

Because archaeology is an assemblage of specialized techniques and methods used by several independent disciplines and subdisciplines, it does not necessarily have a common conceptual framework of its own. It can be structured only within various methodological frameworks or systems designed to deal with specific aspects of culture and society on the conceptual bases of the relevant disciplines concerned. The particular methodological framework outlined here is one for the acquisition and interpretation of archaeological data, by way of defining, characterizing, and relating prehistoric social groups.

The central concept of our methodological framework is the definition of an archaeological settlement; the focal point of our operations is typology. The dichotomies of objective vs. relative types and of function vs. style are also fundamental to the framework.

To lay in building materials for our models, we categorize relative types– on the basis of the "within" settlement and "beyond" settlement distinction. We then use these materials to build two kinds of structural models: microstructure and macrostructure. The operational process for the former is termed microarticulation, and that for the latter, macroarticulation; microarticulation is an analytic and reconstructive process, macroarticulation a comparative and correlative synthesis.

Under this view, the conventional methodology of archaeology, formulated as it is primarily for the acquisition and interpretation of artifacts, is inadequate for the acquisition and interpretation of data suggestive of cultural and social grouping and structure. This new framework, however, does not supplant the existing frameworks in studies where it does not apply: it represents simply a realignment of emphases and vantage points for a specific purpose or set of purposes. Artifacts are regarded, under this view, not as closed systems in themselves, but as elements of greater systems and as indicators of relationship; residential residues are considered not simply as indications of food habits, architectural patterns, or trash-throwing customs, but as contexts of social and cultural activities; and decorative arts are viewed both as integral elements of the intellectual and/or practical life and as horizon and tradition markers.

The new framework does not so much conflict with, as it does supplement and complement, the existing archaeological methodologies formulated for other purposes. There is no reason, then, to take an alarmist view and to suppose that if this system is adopted, all the rest now flourishing in archaeology will be relinquished into the dustbin. On the contrary, it is imperative that this and other systems of archaeological methodology continue to serve together and to draw from each other such inspiration and practical guidance as they can–imperative, that is, that they not retreat into carping isolation.

References

GREENBERG, J. H.
1953 "Historical linguistics and unwritten languages," in *Anthropology Today*, A. L. Kroeber, editor (Chicago: The University of Chicago Press): 267-76.
HOUSEHOLDER, F. W., JR.
1959 "On linguistic terms," *Word*, Vol. 15:231-39.
JAKOBSON, R.
1961 "Linguistics and communication theory," in *Proceedings of Symposia in Applied Mathematics*, Vol. 12: 248-49.
KLUCKHOHN, CLYDE
1960 "The use of typology in anthropological theory," in *Selected Papers of the Fifth International Congress of Anthropological and Ethnological Sciences*, A. F. C. Wallace, editor (Philadelphia: The University of Pennsylvania Press): 134.
PIKE, K. L.
1954 *Language in Relation to a Unified Theory of the Structure of Human Behavior*, Part I (Glencoe: The Free Press).
ROUSE, IRVING
1960 "The classification of artifacts in archaeology," *American Antiquity*, Vol. 25: 313-23.
STEWARD, J. H.
1954 "Types of types," *American Anthropologist*, Vol. 56: 54-57.
WILLEY, G. R., and PHILIP PHILLIPS
1958 *Method and Theory in American Archaeology* (Chicago: The University of Chicago Press).

II

IRVING ROUSE

Prehistory, Typology, and the Study of Society[1]

In the paper preceding this one, K. C. Chang has proposed a "science of prehistoric society" as a new approach to the interpretation of archaeological remains, an approach based on the concept of the settlement. In so doing, he overlooks, it seems to me, an ongoing science of prehistoric archaeology—which I shall call "prehistory" for reasons to be given later—with its own practitioners and its own common ground of concepts, methods, and objectives. Moreover, prehistorians have long included society among their prime interests and have developed a number of concepts for studying it. In this paper, I shall compare the science of prehistory with Chang's science of prehistoric society, by contrasting their strategies and their pertinent concepts.

The Science of Prehistory

Archaeology Let us first inquire into the nature of archaeology, since the word is frequently coupled with the word "prehistory" in the phrase "prehistoric archaeology." According to one dictionary (Onions, 1956, p. 92), it is: "1. Ancient history generally; systematic description and study of antiquities. 2. The scientific study of the remains and monuments of the pre-

[1] When invited to contribute to this volume, I suggested several topics to its editor, K. C. Chang, and we finally settled on "The Place of 'Peoples' in Prehistoric Research," which I was preparing to read at a meeting of the Prehistoric Society during the course of a sabbatical year in London. However, Chang's reaction to the first draft of my "Peoples" paper, which I sent him for criticism, was such as to suggest that we had differed in our approach to "Settlement Archaeology." I therefore asked to see his introductory paper, "Toward a Science of Prehistoric Society," and discovered to my dismay that it conflicted with mine. Believing that the reader would be confused if the two papers were set side by side in the same volume without some explanation of the differences between them, I withdrew mine and have published it elsewhere (Rouse, 1965). I wrote Chang that I preferred to withdraw entirely from the volume but that I would, if he insisted, honor my promise to participate by preparing a critique of his paper, in an attempt to explain our points of disagreement. He has asked me to do so, and this paper is the result.

My thanks are due to the Guggenheim Foundation for a fellowship that enabled me to spend my sabbatical in London, exposing me to ideas I would not otherwise have been able to incorporate in this paper. I am indebted also to Chang, for his patience and encouragement, to Harold C. Conklin, for advice about my linguistic analogies, and especially to Peter Ucko and Michael D. Coe, who read and criticized earlier drafts of the paper.

historic period." These are two very different meanings; in the first, archaeology is regarded as the study of historic antiquities and, by implication, is included among the humanities, whereas, in the second, it is defined as the study of prehistoric remains and classified within the sciences.

How are we to reconcile the two definitions? The customary solution is to limit "archaeology" to the qualities common to both definitions and to relegate to other terms the qualities not held in common. Archaeology then becomes the body of methods that have been developed for excavating both historic and prehistoric remains, for restoring and preserving these remains, and for presenting them objectively, whether as monuments, in museums, or in publications. An archaeologist is a technologist, skilled in carrying out these tasks. As such, he must be distinguished from the scholar or the scientist who uses the remains for purposes of interpretation. The two may well be embodied in the same person, but they perform very different operations. Archaeologists are alike in their manner of recovery, preservation, display, identification, and description of their findings, but when they come to interpret the remains they part company, joining one or another group of specialists: classicists, medievalists, and historians proper, who interpret the remains of "Western" civilization; Sumerologists, Egyptologists, Sanskritists, Sinologists, etc., who deal with the remains of "Oriental" civilizations; anthropologists, who are concerned with the remains of prehistoric civilizations and cultures; and art historians, who specialize in the aesthetic significance of the remains. There are, in fact, as many groups of archaeological interpreters as there are academic disciplines concerned with the history and prehistory of man.

In this paper, then, I shall distinguish the technological and descriptive operations of archaeology from the interpretive operations carried out within the confines of the various academic disciplines. In the past, this distinction has been obscured by the tendency of the archaeologist to act as both technologist and academician, but the roles are rapidly diverging. Not only is there a growing number of "amateur" archaeologists, who are more interested in the collection of artifacts than in their interpretation, but also many professional archaeologists are beginning to specialize in salvage work, i.e., in the recovery of remains threatened with destruction, without specific regard to the interpretive significance of the remains. Still other professionals, e.g., the archaeologists in our National Park Service, are devoting themselves to the restoration and display of remains, either in museums or in the form of monuments, again with little or no attempt to produce new interpretations.

Moreover, the technological operations of archaeology are no longer easily mastered by the nonspecialist. More and more techniques of great complexity are being adopted from the natural sciences, and a specialized literature is developing around these techniques; see, e.g., the recently established journal *Archaeometry* (Hall and Aitken, 1958-). It is becoming increasingly difficult, if not impossible, for the specialist in academic interpretation to stay abreast of developments in the technology of archaeology.

Assuming a continuation of these trends, I would suggest that the people interested in archaeology as technology will eventually become sufficiently numerous and specialized to be recognized as a separate profession, bearing the same relationship to interpretive archaeologists that engineers and applied scientists bear to pure scientists. They will have representatives on the staffs of our major universities who, like engineers and applied scientists, will be accorded separate faculty status, teaching practical methods rather than academic interpretation.

Archaeology is comparable in this respect to linguistics. There is now a professional body of linguists, skilled in the methods of analyzing languages, who teach the use of these methods and conduct research to develop new methods, without specific regard for the languages the methods may be applied to. But the methods are also employed by scholars who regard themselves as members of other, interpretive disciplines–Romance languages and literature, Germanic studies, English studies, classics, or anthropology, for example. These scholars do not consider themselves professional linguists, except in a secondary sense; they are instead Romance, Germanic, English, or classical scholars, or anthropologists. They do not study linguistic methods for their own sake but use them to solve the problems of a particular academic discipline. Just so, I believe we must distinguish between (1) an emergent group of professional archaeologists, whose aim is to recover, restore, display, and describe archaeological remains; and (2) those historians, classicists, Egyptologists, anthropologists, art historians, etc., who use archaeological techniques and data in order to solve the problems of their particular disciplines.

In some American universities, it is now possible for an undergraduate student to major in linguistics as a technological subject, with a minor in one of the interpretive subjects, such as Romance studies, Sinology, or anthropology; or to major in one of the interpretive subjects, with a minor in linguistics. It is likewise possible for a graduate student to obtain a Ph.D. either in linguistics, considered as a technological subject, or in one of the academic subjects, such as anthropology, with a specialty in the use of linguistic methods. Continuing with the analogy, I would predict that our universities will eventually come to offer undergraduate majors and doctoral programs in archaeology, considered as a technological subject, and that such majors and doctorates will serve to complement the present academic programs in which archaeological methods are used for purposes of interpretation, such as classics and anthropology.

To complete the analogy, I should note that linguistics owes its recognition as a separate discipline not only to the development of a body of techniques for analyzing languages, but also to the success of scholars in basing those techniques upon theories about the nature of language. It is impossible to analyze languages adequately without the use of concepts that enable one to go beyond speaking, listening, and reading, in the process of thinking about words and their meaning. Just so, archaeologists cannot be concerned simply with the techniques of recovering remains. They, too, have had to develop a body of concepts that express the nature of the remains and make it possible to think about them in an abstract manner, instead of simply reacting to visual impressions of them. These concepts are as much a part of method as are the techniques of manipulating remains.

Neither the linguist nor the archaeologist, then, can be simply a technician; each must be well versed in theory, the former in the theory of language and the latter in theories of human remains. For the archaeologist, this means primarily the theory of material culture, especially of artifacts and structures, since most of the remains are of this kind; but he must also know about burials, plant and animal remains, soils, and all other kinds of materials and recorded behavior encountered in his sites.

Summarizing the argument to this point, we may say that the student who wishes to work with archaeological materials is faced with an important fundamental choice. He must decide whether (1) to make a career of archaeology itself or (2) to enter one of the academic disciplines in which archaeological data are acquired and used for the purpose of interpretation. If he chooses the first alternative, he may expect to join the growing ranks of salvage archaeologists, museum curators, custodians of monuments, and others concerned with remains per se. If he prefers the second choice, he must make a choice between Egyptology, Assyriology, Sinology, classics, history, art history, anthropology, or one of the other academic disciplines that make use of archaeological data to solve its problems.

In any case, this is a more complex picture of archaeology than Chang has presented in his opening paper. He overlooks (1) and ignores most of the subdivisions of (2). For him, the student who wishes to work with archaeological materials "must be both a competent technician . . . and a historian or anthropologist" (p. 2).

This pronouncement fails to recognize that some archaeologists design their excavations and laboratory work not to solve problems of history, anthropology, or one of the other academic disciplines, but to recover, conserve, identify, and display remains, utilizing the concepts that have been developed for such purposes. Are we to deny these people the title of archaeologist? I doubt that we could do so even if we tried. It is better, I submit, to accept the fact that they are indeed archaeologists and to tailor our thinking to this fact.

Chang's pronouncement also fails to recognize how widespread the use of archaeological techniques and concepts is among the various academic disciplines. He has perhaps been misled by conditions in American anthropology, where it is customary to distinguish only between prehistoric and historic archaeology. In the Old World, every historical discipline, from Sumerology to medieval studies and even modern "industrial" history, now has its archaeologists, for it is recognized that remains are still being laid down and that the archaeological record therefore extends into the present (Daniel, 1962, pp. 5-6). From this point of view, even the artifacts collected by ethnologists and folklorists are archaeological because, as they are removed from their cultural context, they become, in effect, remains.

Prehistory For the purposes of this paper, we need consider only the use of archaeological techniques and concepts within the discipline of anthropology. It is customary in the United States to divide the discipline into four parts: cultural anthropology (including both ethnology and social anthropology), physical anthropology, linguistics, and archaeology. The third of these might better be termed "linguistic anthropology," in order to distinguish the use of linguistic methods to solve anthropological problems from the technological discipline of linguistics, to which I have referred above. Similarly, the phrase "prehistoric archaeology" is frequently used to differentiate anthropological archaeology from the archaeology of other disciplines. The phrase is sometimes applied to the results achieved by archaeological anthropologists, but there seems to be an increasing tendency to reserve "prehistoric archaeology" for the methods and to apply the term "prehistory" to the results. For example, Hole and Heizer, in *An Introduction to Prehistoric Archaeology* (1965), deal with method, whereas Daniel, in *The Idea of Prehistory* (1962), is concerned with results. Since this trend is consistent with the definition of "archaeology" developed above, I shall follow it here.

Prehistory may be defined as the results achieved by "application of archaeological techniques and concepts to non-literate societies in antiquity" (Piggott, 1959, p. 96). The phrase "non-literate societies" is the key to this definition. It implies that "archaeological techniques and concepts," i.e., archaeological methods, are applied in accordance with the aims of anthropology and in the light of the knowledge that anthropologists have acquired by the study of modern, nonliterate societies. In other words, prehistorians must be anthropologists as well as archaeologists, able not only to handle archaeological remains but also to fit the remains into an anthropological context.

By contrast, the members of the other subdisciplines of anthropology are each concerned with a different kind of data – cultural anthropologists with the information they collect about observable contemporary societies, physical anthropologists with man as a biological organism, and linguists with languages. Each subdiscipline has had to develop its own strategy and its own methods in order to handle its own distinctive kind of data.

This is not to say that members of one subdiscipline do not frequently cross over into another subdiscipline. Linguists, for example, after having developed their own strategy and methods for the study of languages, increasingly tend to expand from the subject of language into the kinds of data studied by cultural anthropologists, in order to correlate language with culture. But linguists have been successful in doing this only because their studies of language per se have reached the stage where they provide a solid base upon which to investigate the relationships between language and culture.

In like manner, prehistorians, whose methodology and strategy are designed to study archaeological remains, are beginning to expand from that field into cultural anthropology, i.e., to reconstruct nonmaterial culture from the remains in order to fill out the picture of a culture, as it is observed in contemporary societies. But prehistorians will be able to do this, in my opinion, only to the extent that they can build upon the results obtained within their own subdiscipline. Like linguists, they must first draw conclusions from their own kind of data, archaeological remains, before they can hope to use the remains to reconstruct nonmaterial culture, as it is studied by cultural anthropologists.

Chang has not taken this prerequisite into consideration in his paper. His "science of prehistoric society" is clearly designed to bridge the gap between the subdisciplines of prehistory and cultural anthropology, and he performs a valuable service in calling attention to the need for such a bridge, but he proposes to effect it by a new kind of study, a kind not based on the strategy and methods of the prehistorians. He should not, in my opinion, have presented his science of prehistoric society as a thing apart but should have developed it out of the extant science of prehistory.

Chang goes wrong, it seems to me, in assuming that anthropology can be organized into such fields of study as society, artifacts, and religion (p. 1), which cut across the different kinds of anthropological data and across the subdisciplines that have arisen to study these kinds of data, viz., prehistory, cultural anthropology, physical anthropology, and linguistics. On the contrary, I believe that prehistorians and cultural anthropologists, for example, must work out their own peculiar approaches to society, to artifacts, to religion, etc., on the basis of the kinds of data available to them; must produce their own conclusions within each of these fields; and should only then proceed to correlate their respective conclusions with those in the parallel investigations. In an attempt to demonstrate this point, I shall now compare the strategy and methodology of prehistory with those Chang proposes for his science of prehistoric society.

In another paper (Rouse, 1966), I have expressed the strategy of prehistory in terms of four questions, as follows:

(1) What is the nature of the archaeological remains under study?

(2) Who produced them?

(3) When and where were they produced?

(4) How did they change?

Since Chang deals primarily with the first two of these questions in his paper, I shall concentrate upon them. Following his example, I shall also restrict myself to artifacts, though nonartifactual remains are likewise pertinent to the study of society.

WHAT IS THE NATURE OF THE REMAINS?

This question focuses attention on the remains themselves and poses the problem of their cultural significance. As I see it, four steps are required to solve the problem:

a. Recovery of the Remains. First, the prehistorian must obtain an adequate sample of the remains. This may require one or more of the following kinds of research: site survey, excavation, collection of materials from the surface of the ground, and search of museum collections for specimens of the proper kinds. In designing this research, care should be taken to obtain as great a variety as possible of artifacts, structures, etc., in order to obtain the total range of cultural remains.

b. Classification of the Remains: Once recovered, the materials must be classified, in order to convert them from raw data into conceptual units. There are two ways of doing this–taxonomic and analytical classification (Rouse, 1960). In taxonomic classification, all artifacts that are alike are grouped together as a class, and the class is given a name and defined by listing its distinctive attributes. It is customary in American prehistory to refer to these diagnostic attributes as a "type" (e.g., Krieger, 1944). The same procedure is followed in analytical classification, but the artifacts are first broken down into their distinctive features and it is these features, rather than the artifacts as complete objects, that are grouped into classes. The series of attributes diagnostic of each class of features is termed a "mode" (e.g., Ford, 1962, p. 16). The petaloid celt is an example of a type, and the human face design, of a mode. Such a design may occur not only upon celts but also upon artifacts of other types, e.g., pottery vessels, since modes cut across types. The two are different kinds of categories, both of which must be exploited to determine completely the nature of artifacts and other cultural materials.

c. Reconstruction from the Remains. The next step is to reconstruct the manner in which the artifacts were made and used. This is done by a process of inference, combining study of indicative attributes of the artifacts of each type (e.g., Semenov, 1964) with analogies to the manufacture and use of comparable artifacts and features among contemporary peoples (e.g., Ascher, 1961). It is also advisable to study the circumstances under which artifacts were found, e.g., by investigating workshop areas in which byproducts of the manufacturing process are recoverable.

d. Interpretation of the Remains: For complete understanding of artifacts and other kinds of cultural remains, the prehistorian must also investigate the factors that have influenced their nature, manufacture, and use. These include the availability of materials, the effects of one part of the artisan's procedure on another, the aesthetic qualities of the artifacts, and the needs of the society under study.

Chang would presumably not include the question "What?" in his science of society, since he lists the study of artifacts as a separate field (p. 1), but he would agree, I am sure, that some knowledge of artifacts is a necessary prerequisite for the study of prehistoric society. I would myself argue that, optimally, all four of the above steps should be performed, in order to provide the broadest possible base for societal study. Chang, on the other hand, seems to feel that only steps *b* and *c* are necessary, for he discusses only parts of these, under the headings of "Objective and Relative Types" and "Function and Style," respectively. I shall use the same headings in my critique of his discussion.

Objective and Relative Types (pp. 4-6) Chang does not explain what he means by artifact type, but, insofar as I can tell, he is not following the normal usage in prehistoric archaeology, as given above. The examples he gives, such as shell temper, are all modes rather than types, and nothing in his theoretical discussion leads me to believe that he is referring, for example, to a pottery type that might incorporate the mode shell temper. Hence, in attempting to understand his distinction between objective and relative types, I find it necessary to substitute "mode" for "type" as follows:

"...An *objective* [*mode*]..may be defined, as consisting of actual variations selected from archaeological assemblages...according to cross-cultural and cross-social criteria that are, to the best of our knowledge, universally valid and applicable. The color of pottery, for example, may be classified according to a color-scale supplied by physicists, and the floor plans of dwellings according to the measures and geometric forms that exist in all parts of the world. A *relative* [*mode*], on the other hand, includes only those variations that cluster around a common modal standard of behavior, in contrast with and relative to other variations clustering around other modal standards, within a single cultural or social system" (p. 4).

Reformulated in this way, Chang's dichotomy between objective and relative types makes better sense to me, but is still not entirely satisfactory. I have found it necessary to introduce two additional ideas–description and dimension. By description is meant the process of giving a verbal picture of the artifacts, as opposed to grouping them into classes characterized by types or modes. Lathrap (MS) has defined dimension as a range of variation in the corresponding features of a number of artifacts, e.g., a range in color, in hardness, or in geometric motifs, from one artifact to another.

Let us assume that a prehistorian has divided a collection of artifacts into classes, using the taxonomic procedure, so that each class comprises all the artifacts of a single type. Two additional procedures are then open to him.

He may simply describe the artifacts of each type; or he may analyze the artifacts of all types together, in terms of their various features, and classify the corresponding features in order to produce modes. In either case, he will proceed dimension by dimension, considering, e.g., the dimensions of material, such as color and hardness, then the dimensions of shape, such as bases and rim profiles, and then the dimensions of decoration, such as techniques and design motifs.

If the prehistorian is doing description, he will make use of scales of color, as worked out by physicists, of hardness, as devised by mineralogists, and so forth. He will also deal with geometric figures and various other descriptive criteria of more or less universal applicability. These criteria will enable him to express the range of variation along each dimension in an "objective cross-cultural and cross-social" manner, and hence he will be working with "objective types" as Chang has defined them.

If the prehistorian is doing analytical classification, he will not describe the range of variation along each dimension in this manner but will instead segment the dimension into units by grouping together all features which are enough alike that they may be said to "cluster around a common modal standard of behavior." In other words, he will be producing modes, or as Chang calls them, "relative types."

A further analogy to linguistics may be helpful at this point. By using the method of physics, linguists are able to measure and describe sounds along all the dimensions utilized in speech. But these measurements are not in themselves meaningful units of linguistic study, for each language cuts up the dimensions of sound in a different manner. Hence, the linguist must formulate a different, finite set of units to account for the phonology of each language. Just so, the prehistorian may describe the range of variation of his artifacts within each of their dimensions by means of "cross-cultural and cross-social criteria," but this will not of itself provide him with meaningful units of study. To obtain such units, he will have to turn to analytical classification, using it to divide each dimension into modes.

Allchin (1960, pp. xviii-xxiv) has implicitly recognized this difference by contrasting the study of archaeological "objects *qua* objects" with the study of objects "as things for interpretation and therefore potential culture traits." In Chang's terms, Allchin is distinguishing objective and relative study of artifacts; in mine, he is distinguishing description from classification in order to produce types and/or modes.

To sum up, Chang's "objective types" are not types at all, as this term is ordinarily used in the literature of prehistory, nor are they modes. Instead, they are criteria of description obtained from physics, mineralogy, geometry, etc., or from the general language of description. Chang's "relative types" are modes. Each consists of the attributes distinctive of a class of artifact features, and each therefore conceptualizes its class in the same way that a type conceptualizes its class of artifacts, providing the prehistorian with meaningful units of research.

Function and Style (p. 6) Chang's second dichotomy seems to me straightforward, and I have had less difficulty in understanding it. I assume that Chang is using "function" and "style" in the dictionary definitions of these words–function as "the action for which a...thing is specially fitted..." and style as "the manner of expression characteristic of a period...or identifiable group [of people]" (Gove *et al.*, 1961, pp. 920, 2271). Thus he focuses attention not on the nature of the artifacts and their features–as in forming types and modes–but on the manner in which the artifacts of each type and the features of each mode were made or used, and on their chronologic or ethnic significance.

The one example Chang gives is of a mode–shell temper (p. 6). Applying the dictionary definitions to this example, we may say that shell-tempering material was included in potsherds primarily in order to prevent the vessels from cracking during the drying process, and that it is therefore indicative of part of the behavior of making the vessels. But tempering material may also have been included in order to give the vessels a distinctive appearance, i.e., for stylistic reasons. Hence, each mode may, in Chang's terms, have both "a function or cluster of functions, and a style or cluster of styles" (p. 6).

This is true of types as well as modes. For example, the pottery vessels just discussed may have had several different functions, such as cooking and the storage of food, and they may have shared a distinctive style, such as angularity and simplicity of shape and decoration.

Chang might have noted that the relative degree of functional and stylistic significance varies from one type of artifact or one mode of feature to another. Most Paleolithic backed blades, for example, have been made in the simplest possible way; i.e., almost all their features are designed to give them utility rather than style. By contrast, most pottery vessels abound in features of shape and decoration which are not essential for the use of the vessels but which have been included as a means of expressing style.

The same variation is to be found on the level of modes. For example, the bodies of pottery vessels are generally designed for use as some kind of container, whereas rim profiles have less functional significance. The profiles are more likely to have stylistic significance, because they tend to vary from time to time and from community to community.

It seems to me that Chang has in fact made a significant advance in the methodology of prehistoric archaeology by distinguishing between types and modes, on the one hand, and function and style, on the other. Previous writers, myself included, have tended to confuse these two. For example, Steward (1954, pp. 54-55) has distinguished three kinds of types as follows:

a. Morphological Types. These are "based solely on form–on physical or external properties. When the use or cultural significance of an object...is unknown, a descriptive label is necessary." Steward mentions "stone balls" as an example.

b. Functional Types. These are "based on cultural use or role rather than on outward form or chronological position. The same materials may be treated in terms of functional type or of morphological type. When preoccupation is with the latter, a monograph is likely to describe artifacts under major headings such as 'Stone,' 'Bone,' 'Wood,' and the like. A functional treatment uses such categories as 'Weapons,' 'Food Preparation,' 'Clothing,' etc."

c. Historical-Index Types. These are "defined by form but, whereas the morphological type is considered as a characteristic of the culture, this [kind of] type has chronological, not cultural significance. It is a time-marker." Pottery types are the classic example.

Only the first of these three categories fits the definition of type given above, for it is the only one in which artifacts are grouped into classes and the classes defined in terms of attributes per se. In *b*, the classification is instead effected in terms of the behavior associated with the artifacts, and in *c*, of the stylistic significance of the artifacts. I agree with Chang that it is better to limit the term "type" to *a* and to consider *b* and *c* separately as "a function or cluster of functions, and a style or cluster of styles" (p. 6), for two reasons.

First, Steward's concept of functional type is difficult to apply, because artifacts of the same type may have performed several different functions and these functions may have changed during the life of a given artifact. In the West Indies, for example, many stone celts appear to have been used as axes until the cutting edges were too worn to be resharpened any more, and the same tools were then pressed into use as hammers. How are we to classify these tools–as axes, as hammers, or as ax-hammers? It is better, I believe, simply to call them celts, and to discuss their uses as a separate issue.

It also seems to me advisable to distinguish types from their functional and stylistic significance because the three belong in different parts of the strategy of prehistory, as I have outlined it above (p. 15). Types are produced by classification, which is step *b* in the procedure of answering the question "What?" whereas function is determined by reconstruction, which is step *c* in the same procedure (see pp. 16-17). Style does not enter into this procedure at all; instead, it is pertinent to the procedures for answering the questions "Who?" and "When?," for, as we have seen, style expresses the ethnic and chronologic significance of the artifacts, rather than their inherent nature.

So far as I am concerned, this last point explains the argument between Spaulding (1953) and Ford (1954) to which Chang refers in his paper (p. 4). When Spaulding claims that types are inherent in artifacts, he is basing his claim upon the procedure of classification that I have described above, in which artifacts are grouped into classes on the basis of their distinctive attributes, with the result that those attributes, which are inherent in the artifacts, constitute the type. When Ford argues, on the contrary, that types are imposed upon the artifacts, he is in effect stating that he has selected combinations of modes which are stylistically significant and which therefore enable him to answer the question "When?" rather than "What?" Hence, Spaulding and Ford are referring to different kinds of units. In a previous paper (Rouse, 1960, p. 317), I called these two "descriptive" and "historic" types, respectively. In the light of Chang's distinction between type and style, I would now use a different name for the latter, such as "chronological complex of modes."

Shifting from the level of types to that of modes, I made a distinction in the paper cited (1960, p. 315) between "conceptual" and "procedural" modes, the former referring to the features themselves and the latter to the behavior of manufacture and use that can be inferred from the features. In the light of Chang's separation of function from modes, I would now scrap this distinction and limit my use of "mode" to the attributes distinctive of a class of features, as stated above (see also Rouse, 1967).

Who Produced the Remains?

Let us now turn from the question "What were the remains like?" to the question "Who produced them?" and let us turn also from the cultural significance of the remains to their ethnic and social significance. We shall no longer regard a site as a repository of artifacts and other remnants of culture but shall instead view it as the place where a group of people carried out their activities. Our problem is to define the group and to reconstruct its life.

This brings us directly into the field of Chang's science of society, for he states that his science has the purpose of "defining, characterizing, and relating prehistoric social groups" (p. 8). I shall first outline the procedure ordinarily used in prehistoric archaeology for this purpose, and will then compare it with the procedure Chang proposes for his science. The ordinary procedure has four steps, comparable to those for answering the question "What?," as follows:

a. Recovery. Again, the prehistorian begins by locating and examining sites and collections from sites, but he no longer seeks out the sites that are likely to yield the greatest variety of artifacts and structures. Instead, he will search for sites that have been occupied by ethnically homogeneous groups of people. Sites occupied by single groups will be best for his purposes, but he will also be able to utilize sites occupied by successive groups, provided that the remains of each group are clearly separated, e.g., by sterile soil. Occupation units like these are known as "components," and each is considered to be indicative of a single prehistoric community (see, e.g., Willey and Phillips, 1958, pp. 49-50).

b. Classification. The next step is classification, but of components rather than of artifacts or their features. All components that have yielded the same kinds of cultural materials are grouped together in a class, the class is given the name of one of its constituent components, and it is characterized by listing its types and modes. It has become customary in American prehistory to refer to such a class as a *focus*, or a *facies* (e.g., Heizer, 1958, pp. 97-101). Since each of the components making up a focus consists of the remains of a single prehistoric community, the focus itself is the product of a group of communities, which together constitute a people (e.g., Piggott, 1959, p. 81) or a society (e.g., Allchin, 1960, p. xiv). The types and modes present in the focus are variously known as the people's phase, culture, complex, industry, or style (Rouse, 1965, pp. 4-5). The name of each focus is, of course, also applicable to the people who produced its constituent components and to the phase (types and modes) that characterizes it.

c. Reconstruction. The phase performs the same functions in answering the question "Who?" that its constituent types and modes have performed in answering the question "What?" It serves, in the first place, as the unit around which to reconstruct a people's culture. In this respect it is analogous to a skeleton; just as the paleontologist reconstructs the flesh and skin of an animal around its skeleton, so the prehistorian expands from the phase of a people to the other aspects of the culture of these people, using the processes of inference and analogy. The methods of doing this have been well described in the literature of prehistoric archaeology (for one summary, see Rouse, 1965, pp. 8-10), and here I need mention only the twin concepts of Chang's paper. By "settlement pattern" is meant the ecological relationships between a people's components and their environment, and, by "community pattern," the social relationships among the various components. Willey (1953) has shown that these two kinds of pattern provide an effective basis for reconstructing various aspects of a people's culture.

d. Interpretation. Finally, as in answering the question "What?," the prehistorian may attempt to analyze the factors that have affected the nature and functioning of both the phase and the reconstructed areas of a people's culture. These might include adaptation of the culture to the environment, interrelationships between various parts of the culture, the structure of the culture, and its external relationships to other cultures.

The work of MacNeish (1964) in Tehuácan Valley, Mexico, provides an excellent example of this procedure. MacNeish first made a survey of the valley and located 392 sites, of which he selected 30 for excavation. In the excavated sites he encountered 113 distinct occupational zones, each of which comprises a single component. He classified the components into seven successive foci–Ajuereado (7 components), El Riego (24), Coxcatlan (12), Abejas (13), Purron (2), Santa Mária (38), and Palo Blanco (17). He then worked out phases, i.e., the complex of artifact types present in each focus. He used the phases to assign to foci the surface collections from his unexcavated sites, as follows: Ajuereado (4 sites), El Riego (14), Coxcatlan (4), Abejas (8), Purron (0), Santa Mária (53), and Palo Blanco (150). Working both with the excavated materials and the surface collections, he proceeded to reconstruct the settlement and community patterns associated with each phase. MacNeish has graphically expressed these in a series of sketches, one for each phase (1964, Figs. 2-8). In each sketch, the settlement pattern associated with the phase is shown by plotting a few selected components against a background drawing of Tehuacán Valley; and the community pattern is shown by connecting the components with lines and by using symbols to indicate the kinds of activity carried out in each component or the kind of social unit present there. This carries MacNeish through step *c* in the procedure for answering the question "Who?" (see p. 15). He does not go on to step *d* in the article cited, which is only a preliminary report.

To my surprise, Chang has ignored this procedure and its concepts in the text of his paper. As a result, I have had great difficulty in comparing his concepts and procedures with those ordinarily used in prehistoric archaeology, but I shall attempt the comparison, proceeding as before in order of the pertinent sections of his paper.

The Settlement (pp. 2-4) Chang begins with the concept of community. He does not define this concept, but I assume that, for him, a community consists of a group of families living together in a single locality, such as a camp or village. He proposes to group together all the remains that have been laid down by such a community and to call these remains a "settlement." I am not sure whether he intends to limit each settlement to the remains that a community is depositing or has deposited simultaneously (e.g., while living in one place and burying in another), or whether he would include in each settlement all the remains produced by a single community during the entire period of its existence (i.e., in all successively occupied dwelling and burial sites). I assume the latter, since it seems more logical to me. For purposes of this discussion, therefore, a settlement may be said to consist of all the remains deposited by a single community–whether entirely in one place, in separate sites used respectively for habitation, burial quarrying, butchering game, etc., or in sites used successively for each of these purposes. In other words, it is all those space/time components in which a particular community carried out its various activities.

Since settlements are the only grouping of components Chang proposes to use in his science of society, it must be assumed that, for him, they take the place of the concepts of focus and phase, which, as we have seen, are normally used in prehistoric archaeology to classify components. My own experience with settlements has convinced me that they cannot be used for this purpose. I have worked with settlements on three different occasions and on none was I able to group all my components into settlements, as would be necessary in order to make an adequate classification of the components. I shall mention each of these experiences briefly.

a. Refuse and Ball Courts. When conducting an archaeological survey of Puerto Rico in 1936-38, I found both refuse of habitation and ball courts. Often, the refuse and courts occurred together in the same sites, so that it was reasonable to assume that both had been produced by the same community; but in an appreciable number of cases the refuse and the courts were in separate sites, some distance apart. In most of the latter cases, I was unable to pair a particular refuse site with a particular ball court, so as to conclude that both had been produced by the same community, and thus to classify the components into settlements (Rouse, 1952).

b. Refuse and Burial Mounds. When I surveyed the Indian River area of Florida in 1946, I had to deal with both refuse deposits and burial mounds. The two never occurred in the same sites, nor were they close enough together, except in a few cases, for me to presume that a particular refuse site and a particular mound had been produced by the same community and hence to establish settlements (Rouse, 1951).

c. Seacoast and Interior Shelters. Finally, those of us who study the prehistory of New England are faced with a situation in which we know from ethnohistorical evidence that many Indian communities lived on the shore during the summer, in order to fish and to catch shellfish, and moved into the interior during the winter, in order to hunt and to obtain protection from the wind (Rainey, 1956, p. 11). We have been able to identify the middens that were inhabited during the summer and the rock shelters occupied during the winter months, and to observe the differing food remains in each–principally shells in the middens and deer bones in the shelters–but only rarely are the two sufficiently near that we may safely conclude they belonged to the same settlement.

MacNeish seems to have experienced similar difficulty in his Tehuacán research, cited above. As we have seen, he diagrams several settlements for each of his phases, using them to illustrate both settlement and community patterns for that phase (MacNeish, 1964, Figs. 2-8). I assume he has selected the best authenticated settlements for this purpose, but even these do not appear to be completely substantiated. Many are missing one kind of component, and in many the relationships between certain components are so tenuous that MacNeish indicates them with dashed lines.

It would thus appear that the concept of settlement cannot be used as a substitute for focus and phase in the classification of components. Nevertheless, as MacNeish's work shows, it can be used as the basis for establishing settlement and community *patterns*. One need only identify several valid settlements and generalize from them to the patterns.

There is good theoretical reason for this difference: foci and settlements belong in successive steps of the procedure for answering the question "Who?" In the case of foci, components are grouped on the basis of their phases; these consist of types and modes inherent in the remains; and hence focus and phase are truly classificatory concepts, and as such belong in step *b* of the procedure (see pp. 21-22). In the case of settlements, on the other hand, the components are grouped together because they have been produced by the same community; communities are external to the remains and can only be reconstructed from them by means of inference and analogy; and hence the concepts of settlement and community belong in step *c* of the procedure rather than in *b*.

This point is well illustrated by MacNeish's research. Before attempting to reconstruct settlements, MacNeish found it necessary to classify his components into foci in order to form phases. By so doing, he grouped together all the components that had been produced by a single people, and thereby eliminated components that could not possibly have been produced by the same community. This put him in a position to effectively reconstruct settlements from the remaining components. If, on the contrary, he had attempted to reconstruct settlements without first establishing foci and phases, I doubt that he would have accomplished anything, for the number of his components (346) and their variety would have obscured the relationships he was looking for.

My conclusion, then, is that there is nothing wrong with Chang's concepts of settlement and community per se. His mistake is in not also including the concepts of focus and phase in his science of society; and in not acknowledging that prehistorians must form foci and phases, by a process of classification, before proceeding to form settlements and communities, by a process of inference and analogy. Viewed in this way, settlement and community are useful additions to the prehistorian's repertoire of concepts.

Microstructure and Macrostructure (pp. 6-7) Chang defines microstructure as the structure of relationships among the members of a community, and macrostructure as the structure of relationships from community to community. He proposes to study these two kinds of structure in terms of settlements, since settlements are the archaeological expression of communities. This proposal seems reasonable to me, provided the concepts ordinarily used in prehistoric archaeology are also included in the procedure.

MacNeish's work (1964) in Tehuacán Valley may be used to illustrate this. His basic units of study are focus and phase, rather than settlement and community. As we have seen, he has been able to reconstruct only a few predominantly reliable settlements for each focus and phase, but has generalized from these to work out the settlement and community patterns associated with each focus and phase. These patterns constitute the microstructure of the people who lived in the focus and who possessed the phase.

To work out the macrostructure, MacNeish goes beyond the question "Who?" to answer the questions "When?" and "How?" He answers the question "When?" by working out the succession of his phases on the basis of stratigraphic evidence and radiocarbon dates, and by fitting this succession into the regional chronology that prehistorians have established for Mesoamerica as a whole—though this is only implied in his preliminary report (MacNeish, 1964). He answers the question "How?" by fitting the phases into the sequence of Mesoamerican developmental stages: Lithic,

Archaic, Formative, Classic, and Post-Classic (though he uses some variants on this terminology).

Thus, MacNeish works out the macrostructure without reference to the concept of settlement. This seems theoretically correct to me, for reasons that I have presented elsewhere (Rouse, 1967). Here, I need only note that the questions "When?" and "How?," like "What?" and "Who?," must be answered in terms of classificatory units such as types, modes, and phases that are inherent in the remains. Settlements are unsuitable, because they are formed by inferring communities from the remains. If, for example, MacNeish had used his settlements as the basis for chronological and developmental interpretation, he would have been building inference upon inference, which is not sound procedure.

Microarticulation and Macroarticulation (pp. 7-8) Chang defines microarticulation and macroarticulation as the procedures for producing microstructure and macrostructure, respectively; and hence my criticisms of the latter pair apply also to the former. If these criticisms were met, and if the concept of mode were added to that of type, I would have no objection to this section, and indeed would agree that it performs a useful service by calling attention to the study of social relationships, which prehistorians have tended to neglect.

CONCLUSIONS

In the foregoing pages, I have paid an unusual amount of attention to definitions, in order to make up for Chang's failure to do so. This has seemed to me a serious fault of his paper. I do not believe that archaeology and prehistory can claim to be sciences unless and until we are able to agree upon our terminology, with reference to both concepts and procedures, as is the case in the natural sciences. We have made considerable progress in this direction, progress that Chang has ignored. In my opinion, he has weakened an otherwise fine paper by failing to define each of his terms and to relate them to the concepts and practices that are current in prehistoric archaeology. I have tried to do this for him.

One problem of definition remains to be resolved. In seeking to understand Chang's paper, I have found it necessary to distinguish between a people and a society. According to my dictionary (Gove, *et al.*, 1961, pp. 1673, 2126), a people consists of "persons linked by a common factor," i.e., by possession of a common culture, whereas a society is "an enduring and cooperating social group, whose members have developed organized patterns of relationships." A people is an ethnic group, characterized by its own distinctive traits of culture and, to a lesser extent, also of race and language, whereas a society is a social group, held together by a structure of relationships (cf. Kluckhohn, 1965, p. 24).

Peoples (ethnic groups) and societies (social groups) rarely coincide. A single people may be composed of a number of societies, as among the prehistoric Eskimo, with their many independent communities. Conversely, one society may be composed of several different peoples, as is the case with most contemporary United States societies. We have only to look at current trouble spots for two more examples: Cyprus, where the Turkish people are attempting to break away from a society controlled by the Greek people; and Kashmir, claimed by one society, Pakistan, from another society, India, because the people of the region are Pakistani rather than Indian.

From this point of view I would have done better, earlier in the paper, to distinguish between cultural and social anthropology (as in Beattie, 1964, pp. 20-21), instead of following the usual practice in the United States of grouping them together under the heading of cultural anthropology. Then I could have said that cultural anthropologists are concerned with peoples, since they study cultural traits, whereas social anthroplogists are concerned with societies and their relationships. In other words, cultural anthropologists investigate mankind ethnically – as is indicated by the alternative term *ethnology* – whereas social anthropologists investigate him economically, socially, and politically.

It follows from this distinction that prehistorians may answer the question "Who?" in either of two ways, in terms of peoples (ethnic groups) or of societies (social groups). Most prehistorians answer the question by formulating peoples, each characterized by its own phase of culture, whereas Chang proposes to answer it by distinguishing societies, i.e., settlements, each of which is characterized by a different set of social relationships rather than a different phase of culture. Prehistorians have been led to the first answer by practical considerations: cultural traits, which are definitive of a people, survive in archaeological sites, whereas social relationships, which are definitive of a society, do not. Sites contain direct evidences of peoples but not of societies.

Earlier in this paper, I stressed the distinction between classification of artifacts, which yields their inherent nature, and the drawing of inferences from the artifacts. It is a virtue of Chang's paper that he clearly recognizes this distinction by contrasting typology with function and style. Unfortunately, he fails to preserve the distinction when shifting from the question "What?" to the question "Who?" He has overlooked the fact that people are defined in terms of types and modes, which are inherent in the remains, whereas societies are defined in terms of relationships, which can only be inferred from the remains. As a result, he has failed to distinguish foci and phases from settlements and communities.

The prehistorian who has been the most explicit in discussing the study of society has been V. Gordon Childe. It is appropriate, therefore, that I close this critique of Chang's "Toward a Science of Prehistoric Society" with a quotation from Childe's last book, *The Prehistory of European Society* (1958, pp. 9-10):

> . . . in archaeology societies are represented, not by their members' skeletons, but by the durable results of their behavior–by pots and house-plans, personal ornaments and burial sites, the materials they fetched from afar, and so on. Such remains archaeologists divide and classify into *types*, and, when the same types are repeatedly found together at different sites within a limited region, they are grouped together to represent what we term *cultures* [i.e., phases]. Pots, house-plans, and the rest can be reduced to abstract types just because they express, not personal idiosyncrasies, but traditional ways of building pots, laying out houses, burying the dead, and decking the person. And types are repeatedly found together just because the traditions they embody are approved and transmitted by a society of persons who can communicate and co-operate. In this sense archaeologists' 'cultures' [i.e., phases] do really stand for societies.

Before reading Chang's paper, I had believed this to be the only practicable way to study prehistoric society. I still believe it to be basic and indispensable, but Chang's paper has made me realize that Childe himself is not really discussing societies. Rather, he is referring to peoples, formed by classifying the inhabitants of sites in terms of their cultural traits. Once peoples have been established in this manner, the prehistorian can go on to infer societies by studying relationships within and among the peoples. Chang is to be commended for pointing out the need to do this.

References

ALLCHIN, F. R.
1960 *Piklihal Excavations* (Andhra Pradesh Government Archaeological Series, No. 1 [Hyderabad]).

ASCHER, ROBERT
1961 "Analogy in archaeological interpretation," *Southwestern Journal of Anthropology*, Vol. XVII, No. 4: 317-25.

BEATTIE, JOHN
1964 *Other Cultures: Aims, Methods and Achievements in Social Anthropology* (New York: The Free Press).

CHILDE, V. G.
1958 *The Prehistory of European Society* (Harmondsworth, Middlesex: Pelican Books, No. A415).

DANIEL, GLYN
1962 *The Idea of Prehistory* (London: C.A. Watts & Co.).

FORD, J. A.
1954 "The type concept revisited," *American Anthropologist*, Vol. LVI, No. 1: 42-54.
1962 *A Quantitative Method for Deriving Cultural Chronology*, Pan American Union, Technical Manual No. 1 (Washington, D. C.).

GOVE, P. B., *et al.*
1961 *Webster's Third International Dictionary of the English Language, Unabridged*.

HALL, E. T., and M. J. AITKEN, editors
1958 *Archaeometry: Bulletin of the Research Laboratory for Archaeology and the History of Art* (Oxford: Oxford University Press), Vols. I - .
HEIZER, R. F.
1958 *A Guide to Archaeological Field Methods* (Palo Alto: The National Press).
HOLE, FRANK, and R. F. HEIZER
1965 *An Introduction to Prehistoric Archaeology* (New York: Holt, Rinehart, & Winston).
KLUCKHOHN, CLYDE
1965 *Mirror for Man* (New York: Premier Books, No. R255).
KRIEGER, A. D.
1944 "The typological concept," *American Antiquity*, Vol. IX, No. 3: 271-88.
LATHRAP, D. W.
MS "Archaeology of the Yarinacócha Region, Peru," manuscript in the Department of Anthropology, University of Illinois, Urbana.
MACNEISH, R. S.
1964 "Ancient Mesoamerican civilization," *Science*, Vol. CXLIII, No. 3606: 531-37.
ONIONS, C. T., editor
1956 *The Shorter Oxford English Dictionary on Historical Principles* (Third edition; Oxford: The Clarendon Press).
PIGGOTT, STUART
1959 *Approach to Archaeology* (London: Adam & Charles Black).
RAINEY, F. G.
1956 "A Compilation of historical data referring to the ethnography of Southern New England Indians," *Bulletin of the Archaeological Society of Connecticut*, Reprint No. 3.
ROUSE, IRVING
1951 "A survey of Indian River archaeology, Florida," *Yale University Publications in Anthropology*, No. 44.
1952 "Porto Rican prehistory," *New York Academy of Sciences, Scientific Survey of Porto Rico and the Virgin Islands*, Vol. XVIII, Nos. 3-4.
1960 "The classification of artifacts in archaeology," *American Antiquity*, Vol. XXV, No. 3: 313-23.
1965 "The place of 'peoples' in prehistoric research," *Journal of the Royal Anthropological Institute of Great Britain and Ireland*, Vol. XCV, Pt. 1: 1-15.
1966 "The strategy of archaeology," *Bulletin of the Eastern States Archaeological Federation*, No. 25:12-13.
1967 "Seriation in archaeology," in *American Historical Anthropology*, edited by C. L. Riley and W. W. Taylor, Jr. (Carbondale: University of Southern Illinois Press).
SEMENOV, S. A.
1964 *Prehistoric Technology: An Experimental Study of the Oldest Tools and Artifacts from Traces of Manufacture and Wear*, translated by M. W. Thompson (London: Cory, Adams, & Mackay).
SPAULDING, A. C.
1953 "Statistical techniques for the discovery of artifacts types," *American Antiquity*, Vol. XVIII, No. 4: 305-13.
STEWARD, J. H.
1954 "Types of types," *American Anthropologist*, Vol. LVI, No. 1:54-57.

WILLEY, G. R.
1953 "Prehistoric settlement patterns in the Viru Valley, Peru," *Bulletin of the Bureau of American Ethnology,* No. 155.

WILLEY, G. R., and PHILIP PHILLIPS
1958 *Method and Theory in American Archaeology* (Chicago: The University of Chicago Press).

III

JAMES DEETZ

Cultural Patterning of Behavior as Reflected by Archaeological Materials

Any man-made object, whether a bone awl or a guided missile, a spindle whorl or a cyclotron, is the end result of a series of decisions. Whereas organic entities are formed according to a genetic formula present at their moment of conception, objects of human manufacture have as their templates mental models pieced together over time from diverse sources. Orthodox typological methods employed in the analysis of archaeological material concentrate on the *process* by which an artifact has attained its final form rather than on the *reasons* for the object's possession of certain attributes; these methods are thus concerned more with "How?" than with "Why?" In asking *how* a tool was made, the classifier devises a set of criteria for classification which, when combined, produce a cluster of attributes constituting an *artifact type* (Wheat, Gifford, and Wasley, 1958; Krieger, 1944); the artifact type is then employed in the spatial and temporal integration of archaeological complexes. This approach has been successful in such operations, and most space-time frameworks have been achieved through its use in conjunction with modern techniques of archaeological chronology. However, the familiar artifact-type concept has proved singularly obstructive to a realization of the second stated aim of the prehistorian, that of reconstructing the culture of the makers of the object in question.

It is in the viewing of the artifact as the concrete expression of a mental template that we might move closer to the realization of this second goal. Each attribute exhibited by an artifact is present for some reason, and a vast majority of these attributes are employed for reasons of culturally conditioned choice on the part of the manufacturer. In fashioning a projectile point, the maker begins with an appropriate piece of raw material, proceeds through a series of operations, and ultimately produces a usable tool. At each step in the manufacture of this implement, the worker performs certain operations and *does not perform certain others*. He may choose to create side notches, but he could also leave the point unnotched, or make corner notches, or a stemmed base. He makes his decision, from among the available alternatives, for a reason; if this reason can be determined, a link will have been established between the maker and the artifact which may aid in the inference of certain aspects of his culture. It has long been recognized that cultural behavior is patterned, but the reasons for the patterning have not been given adequate consideration in the treatment of archaeological assemblages. Thus, to ask *why* certain attributes appear on a given object is more germane to cultural reconstruction than to inquire into the manner in which the object was made. A certain pottery type might be defined on the basis of rim profile, surface treatment, and design elements used in decoration. Such description is concerned essentially with means of achievement rather than with the reasons for the selection of these three attributes. To say that Turtle Creek Incised is defined by direct rims is also to indicate that the potter produced a direct rim when making this type. It does not ask why a direct rim was chosen in preference to a collared rim, or any other rim profile equally available to the potter but rejected in favor of the direct profile. This approach asks the same questions, and fails similarly to ask the others, of every diagnostic attribute constituting any type defined in this manner.

An inquiry into the reasons for choosing certain attributes in favor of others in the creation of artifacts requires a conceptual scheme and methodology different from those previously employed in archaeological interpretation. Basic to both methodology and conceptualization is the description of each artifact in a discrete and rigorous form, in the most microscopic terms possible; each attribute that makes artifact A different from artifact B must be recorded and must be considered by itself and in combination with all others. The use of such a technique leaves one open to the charge of splitting, in the time-honored lumper-splitter opposition. Such an opposition is actually irrelevant, since splitting and lumping are actually two levels of a single analytical process. It is significant that among anthropologists this opposition has seen its fullest development in the realm of archaeology. Structural linguistics, certainly the most conceptually rigorous discipline within the broad field of cultural anthropology, has never had its opposed camps of lumpers and splitters. If it had, the splitters would probably be those linguists concerned with phonemic analysis, whereas the lumpers would be performing morphemic analysis and synthesis of more complex linguistic forms. But such an opposition could not reasonably have emerged because phonemes and morphemes are parts of a single structural analysis of a patterned cultural phenomenon–an explanation that is germane to the question of an analogous opposition in the area of artifact analysis. It will be shown that the discrete isolation of all attributes in an artifact assemblage is in many ways analogous to the isolation of allophones in a language, and that their subsequent combination into culturally meaningful units is very similar to the isolation of morphemes and their constituent allomorphs. To state the same proposition in different terms, meaningful attribute groupings cannot be derived until their constituent attributes have been considered separately.

To describe the methodology and theoretical considerations employed in this type of analysis, an example will be given that is illustrative of such an approach, and additional examples will be drawn from the literature. Our principal example is an attribute analysis of a sample of rim sherds from a three-component Arikara site in Central South Dakota (the Medicine Crow Site, 39BF2). This study, outlined in detail elsewhere (Deetz, 1960a), demonstrates a relationship between individual design attributes and certain changes in the social organization of the Arikara during the eighteenth century. By treating the attributes separately with respect to the manner in which they formed clusters, it was shown that a high degree of clustering was a function of the regulation of attribute choice within a framework of matrilineal descent and matrilocal residence. When these features of the social structure were altered in later components, there was a corresponding decrease in the degree of clustering, and the attributes exhibited a more random mode of occurrence. Attribute choice was conditioned by training of daughters by mothers, and when this transmission of attributes between generations was disrupted, there was also a change in reasons for attribute choice. Women who once selected certain combinations because they were modal for their lineage and residence group later made their choice with greater freedom, a trend reflected in a lower degree of patterning in the resultant artifacts. Furthermore, the total design vocabulary of the people underwent change, and a somewhat different modal set of attributes was produced in later components.

Bases of Attribute Choice

Since the conditioning of choice is the result of a series of external factors, it should be possible to determine which of these factors are involved in various selections exhibited by the artifact. Although the reason for the selection of every attribute probably cannot be determined, an area of choice conditioning can be defined that will provide further insight into matters of attribute choice. At least five pairs of opposed bases for choice can be postulated. These bases are not complementary, but cut across each other; only within each of the five pairs does mutual exclusion hold.

Functional Choice vs. Nonfunctional Choice The maker of an artifact will select certain attributes because they are essential to the proper functioning of the object. In the manufacture of a stone knife, the selection of a sharp edge in preference to a blunted edge is dictated by considerations of efficiency. In the analysis of Arikara ceramics cited above, it was determined that tabs–small projections on the lips of rim sherds–were in all likelihood functionally significant, since they were associated with square lip profiles in approximately half of all cases, and were rarely found with braced lips. These projections would serve to steady a vessel suspended from a cord passed around its neck and through a pair of strap handles. In many cases, the tabs were at right angles to handles on the vessel's rim. The tabs' low association with lip bracing–a beading along the lip–is also explicable in terms of function, since the brace serves a similar purpose. The selection of tabs is therefore largely a matter of the functional utility of that attribute. In view of the high degree of association with square unbeaded lips, the designation of a type defined by both of these attributes (among others) recognizes this association, but does not explicitly indicate the functional and contingent relationship between the two.

In marked contrast to this type of attribute are those that are nonfunctional. Determination that an attribute lacks function is often a difficult matter, but the difficulty in no way reduces the importance of recognizing a class of nonfunctional reasons governing attribute choice. The selection of herringbone decoration on a ceramic piece, rather than slanted bars or parallel lines, has little or no functional significance, except as herringbone may serve as some form of identification to the owner. Even if the exception were the case, certain choices are made in which functional utility is of minor importance.

Functional reasons for attribute rejection must also be considered. For example, complex designs are not used by Yurok-Karok women in decorating cooking baskets. It might be thought that the rejection of complex designs in this instance can be attributed to the function of the basket–i.e., that fancy designs are reserved for fancy baskets–but this is not the case. Rather, rejection is due to the fact that complex designs create more breaks in the overlay material, and thus render the cooking vessel less watertight (O'Neale, 1932, p. 63). In fact, many of the designs said by the Yurok-Karok to be the most difficult to execute are used *more* frequently on cooking baskets, whereas caps and fancy baskets are more frequently decorated with easy designs.

Imitative Choice vs. Innovative Choice In an imitative / innovative opposition, a choice represents either an imitation of an existing form or varying degrees of departure from the norm. In the relationship between ceramic attributes and kinship change cited above, the meaningful clusters existed because there was a high degree of emulation of mothers by daughters. This could be termed linear imitation, as opposed to generational imitation. The latter led probably to the dissolution of these clusters later in time, since a greater number of design combinations resulted from a synchronic interchange of attributes. Intercultural contact is indicated by an external interchange of attributes between different groups, and imitative attributes serve as an index of the type and intensity of diffusion. Archaeological syntheses abound with statements such as "the cord impression in phase A ceramics indicates contact with the people of phase B, whose ceramics show this trait in a large number of cases." Since imitative reasons for the choice of certain attributes can be put forth to explain such contact phenomena, it follows that the nature of this contact might also be determined. In late Arikara ceramics, those attributes which can be confidently attributed to contact with other groups occur in clusters that are more discrete than the clusters of the Arikara pottery itself. This would suggest that the adoption of the attributes was in the form of complete or near-complete templates, and resulted from the movement of women from group to group, since the total configuration was adopted initially. Subsequently the process of imitation–both linear and generational–took effect, and the clusters can be seen to have dispersed in later components. Innovative reasons for the selection of a given attribute mark the initiation of a new attribute. Thus, innovation of this type is instrumental in contributing to the total attribute vocabulary employed in the creation of any artifact. The Medicine Crow pottery abounds with such attributes, seen on only one or two sherds from a single house, and doubtless represents an individual choice, perhaps never to be repeated. Such innovation could come about through accident, inspiration, or whim. This type of attribute is highly important, since such attributes can form a fountainhead of new artifactual configurations.

Contingent Choice vs. Free Choice Attributes chosen for reasons of contingency are those the selection of which is made necessary by the prior choice of another attribute, as opposed to attributes freely chosen. In the analysis cited here as an example, a number of contingent attributes were isolated. One of these, parallel-line decoration on the lips of the Medicine Crow pots, is contingent on the prior selection of one of a number of thickened lip profiles, since the typical design, three or more parallel lines, could not be achieved on the earlier, more narrow, square lips. Thus this design element appears only when another attribute–thickened or otherwise expanded lip surfaces–also appears.

An excellent example of a contingent attribute is provided by the bore diameter of seventeenth- and eighteenth-century English clay tobacco pipes. Harrington (1954) notes that during the period 1590 through 1850, bore diameters of the stems of these pipes decreased from 9/64 to 4/64 inch at a rather linear rate. This was not the result of a free choice of diameter, but rather was contingent on two other attributes of these pipes – stem length and stem diameter. Stems became longer and slimmer during this period, and as a result the wire used to bore the stem – wire inherited by a boy from his father as part of the pipemaker's tool kit – was too thick to ream the thinner stems that had become fashionable. Thus, a finer wire had to be selected, in order to effect the reaming without breaking the stem, and as a result the bore diameter decreased.

One other example from seventeenth-century colonial archaeology is pertinent here. Bricks used at both Jamestown and Plymouth underwent rather similar changes during the course of the century. In each instance, bricks became thicker, wider, and shorter. The increase in thickness and width can probably be attributed to the use of inferior mortar, since both the Plymouth and Jamestown colonists used a mortar manufactured from clam and oyster shells. With poorer mortar, a wider bearing surface is desirable, hence the widening of the bricks. Moreover, for a given number of mortar joints, thicker bricks make a higher wall. Given such changes, if one wished to maintain the brick's weight at a constant figure, its length must be reduced. It is significant that in the case of the Plymouth bricks, in spite of a change of 1/2 inch in thickness and 1 inch in length, the cubic content and weight remained unchanged (Deetz, 1960b, p. 5). That brick weight can be of considerable importance is indicated by a strike of Baltimore bricklayers in the eighteenth century, brought on in protest of a minor change in brick dimensions that effectively increased their weight. Thus, in this case, brick length is an example of a contingent attribute governed by two other functional attributes.

A final example of a contingent attribute is provided by the designs of Pomo diagonally twined basketry. Selection of a particular technique of twining, known as *shuset* (Mason, 1904, pp. 455-56, Fig. 20), produces a design vocabulary characterized by diagonal elements. This twining technique, a form of twilled twining, automatically sets diagonal elements into the body of the basket if weaving materials of contrasting colors are chosen. The same relationship holds between simple twilling and diagonal design elements. Once the technique is chosen, the form of the design is completely contingent on the weave, and perfect correlation between technique of manufacture and elements of design obtains.

Expedient Choice vs. Patterned Choice Certain attributes may be chosen purely for expediency, whereas others are chosen because the patterning of cultural behavior dictates their choice. The manufacture of a flint knife may be achieved simply by flaking the edge of a particularly suitable flake to fashion a cutting edge. Such an implement is no less effective than the knife that has been fully flaked over all its surfaces as a result of choices made out of regard for patterned imitation. Reasons of expediency for the choice of a given attribute are much like innovative reasons, but this mode of selection is keyed to the immediate circumstances of making rather than the maker's inventiveness. A large portion of Chumash chipped-stone artifacts have attributes that were chosen primarily for expediency: flakes of a wide variety of shapes have one edge worked to a usable form, but beyond this single edge, there is little that reflects patterned behavior in these tools. Patterned choices are primarily a function of the desire to imitate, and it is the repetition of attribute groups that produces the patterns observable.

Technologically Conditioned Choice vs. Nontechnologically Conditioned Choice In many cases, the choice of a given attribute is limited by the material selected for the manufacture of a given object. Thus, chopping tools of the Anyathians of Paleolithic Burma (Movius, 1956, p. 90, Figs. 121-25) are roughly rectangular, since the raw material utilized is fossil wood, which fractures only along certain lines and planes. External factors also influence attributes of this type. The initial development of stoneware in Northern Europe was in part a function of the hardwoods there present, which when burned yielded temperatures of adequate intensity to produce hardpaste pottery. Attributes that are a function of limitations of the materials and technological processes used are of a relatively low order of reliability in constructing typologies, since there are too many independently variable external factors involved. In the Medicine Crow pottery, attributes such as color, hardness, and thickness are so clearly a function of the technology that they were purposely omitted from the analysis. Of course, even attributes that result from this type of selection conditioning may have a social meaning, since the technology is passed through the generations by a person-to-person mechanism. In contrast to those attributes chosen because of limitations dictated by material and technological sophistication are those that are in no way conditioned by these factors. These will include all of those attributes chosen for previously stated reasons.

Operations Yielded by the Foregoing Concepts

From the foregoing it can be seen that the attributes forming any given typological configuration are likely to have been of such diverse origin, and of such variable significance to the maker, that any multiattribute typological construct will probably be artificial and of a relatively low order of utility in cultural interpretation. Only by viewing each constituent attribute in terms of its possible significance and its reasons for selection over others in its class can one approximate the significance of the mental model or template employed by its maker. Even under these circumstances, to make such a determination in every instance is impossible, but a significant percentage of instances can be so treated, and these represent an important advance in the direction of finer and more meaningful *cultural* interpretation. An approach to archaeological analysis along the lines of the concepts outlined above makes possible a variety of operations heretofore relatively unavailable to the prehistorian.

Analysis of Change in Nonmaterial Culture Artifacts can be treated as indicators of certain aspects of change in nonmaterial culture. The Arikara case, in which attribute variation formed a reflection of kinship change, is illustrative of this application of the method, and any other sex-associated aspect of material culture will probably behave similarly upon the disruption or reinforcement of the social channels of technological-knowledge transmission.

Analysis of Intercultural Contact The nature of intercultural contact can be demonstrated more precisely by inspection of the attribute configurations of donor and receiver cultures, in instances where these can be postulated. At least four modes of occurence of such configurations can be suggested and demonstrated in the available literature.

Migration or Conquest. The first of these modes is characterized by major coherent configurations in which a high number of attributes are found in repeated association in both donor and receiver cultures. A majority of items in both entities show convergence and/or identity. This is expectable in the event of template movement, which can take place only through population movement, since the people are the vehicles of the templates. If the artifacts exhibiting these repetitive configurations can be shown to be normally the products of both sexes, this mode of occurrence should indicate migration and/or conquest by both sexes. If the convergence seems sex-linked in terms of industries, probably with male manufacturers, then a military conquest or selective migration can be postulated, without a supporting female population. Conversely, migration and conquest cannot be confidently postulated in situations where template convergence cannot be demonstrated, since this is the primary requirement for such proof. Even if a majority of the attributes of the donor assemblage are repeated in the receiver culture, major population translocations cannot be postulated if there is not an equally high number of identical configurations.

Limited Mobility. The second mode is characterized by minor coherent configurations, occurring only in certain industries. These industries are likely to be identifiable, in most cases, with a single sex. Such a mode should indicate regularized exogamy, slave trade, or any other mechanism that produces limited mobility of members of one sex between cultures. If single sex association is low, limited mobility of both sexes may be indicated. Whereas, according to the first model, cases of migration or conquest will show a high number of substitutive changes in artifact assemblages, this second mode should normally show additive change only, since wholesale population and hence template displacement is lacking.

Stimulus or Secondary Diffusion. A third mode is characterized by a lack or insignificant degree of recurrent association in receiver and donor cultures. Similarities exist only on the attribute level, and the method of employing these attributes may be quite different in each assemblage. This mode of occurrence is indicative of the process usually referred to as stimulus or secondary diffusion, specifically indicating such processes as visiting, limited social intercourse, and unstructured, temporary exchange of people between groups.

Trade. A fourth mode of contact, with somewhat different indications than those indicated above, is that of trade. Under conditions of primitive trade, one would normally expect movement of objects from culture to culture without an accompanying movement of templates. The presence in the receiver culture of these objects sans templates may affect the templates of the receivers, but in a manner different from those previously discussed. Since only the objects are transmitted, the choice conditioning that has created the templates does not follow. One would expect, in such circumstances, configurations in which identity is often irrational, in cases where it is used at all. Such instances as the reproduction of casting seams on flint, and clay copies of metal tools, in Neolithic sites in Europe and the Near East, are relevant.

Analysis of Technology The method outlined above also permits a more precise reconstruction of a given technology in terms of the templates used in production. We can more closely approximate the significant construct as it existed in the mind of the maker, rather than derive what may well be a totally artificial device. This approach has been applied to a sample of Chumash stone artifacts with considerable success. Although a full description of the process involved in this application is beyond the scope of this paper, the method and preliminary results should be summarized. A large sample of chipped stone, including waste flakes, cores, and tools, from a historic Chumash site in inland Santa Barbara county, California, was used for this study. The sample was progressively subdivided according to a series of attribute classes that represent choice conditioning of the types described above. Through this method, it is possible to describe the modal technique used in the manufacture of stone tools, as well as less frequently employed methods. The sample was subdivided first according to flake derivation (interior or exterior of raw material block), and then progressively, according to flake fragmentation (complete flake, or proximal, medial, or distal segment), working (use of flaking or pressure flaking on one, two, or three edges), bifacial or unifacial chipping, weight, color, and size. Each level of this breakdown represents a choice that faced the chert knapper. By cross-checking from level to level for significant configurations and high or low degree of association in various areas, it is possible to suggest the choice conditioning that obtained in many cases. For example, since most proximal flakes appear in the earlier-divided category of outside flakes, the latter would seem to have been normally selected for derivation of proximal flakes from which to fashion certain tools. Later in the breakdown, similar tools are seen in differently derived categories, which would seem to indicate more than one mode of manufacture. In this case, as with any application of this technique, an initial breakdown of choice types should be kept in mind. High association of attributes indicates choices in the realm of contingent, patterned, imitative, and functional reasons, and, to a lesser degree, technologically conditioned reasons. Low association, on the other hand, indicates innovative, nonfunctional, expedient, or nontechnologically conditioned choice. Within each of these categories, there are usually adequate indications of precisely which type of choice reason is involved. Although this process may seem to inject a subjective element into the analysis, it appears for the first time at this level, and is therefore insulated by a series of earlier, explicitly objective divisions. Contingent reasons for choice are self-evident in most cases, as the examples cited indicate. Choices arising from imitation and patterning, extended to relatively complete configurations and thus producing high associations within certain attribute clusters, are the result of similar cultural dynamics, and produce similar interpretive results. In the areas of functional and technological significance, one can normally make determinations with little difficulty. Innovative attributes are usually determined by their rarity, and expediency as a basis for choice is therefore the only remaining cause of low associations. Most choices in the Chumash sample seem to be a function of expediency. The presence of similar tools in different final categories (i.e., multiple manufacturing methods) indicates a low degree of patterning in the production of specific objects. Frequent use of medial flakes for tool manufacture is indicative of a functional-technological basis for this selection, since thicker, more even segments normally derive from the centers of flakes. Although the mean weight of used vs. discarded flakes differs by as much as 300 per cent, with utilized flakes being heavier, the mean length difference between categories is of the order of 5 to 10 per cent. Thickness in this case seems to be the most important flake attribute governing choice of suitable blanks for tool manufacture. The relatively low degree of consistent patterning indicates that the templates involved in this assemblage are of extremely variable dimensions. As a result, one can postulate a low order of traditional or imitative choice conditioning, with most choices being made according to the needs of the moment. Since the Chumash of inland Santa Barbara county may well be coastal people using this area as a seasonal food-gathering zone, rather like the Shoshonian family band model (Steward, 1955), this result would be completely expectable. The same analysis applied to samples from coastal sites may produce more patterned, more traditional results. In any case, standard typologies derived from material such as this will produce categories with close internal similarities, but little social significance. The complete analysis of this material has yet to be accomplished; when it is, there is reason to expect a more succinct statement of the social implications of the technology employed, on the basis of the extremely promising preliminary results.

Analysis of Seriation Another use of the method herein described is in more precise and more meaningful seriation. If ceramic types are further reduced to their constituent attributes, this method of analysis permits formulation of a statement concerning the trends in attribute popularity that are reflected in typological succession. Two firmly defined and fully accepted pottery types, Talking Crow Ware (Smith, 1951) and Stanley Braced Rim Ware (Lehmer, 1954, pp. 42ff) account for most of the Medicine Crow pottery. Viewed at the type level of classification, ceramic changes at the Medicine Crow site involve the increase of Stanley Ware at the expense of Talking Crow Ware, a simple two-type seriation that is repeated in Arikara sequences from the entire Missouri Basin in South Dakota during the eighteenth century. However, the change involved from one type to another, which is usually considered to be a simple case of gradual substitution, can actually be seen to be a very complex development at the attribute level. Those attributes that are characteristic of Stanley Ware were positively selected for a series of different reasons. Some of the change involved is a function of contact with other groups in the vicinity and the subsequent adoption of their attribute configurations; others result from internal change, a function of contingency, as in the case of thickened lips and certain designs cited above, or from accelerated innovative choice and combination, due to the removal of the cultural restraint formerly provided by matrilocality and matrilineal descent. The change at Medicine Crow is a relatively smooth and gradual one. In other cases, reduction of types to constituent attributes would suggest that the typological succession was more abrupt and sudden, indicating phenomena other than in-place development of one type into another. In either case, categories derived as multiattribute types may vary considerably in the number of shared attributes, and only a further reduction of these categories will indicate the exact nature of the change in the ceramic sequence, particularly with regard to the cultural dynamics involved.

Conclusion

This paper has done little more than to suggest certain courses to follow in analytical areas as yet unexplored. If the basic postulates are reasonably sound, and if subsequent applications are as fruitful as those already undertaken, there may be much to be learned from these concepts and techniques.

References

Deetz, James

1960a "An archaeological approach to kinship change in eighteenth century Arikara culture," unpublished PhD. thesis, Harvard University Department of Anthropology.

1960b "The Howlands in Rocky Nook, an archaeological and historical study," supplement to *The Howland Quarterly*, Vol. XXIV, No. 4.

Harrington, J. C.

1954 "Dating stem fragments of seventeenth and eighteenth century clay tobacco pipes," *Quarterly Bulletin, Virginia Archaeological Society*, Vol. IX, No. 1.

KRIEGER, A. D.
1944 "The typological concept," *American Antiquity*, Vol. IX:271-88.

LEHMER, D. J.
1954 "Archaeological investigations in the Oahe Dam area, South Dakota," *River Basin Survey Papers*, No. 7, Smithsonian Institution, Bureau of American Ethnology, Bulletin 158.

MASON, O. T.
1904 "Aboriginal American basketry: Studies in a textile art without machinery," *Annual Report*, Smithsonian Institution, 1902.

MOVIUS, H. L.
1956 "The Old Stone Age," in *Man, Culture and Society*, edited by H. Shapiro, (Oxford: Oxford University Press).

O'NEALE, LILA M.
1932 "Yurok-Karok basket weavers," *University of California Publications in American Archaeology and Ethnology*, Vol. XXXII, No. 1 (Berkeley: University of California Press).

SMITH, C. S.
1951 "Pottery types from the Talking Crow site, Fort Randall Reservoir, S.D.," *Plains Archaeological Conference Newsletter*, Vol. IV, No. 3.

STEWARD, JULIAN
1955 "The Great Basin Shoshonian Indians: An example of a family level of sociocultural adaptation," *Theory of Culture Change* (Urbana: University of Illinois Press).

WHEAT, J. B., J. C. GIFFORD, and WILLIAM WASLEY
1958 "Ceramic variety, type cluster and ceramic system in Southwestern pottery analysis," *American Antiquity*, Vol. XXIV:34-37.

IV

ROBERT ASCHER

Time's Arrow and the Archaeology of a Contemporary Community

More than ninety-nine per cent of human biological and cultural evolution happened before history was invented. What can be known about man's behavior before history, therefore, must be learned from the alterations he has made to the natural world in shaping it to his purposes. Traces of man's activity, in the shape of reordered matter, as well as occasional traces of man himself, are the facts of prehistory.

The kind and amount of information we have about early human behavior are strictly limited, for some of the things men did left barely discernible traces and much of what men might have done could leave no traces at all. Moreover, the acts that turned natural objects into archaeological facts are unintelligible to the uninitiated and far from easy for experts in the science and art of prehistory to unravel. If the absence of certain facts circumscribes possible knowledge of the past, facts that are available but formidable to interpret pose a challenge. Thus, the initial question of prehistory can be formulated: How can information be extracted from the results of behavior stored in matter by men remote in both time and culture?

In interpretational astronomy, the evolution of remote stars is reconstructed on the basis of their behavior in different phases of evolution. The astronomer observes the relative brightness of stars, listens to stellar emissions, and draws on the regularities of local physics to infer past astronomical phenomena. To infer the past behavior of men or stars, in archaeology or astronomy, descriptions of known behavior must be introduced. Surely, prehistorians know that they must utilize the present to infer the past, but they do not know what of the present should be observed, and too little is known about the regularities that govern human behavior.

This paper is concerned with the first problem: What of the present should be observed? I am interested in the notion that every contemporary community is destroying as well as renewing itself, and I believe that observations of this process are of heuristic value in making sense out of the remains of the distant past. In developing this idea, I shall first consider disorganization and its relation to archaeology, and then, by way of example, extend the discussion to a particular community. I take for granted that the physical mass of part of a community, or of an entire community, as it moves through time and space, is as profitable a unit for study as is the standard artifact class or some similarly small unit.

Disorganization and Archaeology

"Inhabited" and "Ghost" Phases Ordinarily, the existence of a community is equated with change in the direction of organization. In the terminology of the late Norbert Wiener (1954), a human community is a temporary island, pocket, or enclave of decreasing entropy in the midst of a universe where entropy is inevitably on the increase. From a distance–that is, from the long-term overview of a hypothetical giant–this picture is correct and comforting. A view from close to the ground shows that, in every community, disorganization and organization proceed simultaneously at different rates, and at different rates at different times. From the inception of any community, at every point in its "inhabited" phase, and during its gradual decline, people and nature in combination act as agents of disorganization.

As an example, consider what can happen in the familiar American automobile yard. One such yard, founded in 1956, is located on the outskirts of Ithaca, New York.[1] The yard holds the remains of fifty-six vehicles, thirty-nine of which are passenger sedans, ranging in date of manufacture from 1935 to 1958. The distribution of all the vehicles is such that the older members, in an advanced state of decomposition, are toward one end of the rectangular yard, and the more recent, less decomposed, vehicles are at the opposite end of the yard. Table I (p. 45) shows the major missing parts of ten Chevrolets, constituting one-third of the passenger sedan population. The data imply that ordering (manufacture of automobiles) is followed by reordering (accumulation of automobiles in the yard), and then by disordering and reordering (selective removal of parts and their use elsewhere), and so on.

Because the existence of a community is often erroneously equated with continuous unidirectional change, it is held that when ordering ceases, the community halts. The fault in this view is best revealed by considering "ghost" towns. Towns without people are thought to have taken on static form because nothing novel is added, but observations of such towns over even short periods show that change continues in the absence of people.

[1] The data on the automobile yard were gathered by Mr. Thomas Greaves, a graduate student, and Miss Allison MacLeod, an undergraduate, during a project for a course in interpretive archaeology at Cornell University in the spring of 1966. Subsequently, the author worked at the yard with one of the students. I thank both students for permission to use the data. I also thank the owner of the yard, Mr. Nelson Eddy, for access to his property.

TABLE I
Parts Removed from Ten Chevrolets in an Automobile Yard

0 = Removed + = Remains − = Not Original Equipment

Year of Manufacture	'36	'39	'41	'47	'48	'49	'50	'51	'52	'54
Block	+	+	0	0	0	0	0	0	0	0
Carburetor	+	+	0	0	+	0	0	0	0	0
Distributor	+	+	0	0	0	0	+	0	0	0
Starter	+	+	0	0	0	0	0	0	0	0
Fan	+	+	0	0	0	0	0	0	0	0
Radiator	0	0	0	0	0	0	0	0	0	0
Horn	0	+	+	+	+	0	0	+	0	0
Air Cleaner	0	0	+	0	+	+	0	0	0	0
Battery	0	0	0	0	0	0	0	0	0	0
Headlights	+	+	0	0	0	0	0	0	0	0
Windshield	+	+	+	+	+	+	0	+	+	0
Rear Window	+	+	+	+	+	+	+	+	+	0
Front Bumper	+	+	+	0	+	+	0	+	0	0
Grill	+	+	+	+	+	+	0	+	+	0
Hubcaps	0	0	0	0	0	0	0	0	0	0
Hood Ornament	0	0	0	0	0	+	0	+	0	0
Hood	+	0	0	0	+	+	0	+	0	0
Right Fender	+	+	+	+	0	+	+	+	+	0
Right Door	+	+	+	+	+	+	+	+	+	+
Front Seat Springs	+	+	+	+	0	+	+	+	+	+
Heater	−	+	0	0	−	+	+	+	+	+
Transmission	+	0	0	0	0	0	0	0	0	0
Differential	+	+	0	0	0	0	0	0	0	0
Right Front Wheel	+	+	0	0	0	0	0	+	0	0
Right Front Rim	0	0	0	0	0	0	0	+	0	0
Right Front Tire	0	0	0	0	0	0	0	+	0	0
Driveshaft	+	0	0	0	0	0	+	+	0	0
Radio	−	−	0	0	−	+	−	0	0	0

TABLE II
Rust on Ten Chevrolets in an Automobile Yard

− = Removed 1 = No rust 2 = Light rust 3 = Heavy rust 4 = Holes due to rust 5 = Material decomposed 6 = Material trace only

Year of Manufacture	'36	'39	'41	'47	'48	'49	'50	'51	'52	'54
Roof	3	4	4	3	2	2	3	2	2	2
Hood	3	−	−	−	2	2	−	1	−	−
Trunk	3	3	3	3	3	2	3	2	2	1
Right Rear Fender	4	4	4	4	−	4	4	4	4	3
Right Rear Wheel Well	3	4	4	4	4	4	4	4	4	2
Floorboard	6	5	6	3	4	4	4	4	3	4
Right Front Door Panel (Chrome)	3	3	3	4	4	3	4	2	1	1
Front Bumper	4	3	4	−	3	3	−	3	−	−
Trim	3	2	2	2	1	1	2	2	1	1
Grill	3	2	5	4	3	2	−	2	3	−
Instrument Framing	3	3	5	5	3	3	3	3	2	1

In all "ghost" towns, natural agents are disorganizing matter that was once arranged in patterns by human effort. The fact that all change in "ghost" towns is in the direction of diminishing order, and that the agency is natural rather than human and natural, should not obscure the issue: a community vanishes only when all of the effort congealed in matter is totally disorganized. It is true that ordering ceases in the absence of man, but change in the direction of disorganization is continuous with him and without him.

For illustration, we return to the case of the automobile yard and consider one natural agent of decomposition, namely, rusting. An automobile begins to rust as soon as it is used, and rusting probably is a factor leading to its deposit in the yard. Various stages of rusting could be observed on the automobiles in the sample, as indicated in Table II. In early stages, the metallic surfaces turn reddish-brown and become rough and pitted; in later stages, the metal turns to a scaly, porous mass. As time passes the cars will fall apart and certain information that the automobile might be made to reveal about American culture will be gradually lost. An observer at some far future time will find nothing at all.

Archaeological Phase After the "inhabited" and "ghost" phases of a community's existence, the archaeologist enters to introduce yet another irregularity in the long-term unbroken curve of disorganization.

The romance some find in archaeology derives from the notion that any turn of the shovel can yield the unusual or the unexpected. Although overstated, this notion is essentially correct. But high uncertainty, resulting from the limited predictability of the course of excavation, is more troublesome than it is romantic; the act of excavation, the disturbance of items suspended in the earth, itself produces disorganization. Specifically, disorganization is introduced because contexts, defined as purposeful arrangements in space and time, are not predictable, and awareness of them may postdate their destruction.

To understand this clearly, imagine the excavation of an ancient community that has become a buried cube of large dimensions. At the start of the excavation the perceptual field of the observer is limited to the surface of the cube lying parallel to the ground. The excavation begins by horizontally and vertically partitioning the cube into a number of smaller units, and proceeds by systematically observing, recording, and removing the contents of each unit. Each advance of the shovel uncovers a fraction of the cube; arrangement of all items with each other is possible only at the close of the work. Observations and recordings in any one arbitrary unit are guided by knowledge of other arbitrary units already excavated. It is impossible to observe and record everything, but everything must be removed. Thus, indicators of a context already partially destroyed by removal become evident as the excavation proceeds, when earlier failures in observation and recording can no longer be repaired.

There are, of course, difficulties beyond those inherent in excavation: the recognition of man's purposeful arrangements depends on *distinguishing between* the action of natural agents and the action of human agents. Generally, the elapsed time between the abandonment and the excavation of a community yields a good inverse relationship to the amount of information the excavation can be expected to produce. In areas where rain is heavy, and lightning storms are common, a few decades are enough to decay all contexts. In an even shorter period of time, more subtle changes can occur. Worms, for example, can alter the distribution of objects and produce novel arrangements, as was demonstrated in a series of elegant experiments by Charles Darwin and his son, Horace (Darwin, 1901). Indeed, the heavy use in archaeological literature of the ambiguous term "feature" to describe any apparent patterning of objects is a tacit admission that the contributions of natural and human factors to an archaeological matrix are often indistinguishable.

It is illuminating to review some archaeological situations that have achieved notoriety. A feature common to most of these cases is an exceptional set of circumstances that have served to reduce the magnitude of the problems discussed above. In August 79 A.D., for example, a shower of ashes and pumice from erupting Mt. Vesuvius descended on Pompeii, suddenly and instantly terminating the "inhabited" phase of its existence and sealing it off from agents of natural disorganization. As we would expect, many of the instances similar to this involve the excavation of burials. In general, a burial is a below-ground, spatial-temporal arrangement of a corpse, usually with other matter, and if not a deliberate attempt at creating a durable context, it is nevertheless the ordering activity most resistant to disorganization. Burials that are particularly resistant to decay and rich in content, but have not been attractive enough to invite pilfering, appear with regularity in the annals of popular archaeology.

But Pompeii and instances like it are clearly special cases. In most situations, disorganization is gropingly interrupted by the spade, and in every archaeological situation observation is limited to the results of the process at one point in time. The path of disorganization from "inhabited," through "ghost," and on to archaeological disturbance is irreversible, but it must be figuratively reversed when inferring past human behavior. This creative task can lead to alternate inferences, any one of which might be as plausible as any other. Ideally, the best solution is the one derived from the accurate retracing of the path of disorganization, but because so little is understood about the path, there is no sound basis for the elimination of any solution.

Information about the path of disorganization can be found in data that are becoming but are not yet archaeological. Such data are present in every "inhabited" community. Since this is true, it should be possible and profitable to look at a contemporary community with the aim of learning how it starts to become the past as it moves from the present into the future.

Fig. 1. The oldest section of the Seri community at Desemboque. Two houses once stood in the area depicted.

TRENDS IN A COMMUNITY

Prehistoric man extracted energy from his environment by some combination of hunting, fishing, and gathering. This way of life set upper bounds on the development of, for example, the number of occupational specialties and the size of the population. Today, there are still a few communities with similar means of subsistence; by analogy, these communities parallel the kinds of communities that existed for most of human history. It is thus reasonable, in extending the discussion to a specific community, to select one that fits this general class – the Seri Indian community in the state of Sonora, Mexico (Ascher, 1961a; 1961b).

The Seri live on a strip of coastal desert about seventy miles long and four miles wide, along the Gulf of California. Although the strip is arid, with an average rainfall of less than 10 inches per year, falling mostly in late summer, microclimatic conditions encourage the flowering of desert plant life. The Gulf forms a natural trap for fish and marine mammals, and the waters are rich in marine food. In spite of these resources, the scarcity of fresh water has constituted in the past, and presently is, the critical inhibitor to occupancy by large terrestrial animals, including man.

The Seri are fishermen; secondarily they gather the fruits of the desert; and to a lesser degree they hunt small game. The sea turtle is most important in Seri economy, but other products of the sea are also taken, including

Fig. 2. A 5,000-year-old archaeological midden. In another 5,000 years from now, Desemboque will probably appear similar to the site shown here.

sea lions, crabs, clams, and several varieties of fish. Women and children gather the desert fruits; men do the fishing and hunting. The Seri utilize a number of camps in addition to Desemboque, the main base at the strip's northern extreme. In pursuit of food, fishermen and their families traverse the territory during the summer months, stop at camps, and eventually return to the main base.

Today, 400 years after they were first seen by Europeans, there are about 240 Seri. Until recently, the Seri camped on Tiburon Island in the Gulf, and sometime earlier their land included a large mainland region. The original occupancy, which occurred at least 500 years ago, stemmed either from Baja California, via the Gulf of California; or from the north, via an overland route or routes. There are no reliable figures of past population size, but former territory and length of occupancy suggest that there were once considerably more Seri than today.

Judging from independent studies, spaced at approximately 30-year intervals (Ascher, 1962; Kroeber, 1931; McGee, 1898), Seri-Western relations have been sporadic, with the result that the Seri have been neither converted to Christianity nor displaced by Mexican interests. Major Seri-Western contact is between fishermen and Mexican entrepreneurs who have been purchasing fish and turtles in exchange for cash and equipment since the late 1930's. The strength of Western intrusion can be inferred from declining population alone, and the fact that Seri garbage includes rusty tin cans, worn-out factory-made shoes, and plastic containers is sufficient warning to those who would prefer to view them as a "Stone Age" people.

Now let us turn to a few trends viewed as systematic movements along the path of disorganization.

Smearing and Blending The main base of Desemboque stretches one-fifth of a mile along a small bay, the limits of which, the Seri point out, form natural boundaries. In the 34 years since its founding, the community has been developing north to south along the Gulf frontage such that the entrance to almost every house faces the water. Two conspicuous features on the landscape are wattle-and-daub or cardboard-and-string houses and garbage mounds.

When Desemboque is overlayed with a checkerboard grid system of 25-foot squares, the varying extraorganic matter in the squares reveals a space-time sequence corresponding to the development of the community. Density, that is, is greater in units falling on the newer portions of the community and less in older areas. Another regularity emerges when the squares are compared in terms of uniformity of distribution of matter. The more recent sections of the community show discontinuous distributions, with large gaps, for example, separating house from house, garbage heap from garbage heap, and house from garbage heap. By contrast, on that portion of the landscape where daily activities of the community were once, but are no longer held, there is less dense, but more equal, distribution of decaying matter.

The movement of the Seri community into the past, then, has the effect of smearing or blending. Clear delineations disappear. The rapid deposition of windblown sand in conjunction with degeneration of form by chemical decomposition is partly responsible for this effect. There are also contributing human factors in the first stages of smearing and at every stage in its progression. For example, a Seri, in walking from one point of the community to another, chooses the shorter path, oblivious of the ubiquitous heaps of fishbone and carapace that at least one non-Seri consciously avoided. The results of this combination of factors can be clearly seen in Fig. 1, which depicts the oldest section of the community. In the future, Desemboque may well look like the 5,000-year-old archaeological midden shown in Fig. 2.

Cycling of Serviceable Material A. L. Kroeber, who visited the Seri in 1930, wrote (1931): "The Seri mode of life led to many instabilities with makeshifts often actually more in use, but finished or efficient types of artifacts seemingly latent and sporadically emerging in the stream of their culture." Kroeber's insight is understandable in terms of the recycling of scarce materials in an environment where scarcity is a universal descriptor. The material contents of the Seri community are ordered, disordered, and ordered again, and then again. The cycle cannot, of course, be repeated indefinitely; fresh materials or substitutes must sooner or later be found.

Laminated cardboard, parts from a 1931 automobile, sections of rubber tires, scraps of rubber, ocotillo poles – these and other materials with which the Seri build houses and harpoons – cycle in a spatial-temporal direction. For example, when a Seri dies, his house is dismantled, some of the materials are used to rebuild another house, and some are left behind. If the remaining materials are not necessary at the moment, they will surely be picked up and used at a later time. In this manner, serviceable material gradually catches up with the movement of the community, leaving in its wake rock, fishbone, and scraps of rubber and metal too small to be of use. In general, those materials that are adaptable, or potentially adaptable, tend to contract in space-time and to accumulate in the more recent areas of the community.

Broadcasting What may be organization from one point of view becomes disorganization from another. In the course of one hour, a Seri may dismember a turtle and crack open the bones of some small land mammal. Hundreds of similar prosaisms broadcast the by-products of human workmanship over the surface of the community. Such acts proceed at a much quicker rate than either cycling or smearing, and impart a past-to-present that can be read from both bottom-to-top and across the mass of unserviceable debris.

Let us consider an example. The Seri gather over a dozen varieties of shellfish; of these, half have long seasons, some have short seasons, and a few are taken only when stormy seas whip them close to shore. From the results of *archaeological excavations* in Seri garbage mounds, I was able to infer that one shellfish was the preferred species, and Seri statements, obtained after analysis, corroborated the inference. Flecks of the shell of this mollusk are abundant in breadth, width, and depth, whereas the shell fragments of seasonal species appear in intermittent groups. This positioning applies to other organic residues, and as such provides a useful clue to the constancies and changes in the Seri community over time.

Time's Arrow: Conclusion

I have considered one important phase of the disorganization path – its beginning in the "inhabited" community. The phenomena identified at Desemboque may not be general, but they are probably not unique. It is noteworthy that the distribution and density of automobiles in an American automobile yard, and the removal of parts from the cars, seem to parallel the trends of smearing, blending, and cycling identified in the hunter-gatherer community. It would be of value to seek and report relevant trends in other communities for the heuristics they can provide.

It is Sir Arthur Eddington who is generally credited with coining the term "time's arrow" with reference to the tendency of the universe to move in the direction of the more probable state of disorder and chaos. Many have found meanings and implications in this general process that extend far beyond its rigorous application in thermodynamics. The meaning of "time's arrow" in the present context, being neither philosophical nor rigorously physical, can be simply stated: in time, every community will become first a "ghost" town, then a cube below ground. The problem of the prehistorian is to reconstruct the community from the cube. Since the connection between the archaeological present and the ethnographic past lies along the route of increasing disorder, the advancement of interpretation depends on knowing what happens along that route.

Here we have considered one important phase of the disorganization path – beginning in the "inhabited" community. Such phenomena as cycling and smearing identified at Desemboque may not be general, but they are probably not unique. If trends in other relevant communities are identified, given precise expression, and used, reconstructions may read less like fantasies.

References

ASCHER, ROBERT
1961a "Analogy in archeological interpretation," *Southwestern Journal of Anthropology*, Vol. XVII: 317-25.
1961b "Function and prehistoric art," *Man*, Vol. LXI, No. 84.
1962 "Ethnography for archeology: A case from the Seri Indians," *Ethnology*, Vol. I: 360-69.

DARWIN, HORACE
1901 "On the movement of stones by worms," *Proceedings of the Royal Society*, Vol. LXVIII, No. 446.

KROEBER, A. L.
1931 "The Seri," *Southwest Museum Papers*, No. 6.

MCGEE, W. J.
1898 "The Seri Indians," *Annual Report of the Bureau of American Ethnology*, No. 17, Pt. 1.

WIENER, NORBERT
1954 *The Human Use of Human Beings* (New York: Doubleday and Company, Inc.).

V

BRUCE G. TRIGGER

The Determinants of Settlement Patterns

This paper is concerned with the range of ways in which the concept of settlement patterns can be useful for the interpretation of archaeological data. My primary interest is in the nature of settlement patterns and the relationships they bear to the rest of culture. I shall analyze (1) the relationships that exist between settlement patterns and other aspects of culture, and (2) the ways in which archaeologists can use the knowledge of such relationships to further an understanding of the cultures they are investigating. The first step requires a cross-cultural investigation of (a) the range of factors that correlate significantly with settlement patterns, and (b) the manner in which these factors articulate with one another to produce the settlement pattern of an individual society. Our main interest will be the determinants of settlement patterns, by which we mean those classes of factors that interact with each other to produce the spatial configurations of a social group. This interaction is not simply complementary, since individual determinants may tend toward results that oppose as well as reinforce one another; a settlement pattern may be a compromise among a number of conflicting determinants. And there are, no doubt, other factors that are functionally related to the settlement pattern but whose relationship is dependent rather than determining. These, however, lie beyond the scope of this study.

Before we proceed with our investigation it is necessary to clarify what we mean by settlement patterns. To do this we must here consider some of the work that has been done to date. The concept of the settlement pattern was first put to substantial use in the field of archaeology by Gordon R. Willey in his book "Prehistoric Settlement Patterns in the Viru Valley" (1953). There, Willey delineated changes in the form and distribution of sites in a small Peruvian valley during the course of several millennia, and related these changes to socioeconomic trends and to historical events. In his *Introduction* he described settlement patterns as a "strategic starting point for the functional interpretation of archaeological cultures" that reflect "the natural environment, the level of technology on which the builders operated, and various institutions of social interaction and control with the culture maintained" (p. 1). Since then, a considerable number of studies have been concerned with settlement patterns. Some are basically factual studies aimed at ascertaining the types of settlement patterns associated with a given culture. Others have attempted to use settlement patterns to reconstruct the social (Chang, 1958; 1962) or religious (Sears, 1961) institutions of ancient cultures. Some have concentrated on the layout and house types associated with individual sites (Willey, 1956b); others, on the distribution patterns of large numbers of sites (Trigger, 1962). The cultures studied range from small hunting and gathering ones (Chang, 1962) to complex civilizations (Coe, 1961), and the interpretive approaches used range from simple comparative exegesis to systematic cross-cultural comparisons using ethnographic societies.

One of the chief merits of Willey's definition of settlement patterns lies in its breadth and its clearly functional view of settlement pattern phenomena. The value of settlement patterns for reconstructing prehistoric cultures is seen as a result of the variety of institutions that are "reflected" in the settlement pattern. In another work, he suggested that there was no settlement pattern approach as such, but that settlement patterns should be treated as a class of data available for analysis through a variety of approaches (Willey, 1956a, p. 1).

Despite such a healthy emphasis on variety and on a range of possible uses of data, it seems that in recent years two approaches have dominated settlement pattern studies. The first is primarily ecological and often appears to be based on the assumption that the settlement pattern is a product of the simple interaction of two variables – environment and technology. This sort of ecological determinism has been actively promoted as a determinant not only of settlement patterns but also of culture in general, by Leslie White and his students, and, in archaeology particularly, by Betty Meggers. The ecological approach is primarily an investigation of how the settlement pattern reflects the adaptation of a society and its technology to its environment. In the second kind of approach, settlement pattern data are used as a basis for making inferences about the social, political, and religious organization of prehistoric cultures. Chang (1958; 1962) and Sears (1961) have used the term "community pattern" to refer to "the strictly social aspects of settlement patterning." E. Z. Vogt (1956, pp. 174-75) has even suggested that these two kinds of approaches, along with studies of process, might be considered as separate branches of the study of settlement patterns. These two kinds of study are distinguished not only by approach but also to a large degree by their choice of data. The first kind tends to be concerned with the size and distribution of whole sites, whereas the second concentrates on the patterning within individual settlements. Mayer-Oakes (1959, p. 167) has distinguished between *community types* and *zonal patterns;* Sears (1961, p. 226) between *site* and *areal* patterns, referring to the former as *microcosmic* and the latter as *macrocosmic*. On the analogy of Chang's terms *microstructure* and *macrostructure*, which are used to describe the sociocultural systems of individual settlements and those made up of a number of settlements, respectively, we could also refer to this distinction as one between *microsettlement patterns* and *macrosettlement patterns*.

I believe, however, that archaeologists and others also can conceive profitably of settlement patterns in terms of three levels. The first and most basic of these is the individual building or structure; the second, the manner in which these structures are arranged within single communities; and the third, the manner in which communities are distributed over the landscape. Each of these levels is perhaps shaped by factors that differ in quality or degree from the factors that shape other levels, and hence the separate study of each is likely to shed more light on archaeological cultures than would the study of a single level.

Although work to date has done much to advance the study of settlement patterns, the heavy concentration on only two approaches has not been without its disadvantages. So far, archaeologists have been more interested in using settlement patterns as a basis for interpretations about cultures than in studying the nature of settlement patterns for its own sake. Hence there is little in the way of a systematic understanding of settlement patterns to guide the archaeologist. In the long run, however, settlement pattern data can be used with a full knowledge of their prospects and limitations only when some attention has been given to the nature of this phenomenon in living societies. My aim in the first part of this paper, then, is to assemble a list of the various factors that scholars have suggested play a part in determining the structure of individual buildings, settlements, and overall distributions. This list is based on the work of geographers, sociologists, and historians. Material from both simple and complex societies will be considered, since circumstances peculiar to each may help to point up problems common to settlement pattern studies as a whole. Since this part of my paper is essentially a survey of other people's ideas, my illustrations are drawn from many different parts of the world; in another study, I try to analyze to what degree similar factors have determined the settlement patterns of a single region through time (Trigger, 1965).

DETERMINANTS

Individual Buildings There has been relatively little in the way of a systematic investigation of our most basic unit, the individual structure. Perhaps the most common use that has been made of house types has been in tracing historical connections among different groups. Therefore, much that we say here must be in the form of queries rather than answers. There is great variety in the structures of complex societies – various types of houses, as well as temples, forts, tombs, etc. In the simplest societies, there may be only one, quite uniform, house type and no special-purpose buildings. Yet even this single house type may represent an accommodation to a considerable variety of factors.

Certainly one of these factors is the subsistence regime of the society. Migratory peoples tend to have houses that are either transportable or easy to build, and even semisedentary swidden agriculturalists may be less inclined to invest in buildings than would a completely sedentary population. But in migratory societies, there seems to be an even more specific correlation between house types and the availability of building materials. In areas where such materials can be come by easily, a new shelter can be erected at each camping place, but in deserts or steppe country where such materials are scarce, buildings tend to be of a sort that can be moved from place to place. Examples are the portable tepee of the Plains Indians, the light goat-hair tent of the Arab Bedouin, and the *yurt* of the Mongolian herdsmen. In the *yurt,* insulation against the cold climate is provided by two layers of felt stretched, one on the inside, the other on the outside, on a collapsible wooden trellis (Fitch and Branch, 1960, pp. 141-42).

Thus a house represents an attempt to meet the challenge of an environment with the building materials that the same environment offers. In a short but important study of primitive architecture, James Fitch and D. P. Branch (1960) have noted that the structural design of many primitive buildings "reflects a precise and detailed knowledge of local climatic conditions...and...a remarkable understanding of the performance characteristics of [local] building materials" (p. 134). They suggest that the principal climatic factors to which houses adapt are the diurnal and yearly variations in ambient and radiant temperatures, air movement, and humidity. They find that houses in different regions of the world often show adaptations that are of "surprising delicacy and precision" (p. 136).

The dome-shaped igloo of the Central Eskimo, for example, is built quickly and easily of local material that is readily available. The dome offers minimum resistance and maximum obstruction to winter gales. This shape also exposes as little of its surface to the cold as possible, and can be heated effectively by a point source of heat, such as an oil lamp.

In hot deserts, there are marked differences between day and night temperatures, as well as between seasons. In such regions, buildings with heavy walls of stone and clay absorb heat during the day and reradiate it at night in a manner that helps to flatten out the uncomfortable diurnal fluctuations of the coldest months. Such buildings are common among the Pueblo Indians of the American Southwest, in North Africa, and in the Middle East. Roofs are either of vaulted mud bricks or of mud slabs laid on beams. In moister regions, such as Nigeria, a mud dome is frequently covered with thatch so that it sheds water.

In wet, tropical regions, temperatures vary rather little, but shade and ventilation are essential to comfort. Walls are therefore reduced to a minimum to allow for ventilation, while a large, steeply sloping roof projects beyond the living space as protection against sun and rain. A raised floor also serves to fend off dampness and animals. Houses of this sort can be constructed easily out of available saplings and fibers.

In some of the preceding examples, not only the general structural principles but also the shapes of the houses are adaptations to the environment. The igloo and the sloping roofs of rainy regions are cases in point. The Naskapi house is a conical wigwam braced by a ring of stones and covered with bark or skins. G. I. Quimby (1960, pp. 383-84) has observed that no other shape would be as efficient in an environment where frozen ground and the lack of soil make it impossible to sink poles into the ground. Moreover, certain types of more complex structures, such as houses built around an open court, are less practical in cold climates than in warm ones. Not only is the usefulness of the courtyard, which is normally the center of a good deal of family activity, reduced in a cold climate, but also heating such a house is considerably more difficult than heating a compact one. Climatic factors also may influence the orientation of houses. Doors or windows may face toward the sun, away from an unpleasant prevailing wind, or toward a lake or river. Such practical considerations certainly enter into the Chinese art of *fung-shui,* or geomancy, although there they are embedded in an elaborate system of symbolism and magic (Durkheim and Mauss, 1963, pp. 68, 73).

But a building is more than an adaptation to climate. It also reflects the skills of its builder and his technology. This technical know-how will affect the range of materials that are available, and through the materials the shape and design of buildings. Skill in stone and brickwork permits the erection of larger and more elaborate structures. In different societies, building techniques may develop along divergent paths that, in part, reflect the different materials used. The brick and stone architecture of Europe and Western Asia gave rise to buildings whose weight rested primarily on the walls. In Eastern Asia, however, a tradition of wood architecture was developed in which walls tended to be "hung" on a pole-and-beam construction that supported the roof (Willetts, 1958, pp. 689-723). Specific techniques also make new designs possible. The dome, for example, made it possible to roof over unencumbered spaces of considerable size.

The size and layout of buildings may also reflect the structure of the family. A house occupied by a nuclear family may contain one or more rooms, but the function of these rooms will relate to the needs of a single family. If the house belongs to a lineage, then nuclear family units are likely to be found repeated within the house, although such things as food stores may be common to the whole unit. Chang (1958) has suggested that even in large houses, such as those of the Witoto of South America, which house a whole village, the household can be distinguished by (1) interpreting the use of equipment, (2) distinguishing the partitions that separate households, and (3) identifying separate kitchens. In a polygynous household, on the other hand, each wife may have her own living area and kitchen, but the rooms belonging to the head of the household will be without a kitchen, since he will be fed by his various wives in turn. Alternatively, a polygynous family may have a common cookhouse (Murdock, 1934, p. 559). From archaeological evidence it might be difficult to distinguish a household consisting of a master and his resident servants from that of a lineage, especially if social differences within a society are not strongly marked in material terms. Moreover, although various forms of multi-family houses may be indicative of lineages or polygynous families, similar institutions are also found associated with nuclear family houses and so can go undetected. Particular forms of houses may also be related to forms of family organization. The longhouse as a unit of residence seems closely associated with lineage organizations. Here, the main archaeological problem is to distinguish residential longhouses from buildings such as men's clubs. In Melanesia, some of the latter have not only the outline of a longhouse but also a row of fireplaces down the center, associated not with nuclear families but with particular status groups within the club (Codrington, 1957, pp. 101-05). Any site in which a few "longhouses" are associated with a large number of nuclear family houses should be suspect, and the buildings subjected to careful investigation before functions are assigned to them.

The structures in a community may reflect differences in wealth and rank, as well as various social institutions. The economic egalitarianism of many primitive societies is reflected in uniformity in the design and size of shelters, but with increasing social complexity the design and functions of buildings become increasingly differentiated. Among the Huron, the most important chiefs in a village occupied the largest longhouses, which served as gathering places for meetings and rituals (Trigger, 1963, p. 156). In societies where authority or class divisions are more pronounced, the houses of the elite become larger and more elaborate. In such places as the Marquesas, for example, the elaborateness of the platform on which a house was built reflected the importance of its owner in the social hierarchy (Suggs, 1960, p. 124). In addition to such differentiations in house types, special-purpose structures are more common in a class-divided society. Some of these structures are also residential. Visitors or bachelors may sleep inside the clubhouses that are common in Oceania (Codrington, 1957, pp. 69-115); and in Sparta and more recently in some parts of Hungary (den Hollander, 1960), adult males normally lived apart from their wives and families. The age grade system of the Masai found expression in the special camps where the warriors and unmarried girls of a village would live together until they reached the age when they could establish homes of their own (Forde, 1934, pp. 302-33).

Elsewhere, various special-purpose structures that are not lived in may serve the needs of the community as a whole or of some of its members. The Arab guest house, which is used to feed and accommodate travelers, functions primarily as a meeting place for the men of a tribe or village (Salim, 1962, p. 72), as did the sweat house among the Pomo. The Plains Indians constructed large triple tepees where some of the ceremonies of their men's societies were performed (Forde, 1934, p. 57). Huts or houses may also be built to isolate members of society: among the Indians of the Northwest Coast, girls were frequently secluded for a time at puberty, either in a small hut or behind a curtain. And in complex societies, there is often a considerable variety of public buildings devoted to secular group activities, such as schools, libraries, stadia, public baths, and museums. Once their function has been determined, these buildings permit us to say a good deal about the nature of community life and the values of ancient civilizations.

The specialization of production is also reflected in the individual structure, in the form either of workshops added on to houses or of new buildings that serve as workshops and storerooms. Likewise, the transportation and sale of goods stimulates the growth of marketplaces, stores, and caravanserais. By determining the use that was made of individual buildings, the archaeologist can recover a good deal of solid information about patterns of production and trade in ancient societies.

The religious beliefs of a society may affect house types and may also result in the construction of shrines, temples, or tombs. The royal funerary temples of the Khmer civilization were built as a model of the universe: the central structure with its five towers on a large pyramid represented Mount Meru, the center of the universe; the surrounding walls were the rock wall that surrounded the universe; and the moat beyond was the great ocean (Coe, 1961, p. 71). Mircea Eliade (1960) and others see the house as a representation of a people's conception of the universe. Eliade notes that such "habitation symbolism" is very clear among the subarctic peoples of North America and Siberia. Among them the center post is symbolically identified with the "pillar of the world"; among the pastoralists of Asia, and the "archaic Chinese," the mythico-ritual function of the pillar has been "passed on" to the overhead smoke hole. Special religious buildings include temples and plazas where rituals can be performed. The *kivas*, or ceremonial lodges, found among the Pueblo tribes of the American Southwest are interesting for two reasons: first, the *kiva* may be a retention of an earlier form of round house, long abandoned as a dwelling; and second, the *kivas* were owned by religious fraternities that were associated with the various clans of the community. Sears (1961) has already demonstrated the value of studying temple and tomb complexes as representations of ritual. In this way, much can be learned about the religious practices of prehistoric societies. Nevertheless, the whole field of the relationship between structures and rituals remains to be studied in a comparative fashion on both a world-wide basis and within particular culture areas. In any case, archaeologists must beware equating the study of religious buildings with the study of religion itself. The importance of cult buildings varies a good deal from society to society. Gods may have no temples at all, and ceremonies may be performed in the open or in public places that normally have other uses. To understand religious practices, we must also look for household shrines and cult images and symbols, whatever the architectural complex may be.

Political institutions also affect house styles. In areas where crime is common and police controls ineffective, houses will often tend to be built with an eye to security. The inward-facing house is one example of this sort of building. A few fierce dogs will also provide protection to a house or tent, but this sort of defense would not likely be obvious in the archaeological record. The lack of proper defenses on a higher (community or national) level may result in houses themselves being adapted for such purposes. The towering, thick-walled dwellings found in Southern Arabia were often strong enough to hold off attacks by Bedouin. A more complex political organization will also generate buildings to serve its own needs, such as adminstrative offices, jails, and barracks.

Nor can the influence of secular tastes and fashions be ignored. These are reflected in the design and layout of houses, and may account for the spreading of particular types of buildings into areas for which they were not originally designed and may not even be well suited. The layout of a house may also reflect such tastes as a desire for individual or group privacy. The former will be reflected in the clear division of a house into rooms and the separation/interconnection of the rooms by doors. Secular tastes may also produce special summer or country houses that may differ a good deal from normal ones. Huron women are described as going with their children to live in the fields during the summer, not merely to be nearer their work but also to be away from the crowded conditions of village life (Trigger, 1960, p. 18).

Community Layouts The next level I deal with is the layout of the structures constituting a single community. By a community I mean "the maximal group of persons who normally reside in face-to-face association" (Murdock, 1949, p. 79). In general, a community corresponds to a single settlement and therefore can be identified with the archaeologist's *component* (Willey and Phillips, 1958, pp. 21, 22). However, in areas of dispersed settlement such an equation would not hold, nor would it hold for migratory hunting and gathering peoples who might reestablish their community several times in several settlements in the course of a year, or among whom the community may be forced to scatter into small family groups during at least certain seasons. In these cases, the community, as socially defined, would be associated with more than one settlement or site. The archaeological definition of the aggregate of settlements associated with such a community would depend on ascertaining at what time of year different settlements were occupied and what kinds of settlements are associated with each season. In dispersed patterns, the solution may depend on the definition of whatever nuclei exist in the pattern and on estimations of the size of a community that could be associated with a particular mode of subsistence. Then, on the basis of complementary distributions, the pattern itself could be worked out, at least as a statistical possibility. Despite some violence to the sociological concept of community, I extend the term to cover the whole of large stable units of settlement, such as cities, which, if they cannot be defined as communities, at least represent stable interaction patterns.

The maximum size and stability of a community are quite obviously limited by the environment and the effectiveness of the subsistence technology. The latter includes the means of both acquiring and producing food, as well as storing, processing, and transporting it. The three last factors are often crucially important: effective means of storing food allows the population to expand beyond the numbers that can survive the period of least production; processing allows foods to be used that otherwise would be inedible (e.g., acorns and bitter manioc); and transportation determines the size of the area in which food can be collected and concentrated. These ecological factors play an important role in determining the major types of community pattern as they have been defined by Chang (1962, p. 30). They will determine, for example, whether or not a community can complete its annual subsistence cycle at a single site, and whether a single site can be inhabited permanently, as would be the case with irrigation agriculture, or only semipermanently, as with swidden agriculture. When such sedentary life is not possible, a community may have to occupy a network of scattered settlements in the course of a year. In some cases the annual subsistence region in such a network will remain unchanged from year to year, and even the main seasonal settlements within it will remain unchanged. In other cases the group will exploit and exhaust the ecological potential of one region and will therefore be forced to move on to fresh territory.

Within any region, people will tend to establish their settlements in places that are close to drinking water, sources of food, and, as far as possible, in places that are safe and pleasant. Even the hunters and gatherers of the temperate forests sought to locate their camps on sand banks by the edge of lakes or rivers, where they would be dry, and where the breeze would keep away bothersome insects. Agricultural groups will, of course, seek locations where the soil and weather are favorable to their crops and their methods of cultivation.

Whereas community size and location are influenced to a large extent by ecological factors, the layout of communities appears to be strongly influenced by family and kinship organization–especially, it appears, in primitive societies. These relationships are not necessarily totally independent factors, since kinship relations are at least partly determined by ecological factors that operate through the medium of production.

In a study of circumpolar groups, Chang (1962) has distinguished between communities of a "Siberian" type and those of an "Eskimo" type. The Siberian type is composed of individuals "unilineally determined by descent and / or unilocally recruited by marriage. It is a basic unit of economic cooperation and is strongly integrated as a cohesive body" (p. 33). This type of society often occupies a multidwelling village with individual or multifamily houses laid out in a planned fashion. When there is more than one lineage, each one occupies its own section of the village, and when the community splits up for its seasonal movements it splits according to lines of kinship, with the same groups returning to their winter base year after year. The Eskimo type of community is characterized by the looseness of its organization, by fluctuations in group membership, and by bilateral kinship. Such communities tend to be an incoherent conglomeration of families, each family settling where it likes and moving when new districts offer greater advantages. Even the winter settlements are characterized by this irregularity. Chang's distinction between "Siberian" and "Eskimo" community types is similar in many ways to Steward's (1955) distinction between patrilineal and composite bands. The first type of community, by either distinction, is associated with a more stable and more sedentary subsistence pattern than is the second, and the subsistence is more often based on fishing than on hunting. Chang suggests that the kind of solidarity associated with the Siberian type "tends to call for a symbolic projection of the community structure in the lay-out of the settlement site" (p. 37).

This same theme forms the basis of Chang's (1958) now-classic study of neolithic village patterns, which suggested a high degree of correlation between community plans and village social organization, and postulated land ownership as an important determinant of neolithic community types. In particular, his survey of neolithic societies showed a strong correlation between planned villages and communities composed of a single lineage, and between segmented planned villages and communities composed of more than one lineage. Although there are perhaps more neolithic societies with a scattered homestead pattern than Chang's sample suggests, his conclusions remain valid so long as they are presumed to read: the absence of *x* settlement pattern does not necessarily imply the absence of *y* community type, but the presence of *x* strongly suggests that *y* is present also. The idea that kinship organization is reflected in village plans or in the distribution of communities is not new in anthropology: the relationship between social and geographical space was one of the main themes explored by Evans-Pritchard in *The Nuer* (1940). Nor is this phenomenon confined entirely to primitive societies: in medieval Arab cities, different quarters were sometimes laid out for different tribes; likewise, the city of Tenochtitlan was divided into sections, each with its own temples and schools and belonging to a *calpulli*, probably an endogamous deme (Soustelle, 1962, pp. 7-8).

In complex societies, not only classes but religious and ethnic groups may live in demarcated areas of the community, and such groups may be separated from one another by a wall. In these communities, special sections may be set aside for foreigners or for such ethnic groups as Jews. In such areas, these groups are able to live under the protection of city officials (Sjoberg, 1960, p. 100). Ethnic areas may also be found within modern communities, where they develop as a result of associational patterns rather than formal rules. Although divisions of the community resulting from disparate levels of wealth may be defined fairly easily from the quality and size of dwellings, the more informal ethnic divisions may be hard to trace in the layout of a site. A district populated by prosperous foreign traders could perhaps be distinguished from the local elite quarter by a preponderance of store rooms, by alien house plans, or by evidence of foreign cults. The section of the Spanish settlement of Nueva Cadiz in Venezuela that was inhabited by Negro and Indian slaves was identified by Indian pottery representing various tribal groups and by the lack of such permanent habitations as were found in the European quarter (Rouse and Cruxent, 1963, pp. 134-38). The best hope of identifying ethnic groups at an archaeological site seems to lie in investigating artifacts to discover whether particular symbols or written materials are associated with houses in one part of the site but not in another. But even where these efforts prove fruitful, it is difficult to demonstrate that an ethnic difference–as opposed, for example, to a religious or tribal difference–is involved. The presence of Huron captives in historic Seneca villages is attested in the archaeological record by the presence of many Huron-style potsherds among those of native design. Without historical documentation, however, it is likely that these sherds would have been described as trade sherds and their real social significance overlooked (MacNeish, 1952, p. 46).

In more complex societies, subsistence factors, in the narrow sense, are less important as determinants of the size and location of communities. Trade may provide a source of wealth and stimulate the growth of large cities in remote regions, and the wealth amassed from such trade may in turn serve either to finance the development of novel agricultural systems in areas where they would otherwise be impractical, or to effect the importation of food from distant regions. Settlements may also spring up in wastelands where rare and valuable minerals are discovered: in ancient times, copper smelters were built at Aqaba on the shores of the Red Sea, a region rich in copper but lacking in agricultural potential.

Specialization on a local or village level can develop among relatively simple societies: when a number of villages are linked together in a trading network, for example, they are better able to transcend local limitations in natural resources; and a trading network also fosters greater specialization and better products than does an autonomous village economy. Thus a careful investigation of trade and of the nature of production is prerequisite to estimates of the size and the social and cultural complexity of communities. The archaeologist must determine what goods were present and produced in his sites. Data concerning production relationships can be obtained through study of the layout of workshops and stores within a community. The study should note whether places of work and residence are together or separated; whether the workshops of one trade are in the same part of the community or at scattered points; the degree to which the production and sale of goods are handled as a single operation or as separate functions; the importance of public markets, as opposed to stores; and so forth. Data of this sort, considered together with what can be learned about the social organization of the community from other sources, will permit more detailed and more faithful reconstructions of ancient social organizations.

Graveyards may also provide interesting clues to social and political organizations. For example, status differences can often be traced in graves even better than in house types or village patterns. This is especially true at a neolithic or other collecting level where there may be considerable differences in status but little difference in standards of living. Social relations and kinship may also be reflected in the relationship between communities and their cemeteries. Chang (1963, p. 65) has noted that in the Yangshao phase in North China each village had its own cemetery, but as the population increased and villages split, villages that shared a common ancestry often continued to share a common graveyard, so that the ratio of cemeteries to villages declined. In historic times, the tribes of the Huron confederacy held a ceremony every decade or so in which all the members of the various member tribes who had died in the interim were reinterred in a common ossuary as an expression of political solidarity. A careful cross-cultural study of the relationship between burial practices and social structure might reveal correlations of considerable interest and value.

Little formal work has been done by archaeologists on the significance of special-purpose structures to the community as a whole. Gideon Sjoberg (1960) has noted that in most preindustrial cities the major temples and palaces and the homes of the elite are concentrated in the center of the community. In support of this observation, one can quickly call to mind the location of the agora and the acropolis in Athens, the Roman forum, the temple center of the Sumerian city, or the palaces and temples of a Chinese city like Peking. In the New World, similarly, the center of

Tenochtitlan was occupied by the main temples, palaces, and markets of the city, and Cuzco, the Inca capital, appears to have consisted of palaces, temples, and a ritual square surrounded by villages of royal retainers (Rowe, 1944). But in cities like Tenochtitlan that were organized on a segmental principle, each of the divisions of the city also had a secondary center. Moreover, in some cities the elite center appears to have been at one side or in one corner of the city. In some of the cities of Chou China the elite center was a walled-off corner of the city (Chang, 1963, pp. 180-95), and in the cities of the Indus Valley civilization the citadel was to one side (Wheeler, 1960, p. 18), as was the elite center in the ancient Egyptian town of Kahun (Smith, 1958, pp. 96-98).

The *kind* of buildings associated with such civic centers also provides some indication of the values and orientation of a particular society. In simpler societies, houses are often grouped around a central plaza that may serve as a market, a work area, and a meeting place, and may contain or be bordered by such public buildings as temples or council houses. In the dispersed pattern of the American farming community, such special-purpose buildings as schools, churches, and general stores are foci of public activity. However, as we noted in the discussion of individual structures, the reconstruction of community activities on the basis of the layout of public buildings within the community must be undertaken with caution. For one thing, it may be difficult, from archaeological evidence, to determine the full range of uses that was made of a plaza; and for another, norms may require that various structures important in community life be located outside the settlement, as for example the clubhouses of the secret societies in Melanesia. Temples or cult centers may also be located in sacred spots outside the residential area. The Egyptian pyramid complexes, with their small colonies of attendant priests, were built as the foci of royal mortuary cults. The priests lived near the pyramid and maintained themselves through agriculture and craft occupations (Kees, 1961, pp. 157-60). Monastic communities, with carefully organized routines and often with rigidly laid-out buildings, are still another example of whole communities that are religiously based. Pilgrimage centers like Mecca would be humble desert villages were it not for the tourist industry that sustains the local population.

The development of complex political organization gives rise to similarly specialized communities. Isolated forts and garrison towns are built to guard frontiers or to police the countryside. Royal courts are commonly established within cities, but some constitute independent communities. The king of Buganda, for example, lived in an oval enclosure over a mile long that also housed his guards, retainers, and slaves. The roads leading to this compound were lined with the houses of important chiefs and officials (Murdock, 1934, p. 525). Warfare and defense play important roles in determining the site and layout of communities in many parts of the world. Where warfare is endemic, as it was among the Iroquois, villages were commonly built on hilltops or in the bends of rivers. Where walls or stockades are used for defense, houses are often crowded together to conserve space. When the Roman empire was adequately defended by its armies, cities tended to grow into sprawling agglomerations, but when the defense system collapsed in the third century A.D. the inhabitants of cities such as Barcelona were forced to abandon their suburbs and crowd together behind hastily built walls (Weiss, 1961). Large numbers of pastoralists often camp together for protection, and smaller groups of Bedouin will camp with their tents arranged in a circular fashion (Forde, 1934, p. 317). Similarly, the Masai *kraal* consists of a thorn fence and a ring of houses surrounding a central area where the domestic animals are secured for the night. The central area of a city is often similarly walled off, both to separate it from the city as a whole and so that it can serve as a place of last retreat. In Mexico, temple platforms served the latter purpose, and the capture of the main sanctuary symbolized the capture of a city (Soustelle, 1962, p. 211). The presence or absence of fortifications cannot be considered as direct evidence of the prevalance of warfare, since the effectiveness of such means of defense depends in part on whether offensive or defensive warfare is in the ascendant.

It is also argued that community patterns, like house plans, reflect cosmological conceptions. According to Eliade (1960), communities are often laid out as an *imago mundi.* In Hindu culture, the central feature of any town is regarded as a symbol of the pillar of the universe. When a village is constructed in Bali, a space is left vacant in the center to be used for a cult house whose roof symbolizes the sky. Likewise, Roman cities were laid out according to a divine plan, their division into four quarters being the earthly manifestation of a heavenly prototype (Müller, 1962). In all such examples, either the community is laid out in some general fashion according to a prescribed pattern, or there is a tendency to read such a pattern into an existing plan. In a very interesting paper, Lévi-Strauss (1953, p. 534) has argued that the elaborate layout of a Bororo village—where houses are arranged around a circle according to moieties, clans, and ranked subdivisions of clans—is a reflection not of unconscious social organization but rather of a model of society consciously existing in the Bororos' minds.

Zonal Patterns The overall density and distribution of population of a region is determined to a large degree by the nature and availability of the natural resources that are being exploited. As long as other land is available, settlers tend normally to avoid areas that are naturally poor or where diseases or other dangers are common. Factors such as availability of game have a strong bearing on the size of hunting territories and on the distribution of permanent and transient bases. The attractions of fishing and collecting shellfish and the difficulties of overland travel through bush or jungle may result in concentrations of population along bodies of water (Kroeber, 1953, pp. 143-46). In Ontario, for example, the late Iroquoian occupation, which was based on agriculture, was confined to the warm and fertile regions in the southern part of the province, and to areas that were close to rivers and had light soil. Such populations were notably absent in central southwestern Ontario, which is relatively high and cold and also an area of hard clay soils, few rivers, and flat, forested lands. At best, such areas were used as hunting territories by the neighboring tribes (Trigger, 1962). Similar correlations have been noted between the neolithic Danubian culture and loess soils in Europe (Narr, 1956, pp. 139-40); the Sangoan culture and the tropical forest zone in Africa (Cole, 1954, p. 26); and the eastern Gravettian culture and the mammoth in ice-age Europe (Hawkes and Woolley, 1963, pp. 83-86). In complex societies, fertile regions become centers of population and hence of political and cultural importance. In Japan the main fertile areas have been the Kanto, Nobi, and Kinai plains on the east side of Honshu Island; the chief cities and cultural centers have been located on these plains, and Japanese history has been largely a struggle for control of these areas, and through them, of the country (Sansom, 1958, pp. 5-6).

Because archaeologists and geographers have had fairly good success in reconstructing both prehistoric subsistence patterns and prehistoric environments, the study of the relationship between these two sets of factors has become popular. And since the relationships of production strongly influence many other aspects of culture, even more stress has been placed on the ecological approach to the reconstruction of prehistoric societies (see, e.g., Kehoe, 1964). This is a perfectly legitimate approach so long as it is used in an objective manner, but it should not inhibit anthropologists from following other avenues of research that also may shed light on prehistoric cultures. For example, if we know that a prehistoric society depended on shifting agriculture, it is reasonable to suggest that it had a lineage-based social structure, and if longhouses are excavated the statement becomes even more reasonable. But determining whether the society was matrilineal, like the Iroquois, or patrilineal, like the Tupinamba, is much more difficult. Knowledge about the division of labor may shed some light on the problem (White, 1959, pp. 150-52), and useful correlations may also someday be found between art styles or religious practices and lineality.

As contiguous regions become more interdependent, zonal patterns are modified to an increasing degree by economic factors, as opposed to merely subsistence factors. In particular, trade plays an important role in establishing new communities and in increasing population density. Many of the most densely populated industrial regions of the modern world produce neither enough food to support their own population nor the raw materials needed to support their industries; both are obtained through trade and production. Trade, however, can be important even among very simple societies: among the Alaskan Eskimo, trading partnerships between sea-oriented and inland hunters helped to level off periods of poor hunting for both groups and induced greater community stability (Dunning, 1960, p. 26). In northeastern North America, agriculturalists and hunters occupying contiguous but different ecological zones exchanged their respective products to such an extent that even before the European fur trade began, the Huron villages in southern Ontario were clustered in a small area favorable for this kind of trade. Long-distance trade has been seen as a major factor in the rise of medieval European cities, e.g., Venice (Pirenne, 1925) and the coastal cities of the ancient Levant, e.g., Tyre (Revere, 1957). In the Hellenistic period, a series of cities including Petra, Palmyra, and Hatra, all of which depended on trade, grew up around the margins of the Arabian Desert. Many of the important cities in ancient southern Arabia were built in the desert east of the fertile mountain region but along a major trade route to the north (Bowen, 1958). Even earlier, special colonies were established for trade in foreign regions; examples are the Assyrian *karums* in Anatolia (Ozguc, 1963) and the self-sufficient colonies established by the Greeks around the Black Sea and in the western Mediterranean.

The overall distribution of settlements is also affected by political organization. Internal security may require garrisons or administrative towns in the various sections of the country. Hsiao-tung Fei (1953, pp. 90-100) describes the *ch'engs* or administrative towns in imperial China as instruments of power in the hands of the ruling classes. The emperor's representatives and the state bureaucracy lived in these towns and administered the countryside from them. Landowners, living off the rents from their estates, also frequently lived there for protection. In a centrally organized state, such towns would form provincial nuclei within a milieu of villages and scattered homesteads, and the national capital would be characterized by its greater size and luxury. Although the relative wealth of city states may differ considerably, it is doubtful that a single city state would predominate to the same degree as the capital city in most national states (Lambert, 1964, p. 17). In civilizations where cities are less important, the distribution of shrines or ceremonial centers may reflect political organization. Although little is known about Maya political organization, the distribution of a large number of minor ceremonial centers around the large centers reflects unmistakably subordination of the former to the latter. On the other hand, even without written records, one may presume that such immense undertakings as the Egyptian pyramids of the Fourth Dynasty reflect a powerful central government controlling a vast dominion. This impression is strengthened by noting that the tombs of the nobles in this period are not to be found elsewhere in Egypt but cluster around the pyramid of the reigning king in a fashion as centralized as that of the government they served (Baer, 1960, p. 301).

Warfare is another factor shaping the overall distribution of settlements. Hunting bands may have a strong sense of territory, and so avoid one another. Since most of these groups have little in the way of immovable property they may simply move out of the way or scatter when danger threatens. Pastoralists, on the other hand, may band together in larger groups so as to be able to defend their herds. Agricultural peoples can respond in a number of different ways. Scattered communities may join together to build a common fort to which they can all flee in times of danger. In Bronze Age Palestine, these forts were often the headquarters of a local chief (Albright, 1960, p.205). Where there are a number of small villages, the people may choose to fortify one of the larger ones, which, like the fort, can be used as a place of refuge in times of danger. In most city states the capital serves this purpose.

One feature of warfare may be the development of buffer zones between belligerent factions. Where the population density is low, warring neolithic groups are often separated from each other by lakes or broad stretches of forest. During the Middle Ages, the rich plains of Burgundy, which had been thickly populated, were abandoned because of the repeated incursions of the Vikings (Bloch, 1961, pp.41-42). In large states the defensive system may become an important specialized feature of the overall settlement pattern. The Roman limes and the Great Wall of China were Maginot Lines of their day, designed to keep out the marauding tribes to the north. Both required elaborate constructions and the establishment of garrison communities. Similar frontier defense systems had been built by the Egyptians as early as the Middle Kingdom (Kees, 1961, p.317). Moreover, the need for quick movement of troops and messengers may result in extensive road systems.

Religious factors can also affect the overall settlement pattern. Among the Maya, ceremonial centers served as community and state foci for the population that lived around them. In the Middle East, Judaeo-Christian religious communities, driven by persecution or a desire to escape the world, established settlements in forbidding and lonely regions, which they developed, often with great difficulty, to produce their needs. European monastic orders pioneered settlement in many parts of northern Europe; the Benedictines were active in clearing the forests of the Dauphine and the Ile de France, and were followed in other regions by the Cistercians (Darby, 1956, p. 194). In North America, utopian religious communities had curious and erratic careers, and Mormonism played an important role in the colonization of Utah.

Taste and symbolic factors appear to have a fairly limited role in determining zonal patterns. They are involved to some degree in determining the location of villas or pleasure resorts serving the main centers of population, in the establishment of summer and winter capitals in some tropical countries, and in the preference for suburban living among the more affluent in western cities. It has been suggested that the twelve great cities making up each of the three Etruscan leagues in Italy were not an accidental number but a ritually auspicious one, perhaps in emulation of the league of twelve cities in Ionia (Pallottino, 1956, pp. 131-35). The designation of the twelve cities appears to have taken place after the fact, and hence to have played no role in their foundation or location. In general, social, economic, and political factors seem to find more expression on the zonal level than do ideational ones.

So far, we have been considering settlement patterns as a reflection of a variety of more or less stable conditions. To the factors we have already noted as determinants, we must add the more dynamic factors of migration and population change. These may alter the settlement pattern of a region more or less completely. Homans (1962, pp.127-81) has argued that two contrasting types of settlement in medieval England, the compact village of the central region and the dispersed settlement of Kent and East Anglia, were the result not of geographical or technological variations but of different traditions of land use that were brought from the continent; neither was sufficiently unsuited to the new environment to be forced to change. The rise or fall of population in response to economic factors or disease may also affect the settlement pattern in various ways. Land crowding may be an important factor stimulating migration to urban centers. As a result of wars and bubonic plague, large areas of farmland in Central Europe reverted to thick forest between 1350 and 1450 (Darby, 1956, p.198).

INTEGRATION

It is clear that settlement patterns represent responses to a number of different kinds of factors that influence them in different ways and degrees on different levels. For example, ecology, warfare, and religion have an influence on individual structures, community plans, and zonal patterns, whereas symbolic factors tend to affect only the first two of these levels. Certain factors leave a very clear imprint on one or more of these levels: war may result in fortified houses, walled settlements, or large defensive works, and trade may be reflected in special buildings and communities. At the same time, these factors may also be reflected indirectly, in terms of the prosperity or lack of prosperity associated with them.

If we conceive of the settlement pattern as an outcome of the adjustments a society makes to a series of determinants that vary both in importance and in the kinds of demands they make on the society, we must consider not merely the range of factors affecting settlement patterns but also the manner in which different factors interact with one another to influence a particular pattern. Factors vary in importance according to both the local situation and the temporal relationship that they have to one another.

We have already noted that primitive agricultural communities threatened by attack may respond in a number of different ways. A number of different solutions then, are possible to the same problem. In other situations the range of choice may be considerably more restricted. Let us consider a shift in the settlement pattern of the Shukriya Bedouin, one that is especially interesting because it was brought about primarily by political changes rather than economic or environmental changes. The Shukriya, an Arabic-speaking people, live in the Butana Desert, east of Khartoum in the Sudan. In the last century their camps and their herds were menaced constantly by raiding parties. In self-defense, they began to move about in groups that were two to three hundred tents strong. But because the sparse, scattered desert pastures could support the correspondingly large herds for no more than 15 to 20 days, the groups were forced to move frequently from one place to another. With the establishment of British rule, the threat of raids was lifted, and the large tribal groups broke up into smaller family units, each able a to occupy pasture year-round without exhausting it. As a result, these smaller groups tended to become sedentary; some even took to agriculture in a small way (Crowfoot, 1920, pp. 86-87). On the basis simply of residence, two alternatives always had been open to the Shukriya: large groups could exhaust individual pastures one by one and move on, or smaller groups could occupy a larger number of pastures simultaneously, each group remaining on the same pasture throughout the year. But was this choice really open to the Shukriya? The answer would seem to be No, inasmuch as the fear of raids necessitated a defense best achieved by staying together. Moreover, even if neighboring tribes had agreed to remain at peace, it is unlikely that conflict could have been avoided prior to British rule; slow increases in population would have begun to tax the grazing areas, and new outbreaks of fighting would have resulted. The same British rule that brought peace also provided the Shukriya new opportunities in a national economy. Conflict and a subsequent need to band together for defense would appear characteristic of pastoral economies in areas where pasturage is limited. A culture wherein a potential variety of settlement patterns is limited by a restricted range of possibilities in one or another of the culture's apects can be said to exhibit a principle of functional limitation.

A variation on this pattern is one in which a form of settlement may be highly desirable in some respects but unfavorable in most others. For example, an area well-placed for trade may be ill-equipped to support a large population. Nueva Cadiz has already provided another example. The town was founded on an island off the coast of Venezuela. The island was close to pearling areas and protected from the Indians on the mainland. On the other hand, both food and water had to be imported. As a result, the colony survived only as long as the pearl fisheries were profitable. Similarly, the city of Samarra was founded in 836 A.D. by the Caliph Mu'tasim, on a site removed from the major trade routes of the Middle East but considered to be a safer residence for the Caliph than the turbulent city of Kufa. Despite the removal of many merchants and artisans to the new site, the city endured for less than fifty years before it was abandoned and its inhabitants drifted back to the "natural" centers of population in Mesopotamia. Likewise, the city of Akhetaton, which was founded in honor of the new god of the Egyptian Pharaoh Ikhnaton, was inhabited for only 17 years. The trading cities in Arabia and desert mining outposts like Aqaba flourished in regions poorly suited for agriculture. Each of these communities was abandoned when the function it was designed to serve had ceased to be important. In other cases, the determination of a settlement pattern may involve a choice between opposing considerations: modern cities, for example, are utterly vulnerable to bombing attack, and therefore a liability to their military defenders, but they are essential for efficient industrial production. In such cases, the course of development reflects the relative importance attached to different functions: advantages gained through trade may make a large investment in land development worthwhile, or the agricultural worth of an area may justify elaborate defenses. We may call this the principle of hierarchical resolution of conflicting tendencies.

When a problem may be solved by one of several alternatives, the solution may be determined by the resolution of a previous problem. A city, for example, is functionally distinguished from a town or village in that it contains a high concentration of the facilities needed for the specialized functions characteristic of complex societies, such as temples, administrative buildings, the residences of the elite, workshops for artisans, and defense facilities. It is evident, however, that some early civilizations, such as those of ancient Egypt and Peru, and of the Maya, existed without true cities. In such societies the main temples might be located in one place, forts in another, and the royal court in still another. Craftsmen, both full- and part-time, could live in the scattered villages and exchange their produce through joint marketing places or through a state-operated redistribution network. Such a settlement pattern, though clearly workable at a certain level, is nevertheless cumbersome, and one would expect that with increased cultural complexity there would be a tendency for different functions to converge toward a common intersection. The pattern of convergence may differ considerably from one society to another. A fort may become the residence of a chief and his retainers; as immovable property accumulates, the well-to-do may move into the fort, so that a town begins to develop; and artisans may settle in the town so as to sell their wares to the townsfolk and to farmers who come to trade and to worship at local shrines. In other cultures, the cult center may serve as a fort or marketplace and in this way become the nucleus of a city. In Shang China the city apparently consisted of a walled elite center surrounded by villages that were probably self-sufficient in terms of subsistence and local handicrafts, but because many of these villages were also centers of particular occupational specialties, the whole tended to be bound together as a unit (Chang, 1963). In the Chou Period, probably largely as a result of warfare, these specialist villages tended to cluster close to the elite enclosures, producing finally a true city. Even without the stimulus of war, a court may attract public servants, attendants, and the merchants and menials who serve them, as well as temples and state buildings. If such nuclei attract trade, or serve as forts or administrative centers, they may eventually become viable cities, whether or not the courts remain.

There is considerable variation in the rate and degree of this concentration in different areas. In Mesopotamia, large urban communities arose at an early period within a context of warring states. In Egypt, where a strong territorial state was early established, there was no need for fortified towns, and less of a tendency for these functions to coalesce around common centers (Frankfort, 1956). In Mexico, cities seem to have developed quite early. This tendency was stimulated perhaps primarily by the growth of interregional trade. In the lowland Maya region, this tendency seems to have been much weaker. Thus, a flourishing center, whether established first for political, economic, religious, or defensive reasons, or for a combination of these, may gradually take on other functions until it becomes an important and diversified center of population serving the needs of a complex society. The basic patterns of growth within a given culture may be directed by local circumstances or by general configurations of development. This sort of development can be seen as illustrating a third principle, that of the convergence of functions.

Conclusions

In the foregoing, I have ranged rather widely in time and space. I should like now to emphasize several points concerning the nature of a settlement-pattern approach to the study of prehistoric societies.

Habitation, Community, Society I have defined three "levels" that are the object of settlement-pattern studies–the individual structure, the layout of communities, and the manner in which communities belonging to a culture or society distribute themselves over the landscape. The patterns displayed at each of these levels can be viewed as being functionally related in some way to all aspects of a culture and therefore able to shed light on a variety of problems. But, in fact, each level displays tendencies especially appropriate to the study of particular aspects of society: individual structures furnish information about family organization, craft specialization, and perhaps the relative importance of different aspects of the social structure; the layout of shrines or temples may elucidate religious rituals; community plans have yielded useful information about lineage organization and a community's adaptation to its physical and cultural environments; and areal patterns reflect a good deal about the social and political organization of complex societies, as well as about trade and warfare. Problem-oriented approaches exploiting the potentials of each of these levels simultaneously would seem to be highly desirable–though the study of settlement patterns must of course be aided by the study of artifacts, which often yield supplementary data about subsistence patterns, warfare, trade, beliefs, and division of labor.

Diachronic and Synchronic Vantage Points Second, I have observed that the interpretation of various aspects of the settlement pattern can be meaningful from a diachronic, as well as a synchronic, vantage point. Many aspects of a settlement pattern can be interpreted using functional ethnographic correlations, but other aspects may be understood only as the result of a historical process of development. For example, the development of Mesopotamian civilization from a neolithic base, through a system of city states, to the level of empire or national state is quite different from the direct transition of Egypt from a neolithic base to a large territorial kingdom. Although ecological differences have been suggested as the primary cause for their dissimilar development (Coe, 1961, p. 84), it seems to me that the explanation lies largely in the nature of their social and political development. In Mesopotamia, social, political, and economic institutions tended to grow in complexity concurrently, and in this way villages or groups of villages grew into city states with multicentric sources of power. In Egypt, where a large territorial state was established while the country was at a relatively primitive stage of cultural development (an analogy might be drawn with Shaka's Zulu empire), further economic and cultural progress took place under the aegis and control of the royal court and the government administration. Membership in the elite culture was long restricted to this administrative elite, and the development of cities as independent nuclei of an elite culture was inhibited. In the course of time, with Egyptian society becoming less court-centered and Mesopotamia moving toward national state configuration, there was a marked degree of convergence between the two cultures. The diachronic study of settlement patterns in a region can shed light on the development of social and economic institutions, and may provide similar genetic explanations for cultures that are not as well documented.

Universal and Limited Correlations In the interpretation of prehistoric settlement patterns, two kinds of correlations are of value. The first are functional correlations of universal applicability; examples of this sort are found in Chang's "Study of the Neolithic Social Grouping" (1958). Correlations of the second kind are those limited in their applicability to a particular area. Within such an area the nature of artifacts or aspects of the settlement pattern may be worked out by analogy with related ethnographic cultures. This method is limited in time and space, and is further dependent on the degree of cultural continuity in a particular area: for example, many features in Eskimo, Pueblo, or Polynesian archaeological sites can be identified by comparison with the modern cultures in the area. Even particular mythological figures can be identified in the pre-Columbian art of the southwestern United States. Through cultural persistences of this sort, the identification of structures and their use in various parts of the world may be accomplished at least as effectively–and perhaps more so–as they might be through universal correlations. If the more limited correlations are less universal (i.e., less scientific), they are no less valuable to cultural historical studies, and are therefore no less deserving of serious attention.

References

ALBRIGHT, W. F.
1960 *The Archaeology of Palestine* (Harmondsworth: Penguin Books Inc.)
BAER, K.
1960 *Rank and Title in the Old Kingdom* (Chicago: University of Chicago Press).
BLOCH, MARC
1961 *Feudal Society* (Chicago: University of Chicago Press).
BOWEN, R. L.
1958 "Ancient trade routes in South Arabia," *Archaeological Discoveries in South Arabia,* R. L. Bowen and F. P. Albright, editors (Baltimore: Johns Hopkins Press).
CHANG, K. C.
1958 "Study of the Neolithic social grouping: Examples from the New World," *American Anthropologist,* Vol. LX:298-334.
1962 "A typology of settlement and community patterns in some circumpolar societies," *Arctic Anthropology,* Vol. I:28-41.
1963 *The Archaeology of Ancient China* (New Haven: Yale University Press).
CODRINGTON, R. H.
1957 *The Melanesians* (New Haven: HRAF Press).
COE, M. D.
1961 "Social typology and tropical forest civilizations," *Comparative Studies in Society and History,* Vol. IV:65-85.

COLE, SONIA M.
1954 *The Prehistory of East Africa* (Harmondsworth: Penguin Books Inc.).
CROWFOOT, J. W.
1920 "Old sites in the Butana," *Sudan Notes and Records,* Vol. III:85-93.
DARBY, H. C.
1956 "The clearing of the woodland in Europe," *Man's Role in Changing the Face of the Earth,* W. L. Thomas, editor (Chicago: University of Chicago Press):183-216.
DEN HOLLANDER, A. N. J.
1960 "The Great Hungarian Plain: A frontier area," *Comparative Studies in Society and History,* Vol. III:74-88; 155-69.
DUNNING, R. W.
1960 "Differentiation of status in subsistence level societies," *Transactions of the Royal Society of Canada,* Vol. LIV, Section II:25-32.
DURKHEIM, E., and M. MAUSS
1963 *Primitive Classification* (Chicago: University of Chicago Press).
ELIADE, MIRCEA
1960 "Structures and changes in the history of religions," *City Invincible,* R. M. Adams and C. H. Kraeling, editors (Chicago: University of Chicago Press):351-66.
EVANS-PRITCHARD, E. E.
1940 *The Nuer* (Oxford: Clarendon Press).
FEI, HSIAO-TUNG
1953 *China's Gentry* (Chicago: University of Chicago Press).
FITCH, J. M., and D. P. BRANCH
1960 "Primitive architecture and climate," *Scientific American,* Vol. XXIII, No. 6:134-44.
FORDE, C. D.
1934 *Habitat, Economy and Society* (London: Methuen & Co., Ltd.).
FRANKFORT, HENRI
1956 *The Birth of Civilization in the Near East* (New York: Doubleday and Company, Inc.).
HAWKES, JACQUETTA, and LEONARD WOOLLEY
1963 *Prehistory and the Beginnings of Civilization.* (New York: Harper and Row).
HOMANS, GEORGE C.
1962 *Sentiments and Activities* (Glencoe: The Free Press).
KEES, HERMANN
1961 *Ancient Egypt: A Cultural Topography* (Chicago: University of Chicago Press).
KEHOE, ALICE B.
1964 "A worm's-eye view of marriage, authority, and final causes," *American Anthropologist*, Vol. LXVI: 405-07.
KROEBER, A. L.
1953 *Cultural and Natural Areas of Native North America* (Berkeley: University of California Press).
LAMBERT, W. G.
1964 "The reign of Nebuchadnezzar I," *The Seed of Wisdom,* W. S. McCullough, editor (Toronto: University of Toronto Press): 3-13.
LÉVI-STRAUSS, CLAUDE
1953 "Social structure," *Anthropology Today,* A. L. Kroeber, editor (Chicago: University of Chicago Press): 524-53.
MACNEISH, R. S.
1952 "Iroquois Pottery Types," *National Museum of Canada Bulletin*, No. 124.

MAYER-OAKES, W. J.
1959 "A developmental concept of pre-Spanish urbanization in the Valley of Mexico," *Tulane University Middle American Research Records*, No. 18, p. 2.
MÜLLER, WERNER
1962 *Die Heilige Stadt*. (Stuttgart: Kohlhammer Verlag).
MURDOCK, G. P.
1934 *Our Primitive Contemporaries* (New York: The Macmillan Company).
1949 *Social Structure* (New York: The Macmillan Company).
NARR, K. J.
1956 "Early food-producing populations," *Man's Role in Changing the Face of the Earth*, W. L. Thomas, editor (Chicago: University of Chicago Press): 134-51.
OZGUC, TAHSIN
1963 "An Assyrian trading outpost," *Scientific American*, Vol. CCVIII, No. 2: 96-106.
PALLOTTINO, M.
1956 *The Etruscans* (Harmondsworth: Penguin Books, Ltd.).
PIRENNE, HENRI
1925 *Medieval Cities* (Princeton: Princeton University Press).
QUIMBY, G. I.
1960 " Habitat, Culture, and Archaeology,"*Essays in the Science of Culture* (G. E. Dole and R. L. Carneiro, editors (New York: Thomas Y. Crowell Company): 380-89.
REVERE, R. B.
1957 "No man's coast: Ports of trade in the eastern Mediterranean," *Trade and Market in the Early Empires*, K. Polanyi, editor (Glencoe: The Free Press).
ROUSE, IRVING, and J. M. CRUXENT
1963 *Venezuelan Archaeology* (New Haven: Yale University Press).
ROWE, JOHN HOWLAND
1944 "An introduction to the archaeology of Cuzco," *Papers of the Peabody Museum of American Archaeology and Ethnology*, Harvard University, Vol. XXVII, No. 2.
SALIM, S. M.
1962 *Marsh Dwellers of the Euphrates Delta*, London School of Economics Monographs on Social Anthropology, No. 23.
SANSOM, GEORGE
1958 *A History of Japan to 1334*. (Stanford: Stanford University Press).
SEARS, W. H.
1961 "The study of social and religious systems in North American archaeology," *Current Anthropology*, Vol. II: 223-46.
SJOBERG, GIDEON
1960 *The Preindustrial City* (Glencoe: The Free Press).
SMITH, W. S.
1958 *The Art and Architecture of Ancient Egypt* (Baltimore: Penguin Books, Ltd.).
SOUSTELLE, JACQUES
1962 *The Daily Life of the Aztecs* (New York: The Macmillan Company).
STEWARD, J. H.
1955 *Theory of Culture Change* (Urbana: University of Illinois Press).
SUGGS, R. C.
1960 *The Island Civilizations of Polynesia* (New York: Mentor Books).

TRIGGER, B. G.
1960 "The destruction of Huronia," *Transactions of the Royal Canadian Institute,* Vol. XXXIII, Pt. 1, No. 68: 14-45.
1962 "Settlement as an aspect of Iroquoian adaptation at the time of contact," *American Anthropologist,* Vol. LXV: 86-101.
1963 "Order and freedom in Huron society," *Anthropologica* N. S. V: 151-69.
1965 *History and Settlement in Lower Nubia*, New Haven: Yale University Publications in Anthropology, No. 69

VOGT, E. Z.
1956 "An appraisal of *Prehistoric Settlement Patterns in the New World,*" Viking Fund Publications in Anthropology, No. 23:173-82.

WEISS, A. H.
1961 "The Roman Walls of Barcelona," *Archaeology*, Vol. XIV: 188-97.

WHEELER, MORTIMER
1960 *The Indus Valley Civilization* (Cambridge: University Press).

WHITE, L. A.
1959 *The Evolution of Culture* (New York: McGraw-Hill Book Company).

WILLETTS, WILLIAM
1958 *Chinese Art* (Harmondsworth: Penguin Books, Ltd.).

WILLEY, G. R.
1953 *Prehistoric Settlement Patterns in the Viru Valley*, Washington: Bureau of American Ethnology, Bulletin 155.
1956a (editor) *Prehistoric Settlement Patterns in the New World,* Viking Fund Publications in Anthropology, No. 23.
1956b "Problems concerning prehistoric settlement patterns in the Maya lowlands" (in Willey, 1956a).

WILLEY, G. R., and PHILIP PHILLIPS
1958 *Method and Theory in American Archaeology* (Chicago: University of Chicago Press).

VI

SHERBURNE F. COOK
and
ROBERT F. HEIZER

Relationships among Houses, Settlement Areas, and Population in Aboriginal California [1]

In studies of primitive societies, the formulation and expression of quantitative relationships between population and elements of space have received only casual attention. Nevertheless, some system of numerical constants or similar indices of general applicability would be very useful for the comparison of different cultures and settlement patterns. Some insight might also be obtained with respect to the factors underlying whatever distinctions are found to occur.

[1] Because several years have elapsed since this paper was written, the authors feel it necessary to state that they would not today write this paper in quite the same way because additional information and alternative approaches have in the interval become available. With reference to California we point to the excellent monograph of A. K. Brown (1967), which deals with the aboriginal population numbers of the Chumash tribe of the Santa Barbara Channel region. If Brown's work had been available in 1963-64, we would have been able to make good use of it. To attempt now to give it consideration would require changing some of the detailed data in the paper, and it is our experience that when one tries to make such adjustments in a paper already written errors are inevitably introduced. We have, therefore, chosen not to make alterations of the original data. Some of the tribal areas named here, and delineated in Fig. 1, would be altered to conform to the more accurate maps that have been drawn up and published in Heizer (1966). While such adjustments would be minor ones, to have made them would also require modification of the tables, and for this reason we have elected to let the paper stand as originally written.

The acquisition of emeritus status by one author (S.F.C.) and the decision of the Committee on Research at Berkeley to consider the research of the other author as unworthy of further support have made revision or rewriting seem a greater effort than is practicable. As a result, what follows has not merely an aboriginal flavor, but also an archaeological tone.

Partial support for the research reported here was provided by the National Science Foundation (Grant G-23734). The Wenner Gren Foundation for Anthropological Research has, through earlier grants to the authors, significantly encouraged the realization of this paper. Some of our ideas on the subject were developed in 1964, when both authors held the appointment of Research Professor in the Miller Institute for Basic Research in Science.

Several years ago Cook and Treganza (1950) examined the maps of seventeen village sites published by Waterman (1920) for the Yurok tribe of northwestern California. An approximately straight-line function was found to exist when the logarithms of the populations, as derived from house counts, were plotted against those of the respective village areas. In other words, the living space increased exponentially, rather than directly, as the population of the villages became larger.

Subsequently, Naroll (1956, 1961, 1962; also Naroll and Bertalanffy, 1956) made significant contributions to the subject. In particular, he found the exponential function to hold when the areas of a series of 18 villages or towns were compared with the corresponding populations. For the space element, in distinction to Cook and Treganza, Naroll used the floor area of the largest settlement within a cultural aggregate. He defined floor area as the total space in a settlement which is under a roof. Clearly we are dealing with different geometrical magnitudes: in one case the area of the whole village, in the other the area covered by roofs. Yet it would appear that the same type of equation can express the relationship of either magnitude with the number of inhabitants. Indeed, Naroll has gone so far as to interpret his area-population data as another instance of the allometric relationship found very widely in the formulation of many types of biological processes. It seems to us, however, that before accepting any broad theory or universal interpretation of the space-population complex, we should reexamine briefly the elementary principles which dictate the type of equation best expressing the interrelationship. Furthermore, it would be desirable to investigate a wider range of raw data than has yet been submitted to the scrutiny of interested students.

We shall assume that the population is the independent variable and that the space occupied is dependent upon the number of occupants. Then, in constructing the graph, we shall plot population on the x-axis, or abscissa, and space on the y-axis, or ordinate. Initially, one would use the given numerical values for both magnitudes. Then the simplest function which could relate space to population would be a straight line, and the equation would be $y = a + bx$, where b denotes the slope of the line and a is the point of intersection of the line with the ordinate.

All other functions, when the numerical values are plotted directly, result in curves. If the data are to be handled by even the most rudimentary statistical methods, it is highly desirable that they be converted to the linear form. With biological processes, this conversion is often accomplished effectively by using the logarithms of the numerical values instead of those values directly. Two such modes of formulation have been found of wide application in the physical and biological sciences, and are of immediate interest in connection with settlement patterns.

Modes of Formulation

In the first of these modes we plot the logarithms of y against the direct values of x. If the graph is then linear, the relationship may be expressed as $y = ab^x$. Here x itself is an exponent. Using ordinary logarithms, we may also write the equation as $\log y = \log a + (\log b)\, x$, or, with natural logarithms, as $\log_e y = \log_e a + bx$. The latter expression is often put in the form $y = a\, e^{bx}$. This is the *exponential* function observed and used generally in following growth in organisms; with a negative exponent, it is the function characterizing radioactive and other types of decay.

It is significant that the processes mentioned, together with many others, involve a change of some magnitude in size, amount, or concentration, and that the independent variable is time. Here we would be dealing with a *rate,* and the exponential formulation is likely to be the most appropriate. On the other hand, when there is no change, no rate, at issue, and interest centers in the association between the magnitudes of two variables at a single point in time, or irrespective of time, it is probable that some other formulation is more suitable.

Such a formulation is that which results when we plot the logarithm of y against the logarithm of x. If the data thus rectified show a straight line in the graph, then $y = a\, x^b$, or, in logarithmic form $\log y = \log a + b \log x$. Here b, not x, is the exponent, and the type of function is better designated *logarithmic* than exponential. The exponent b, of course, defines the slope of the line in the log-log graph, and is the regression coefficient in the statistical sense.

The problem which confronts the student of settlement patterns is whether the linear (direct) plot or the logarithmic plot best expresses the actual data, it being assumed that no secular change or rate is being studied. Very frequently it is not at all obvious at first glance which method is preferable, even though the appropriate graphs are at hand for inspection. We believe that not only under such circumstances but also as a standard procedure, the logarithmic form should be employed. Three reasons for this opinion follow.

First, a direct or linear function associating the two variables may be regarded as merely a special case of the logarithmic function. If $y = ax$, then the exponent of x is 1.0. But this equation may also be written as $\log y = \log a + b \log x$, where b equals 1.0. Conversely, if a log-log plot shows the slope of the regression line b to have the value of 1.0, then the direct plot of the data will also produce a linear relationship. But if b equals any other value, the direct plot will produce a curve, not a straight line. It follows that the logarithmic form includes and surpasses the direct form. The critical constant is, of course, b, and in making comparisons, therefore, b can be a very valuable index. It may be used entirely empirically, within the limits of accuracy of the basic data, without any commitments to interpretation or theory.

Second, data derived from elements of space or from populations are likely to show badly skewed distributions. For example, we may refer to the size of habitation site areas in the territory of the Yuki tribe of Mendocino County, California. The range is from a few hundred to 125,000 square feet. Of 414 sites, 236 are from 0 to 5,000 square feet in area, 85 are from 5,000 to 10,000, 29 from 10,000 to 15,000, and so on. The populations show a similar distortion; when the values of both parameters are plotted, the points are found to be heavily concentrated toward the intersection of the axes, but widely dispersed as higher values are reached. Indeed, in many instances where the direct figures have been plotted, the standard deviation of one or both of the variables exceeds the corresponding mean.

A further consequence of extreme skewing is the undue effect exerted by the very few large areas or populations, which may in fact radically alter the magnitude of derived numerical constants. For example, consider the brief tabulation shown in Table 1 for the data published by Naroll. It will be noted that when the original figures are employed, if the largest settlement (the Inca city of Cuzco) is omitted, the slope of the regression line b has the value $+0.626$, whereas, if Cuzco is included, b equals $+0.083$. This is a very profound influence to be exerted by a single point on a graph.

When the logarithms of both population and area are used, the curves tend to become much more nearly symmetrical, though a completely normal distribution is rare. Moreover, the influence of a few widely divergent points is mitigated. Thus, when the data of Naroll are plotted logarithmically, the slope changes from $+1.044$ only to $+0.858$, according to whether Cuzco is omitted or included.

There is a third reason for using logarithms rather than linear plotting. As already stated, if the variables are related to each other directly, then b is a coefficient of x defining the slope of the regression of y upon x, and the exponent of x is 1.0. Under these conditions, the numerical value of b is determined by the units and the scale employed for the expression of both x and y, and may be altered by changing either the units or the scale (for instance from square meters to square feet, or from hundreds to thousands of people). Here, therefore, b has little value as a numerical index to the inherent relationship between x and y. On the other hand, when the variables are expressed in the form of the logarithms, b is a coefficient defining the slope of the regression of $\log y$ upon $\log x$, and when the logarithms are reconverted to the direct values, becomes the exponent of x. As such, its numerical value is independent of the units and scale in which the variables are expressed and may be taken as describing the function relating x to y.

In dealing with settlement populations and areas, as has been previously suggested, we encounter inevitably a wide range of variability. Probably we shall never encounter a graph in which the points fall perfectly along a line or a curve. Thus it is necessary to evaluate scatter diagrams and to assess and test the goodness of fit of the individual points by conventional methods.

The first and most obvious device is to calculate the correlation coefficient *r*, which furnishes an immediate impression of the extent of association between the two variables. It does not, to be sure, afford any clue to causal relationships, nor does it distinguish between the dependent and the independent variable. On the other hand, the numerical magnitude of the coefficient, taken in conjunction with the number of cases covered, does permit an estimate of the strength, or degree of association. Thus any value of *r* which passes the five per cent, and certainly any that passes the one per cent, level of probability may be considered as establishing beyond reasonable doubt the existence of a valid parallelism between, let us say, population and area.

The second device involves initially the computation of the regression coefficient, *b*. In addition to utilizing the value of this constant as indicating the type of function linking the two variables, we may then determine the standard deviation from the regression line of the points along the *y*-axis, or, as it is otherwise known, the *standard error of estimate*. This term is a direct measure of the average vertical displacement of the observed points above and below the values which would be predicted by *b* from the corresponding values of *x*. If the correspondence is perfect and all points fall exactly on the regression line, the dispersion will be nil, and the standard error of estimate will be zero. For any other condition the standard error will have a real and positive value, and the greater its magnitude, the less perfect the association.

A serious problem immediately arises with the use of the standard error of estimate for evaluating the extent of scatter of points expressing space and population. The standard error is not a pure number, like the correlation and regression coefficients. It states the standard deviation from the regression line in terms of whatever units are employed in plotting the variable *y*. Hence, if we wish to compare the standard errors of estimate produced by plotting points derived from two different settlement populations, it is necessary that the units expressing the *y*-variable be identical. This condition may be satisfied if areas, for example, are given in square feet for both patterns. But we could not compare square feet with square meters. Moreover, if, for a single set of data, we wish to compare the direct form with the logarithmic form, the condition will not be satisfied since the standard errors of estimate will be very different when the logarithms are used rather than the numbers themselves. This requirement of retaining identical units for comparative purposes imposes a severe restriction upon the use of the standard error of estimate.

There is, however, one recourse. We may calculate the *standard deviation* from the *mean* of *y*, which is a measure of the dispersion of the observed values around a single point, the mean, and is contingent upon the units in which *y* is expressed. We now have two standard deviations, one from the mean, the other from the regression line, both based upon the same numerical values. In the *ratio* of the two standard deviations, therefore, the units of expression cancel out, leaving simply a number which can then be compared with other numbers derived in a similar manner, but without reference to the units of expression. In practice, we take the ratio of the standard error of estimate to the standard deviation from the mean of y. The latter must always be a measurable value. The former, if the association is perfect, may approach zero. Conversely, as the ratio increases so does the indicated extent of the dispersion of the points on the graph from the regression line.

To illustrate the type of result that may be obtained from these methods, we have taken the figures published by Naroll for 18 primitive settlements, which show for each settlement the population and the total floor space. The population is expressed as numbers of inhabitants, the floor space as units of 100 square feet (Naroll used square meters). The values of r show a significant correlation for all variants of the data, but are definitely higher with the logarithmic form. The value of b differs materially with the omission of Cuzco when the data are utilized in their direct form, but differs little when the logarithms are used. The ratio of standard error of estimate to standard deviation of y is very high in the direct form, but significantly lower in the logarithmic form. Furthermore, when plotted graphically, it is visibly clear that the logarithmic plot gives a better association of the variables and a closer aggregation of the individual points than the direct plot. These facts alone would justify the use of the logarithms rather than the original direct values.

TABLE 1

Data from Naroll (1961)

	Towns	Form	Number of cases	Mean population	Mean floor space	r	b	Standard Deviation of y	Standard Error of Estimate	Ratio of S.E.E. to S.D.
I	Omit Cuzco	direct	17	2023	2207	0.665	0.626	3341	2642	76.86
II	Include Cuzco	direct	18	13021	3084	0.775	0.083	4998	4995	99.95
III	Omit Cuzco	log-log	17	2.816	2.773	0.888	1.044	0.785	0.367	46.75
IV	Include Cuzco	log-log	18	2.954	2.855	0.879	0.858	0.838	0.411	49.05

Distinctions among Parameters

At this point a more precise definition of the parameters with which we are dealing is desirable. For purposes of this discussion, *population* may be taken simply as the aggregate number of inhabitants without consideration of age, sex, or economic or social status. Furthermore, we may ignore dynamics and consider an area as filled with a maximum, or equilibrium, population at any particular moment of time.

It is possible to distinguish three ranks, or levels, of two-dimensional *space*. The first is *floor space*, that with which Naroll has concerned himself and which he has defined as the area covered by the roof of a house. It is, of course, true that complexities may arise: what is the house?; must it be roofed?; are we to include subsidiary structures or enclosures such as patios? Nevertheless, the underlying concept is reasonably clear; floor space is the space within which a family (or group of families) eats, sleeps, and carries on intimate personal activities. This space may be brought into association with population in two ways. The first way is by determining the amount of floor space occupied per person, which requires a knowledge of the size or area of the dwelling, and the number of persons who constitute the household. It should be emphasized that this calculation does not consider the kinship or social affinities among the persons but only their number. Hence we may bypass all considerations involving kinship and marriage unless an investigation of these factors is necessary to an estimate of numbers.

The other type of association embraces the community as a whole: how is the total floor space in the settlement related to the entire population? This function is, to be sure, an extension of the first, but usually requires that we know also the number of dwellings or its equivalent. It also affords an important approach when, as with archaeological sites, the population itself has disappeared but traces of the dwellings remain.

The second rank, or category, of space covers the entire settlement but does not go beyond it. This space includes that which is devoted to internal domestic affairs and adds what is concerned with interfamily activities—all of the varied social, economic, and ceremonial life of the community. Many names may be applied here, but a term which is simple and noncommittal, and applicable to both modern and extinct settlements of all sizes, is *site space*. Some question may be raised with respect to the limits of this space. Naroll has offered two interpretations of "settlement size," one based upon the dispersion of the dwellings, the other upon population. It is probable that each study is best served by an *ad hoc* definition of site space.

The third category of space is one which is very difficult to delimit rigidly. Here we encounter the entire area in which a human group carries on any activity whatever of a standard and methodical character. This area is often coterminous with the political boundary of a town, state, or nation. It may be circumscribed by rivers, hills, oceans, or degrees of latitude. This area, held for use by the group against other groups, may be designated for convenience *operating space*. Whether or not its relation to population can be expressed by any simple mathematical function has not yet been demonstrated, and we shall not attempt further discussion of the problem here.

KEY TO FIG. 1

Athabascan Family
Oregon group
 1a. Rogue River
Tolowa group
 1b. Tolowa
Hupa group
 1c. Hupa
 1d. Chilula
 1e. Whilkut
Mattole group
 1f. Mattole
Wailaki group
 1g. Nongatl
 1h. Lassik
 1i. Sinkyone
 1j. Wailaki
 1k. Kato

Algonkin Family
Yurok
 2a. Yurok
 2b. Coast Yurok
 3. Wiyot

Yukian Family
 4a. Yuki
 4b. Huchnom
 4c. Coast Yuki
 4d. Wappo

Lutuamian Family
 5. Modoc

Hokan Family
Shastan
 6a. Shasta
 6b. New River Shasta
 6c. Konomihu
 6d. Okwanuchu
 6e. Achomawi (Pit River)
 6f. Atsugewi (Hat Creek)
Yana
 7a. Northern Yana (Noze)
 7b. Central Yana (Noze)
 7c. Southern Yana
 7d. Yahi
 8. Karok
 9. Chimariko
Pomo
 10a. Northern
 10b. Central
 10c. Eastern
 10d. Southeastern
 10e. Northeastern
 10f. Southern
 10g. Southwestern
 11. Washo
 12. Esselen
Salinan
 13a. Antoniano
 13b. Migueleno
 13c. Playano (doubtful)
Chumash
 14a. Obispeño
 14b. Purisimeño
 14c. Ynezeño
 14d. Barbareño
 14e. Ventureño
 14f. Emigdiano
 14g. Interior (doubtful)
 14h. Island
Yuman
 15a. Northern (Western) Diegueño
 15b. Southern (Eastern) Diegueño
 15c. Kamia
 15d. Yuma
 15e. Halchidhoma (now Chemehuevi)
 15f. Mohave

Penutian Family
Wintun
 Dialect Groups:
 16a. Northern
 16b. Central (Nomlaki)
 16c. Southeastern (Patwin)
 16d. Southwestern (Patwin)
Maidu
 Dialect Groups:
 17a. Northeastern
 17b. Northwestern
 17c. Southern (Nisenan)
Miwok
 18a. Coast
 18b. Lake
 18c. Plains
 18d. Northern
 18e. Central
 18f. Southern
Costanoan
 19a. Saklan (doubtful)
 19b. San Francisco
 19c. Santa Clara
 19d. Santa Cruz
 19e. San Juan Bautista (Mutsun)
 19f. Monterey (Rumsen)
 19g. Soledad
Yokuts
 Dialect Groups:
 20a. Northern Valley (Chulamni, Chauchila, etc.)
 20b. Southern Valley (Tachi, Yauelmani, etc.)
 20c. Northern Hill (Chukchansi, etc.)
 20d. Kings River (Choinimni, etc.)
 20e. Tule-Kaweah (Yaudanchi, etc.)
 20f. Poso Creek (Paleuyami)
 20g. Buena Vista (Tulamni, etc.)

Uto-Aztekan (Shoshonean) Family
Plateau branch
 Mono-Bannock group:
 21a. Northern Paiute (Paviotso)
 21b. Eastern Mono (Paiute)
 21c. Western Mono
 Shoshone-Comanche group:
 20d. Koso (Panamint, Shoshone)
 Ute-Chemehuevi group:
 20e. Chemehuevi (Southern Paiute)
 21f. Kawaiisu (Tehachapi)

Kern River branch
21g. Tubatulabal (and Bankalachi)
Southern California branch
Serrano group:
21h. Kitanemuk (Tejon)
21i. Alliklik
21j. Vanyume (Mohineyam)
21k. Serrano
Gabrieleno group:
21l. Fernandeño
21m. Gabrieleno
21n. Nicoleño
Luiseño-Cahuilla group:
21o. Juaneño
21p. Luiseño
21q. Cupeño
21r. Pass Cahuilla
21s. Mountain Cahuilla
21t. Desert Cahuilla

Fig. 1. Native Tribes, Groups, Dialects, and Families of California in 1770 (prepared by the Department of Anthropology, University of California, Berkeley, 1925).

ANALYTICAL APPLICATIONS

We now turn to examine some of the possible relationships suggested above by means of a rather intensive analysis of the specific cultural province of aboriginal northern and central California. For several reasons, this province is particularly suitable for investigation. First, there is a multiplicity of historical, ethnographic, and archaeological sources bearing upon the area. Second, there is a large number of settlements, villages, and other sites–running into the thousands–concerning which at least some information is available. Third, the territory, ecologically and ethnologically, is quite varied in its local aspects. Fourth, the amplitude of the data make California an excellent testing ground for the development of techniques and methods of attack. At the same time, secondary problems of all sorts are brought to light.

In approaching the field offered by native settlements in central and northern California, we are immediately confronted with the problem of scale. In working with the Yurok data, Cook and Treganza (1950) were limited to a string of 17 closely affiliated villages in one small ecological niche–the lower Klamath River and adjacent coast. In another study, we have paid particular attention to the Santa Barbara Channel Chumash and to a local group of tribes in Tierra del Fuego (Cook and Heizer, 1965), but it would be meaningless to attempt a composite graph of area and population for the whole of California, or even a major portion thereof. Consequently, the entire province must be broken down into ecologically or culturally significant areas of smaller dimensions. At the same time, Naroll's method of selecting *one* settlement (the largest) from each of these areas would be uneconomical when the figures for dozens of settlements can be procured. What has been done, therefore, is to divide the entire province into secondary areas or regions in such a way that size to population and other relationships may be studied for the settlements within each region, and also that the regions themselves may be compared with each other. The number and boundaries of these secondary regions will vary with the criterion used, whether that be habitat or tribal affiliation or socioeconomic level.

The three parameters most important to any such investigation are population, floor space, and site space. Data yielding an immediate value for population may be used without further discussion, but such data are not always available, particularly for northern California. If they are not, then an indirect solution is demanded, and is best secured by a consideration of houses and families, or households. The pertinent information may be obtained from ethnographic and historical publications and will include observations and accounts of dimensions of houses, number of persons per family, number of families per house, and number of persons per house. If the number of houses per village is also known, the population can be readily computed. Finally, village or site area can be ascertained, occasionally from contemporary written sources, but usually from archaeological site records.

Thirty Regions in California The task of amassing this information has been accomplished and the numerical material has been set forth in detail, together with discussion of methods, pitfalls, and problems, in a paper published in the University of California *Archaeological Survey Reports* (Cook and Heizer, 1965). A repetition of this discussion here would be superfluous, but the data we must use. Therefore a consolidated summary of the final estimates for 30 regions in California is given in Table 2.

The averages of floor space per house (Column I, in Table 2) are obtained either from written descriptions or from house pit measurements recorded in the files of the University of California Archaeological Research Facility at Berkeley. The number of persons per family (Column II) refers to the nuclear or biologic family of father, mother, and children, although close relatives were occasionally included so as to form an extended family. The value is almost universally taken as 6.0 in aboriginal California. The principal exception is in the case of the northwestern tribes, for which Kroeber (1925:17), after long study, proposed 7.5 persons. The number of families per house (Column III), with a few exceptions, is 1.0. In other words, over most of the state the houses were occupied by single families. The exceptions are for certain regions where multifamily or communal houses are known to have occurred. These regions have been examined in detail in Cook and Hezier (1965). The number of persons per house, or the household number (Column IV), is usually the product of the persons per biologic family and the number of families. But, as we have already intimated, there is evidence in a few cases for believing that each house was occupied by an extended family rather than by a strictly biologic family.

The number of houses per village (Column VI) is generally obtained from house pit counts taken at archaeological sites, although in some instances there exists also valid historical or ethnographic evidence. The house pit method is recognized as subject to error; however, in California, where there has been opportunity to make a cross comparison, the number of house pits has not deviated systematically or seriously from the corresponding number of houses as stated in the written descriptions. Furthermore, it would be very difficult to compare a series of local regions if we were forced to rely exclusively on the relatively few reports submitted by contemporary or secondary observers.

The mean area of villages for each region is based almost entirely on measurements made by survey parties at archaeological sites. From this source, it has been possible to obtain acceptable estimates for nearly 3,000 sites, about half of which have contributed to the figures shown in Column IX, Table 2. Even brief examination of the records makes it evident not only that there is enormous variation in size from site to site, even within

TABLE 2

Estimates of Relationships among Size of Houses, Settlement Areas, and Population for Thirty Regions in Aboriginal California

Region No.	Tribe or Locality	I Floor space per house (mean sq. ft.)	II No. persons per family	III No. families per house	IV No. persons per house	V Floor space per person (mean sq. ft.)	VI No. houses per village	VII No. persons per village	VIII Total floor space per village (mean sq. ft.)	IX Area of village (mean sq. ft.)	X Village space per house (sq. ft.)	XI Village space per person (sq. ft.)	XII Ratio total floor space x 100 to village area
1	Yurok	439	7.5	1.0	7.5	58.5	7.8	60	3,434	25,450	3,263	424	13.5
2	Wiyot	254	7.5	1.0	7.5	33.8	7.6	57	1,930	28,400	3,738	498	6.8
3	Karok		7.5	1.0	7.5		4.1	31					
4	Hupa	400	7.0	1.0	7.0	57.1	10.9	76	4,360				
5	Chilula		7.5	1.0	7.5		7.0	52					
6	Shasta	264	7.0	1.0	7.0	33.0	6.0	48	1,584	18,950	3,158	394	8.4
7	Achomawi	110	6.0	1.0	6.0	18.3	5.3	32	583	14,000	2,641	438	4.2
8	Modoc	118	6.0	1.0	6.0	19.6	5.4	32	637	27,100	5,019	847	2.4
9	Northern Paiute	100	6.0	1.0	6.0	16.7	3.6	22	360	61,500	17,084	2,795	0.6
10	Athabascans	125	6.0	1.0	6.0	20.8	5.0	30	625	6,390	1,278	214	9.8
11	Yuki	100	6.0	1.0	6.0	16.7	6.0	36	600	4,730	788	131	12.7
12	Pomo, coast	150	6.0	1.0	6.0	25.0	5.1	31	765	4,270	840	138	17.9
13	Pomo, interior	900	6.0	2.5	15.0	60.0	15.0	225	13,500	24,750	1,650	110	54.5

TABLE 2 (cont'd.)

Region No.	Tribe or Locality	I Floor space per house (mean sq. ft.)	II No. persons per family	III No. families per house	IV No. persons per house	V Floor space per person (mean sq. ft.)	VI No. houses per village	VII No. persons per village	VIII Total floor space per village (mean sq. ft.)	IX Area of village (mean sq. ft.)	X Village space per house (sq. ft.)	XI Village space per person (sq. ft.)	XII Ratio total floor space x 100 to village area
14	Wappo, valley	940	6.0	2.0	12.0	78.6	15.0	180	14,100	19,350	1,290	107	72.7
15	Wappo, hill	200	6.0	1.0	6.0	33.3	9.3	56	1,860	19,000	2,042	340	9.8
16	Coast Miwok		6.0	1.0	6.0		5.4	32		7,030	1,300	220	
17	Wintu	111	6.0	1.0	6.0	18.5	5.4	32	600	11,200	2,074	350	5.3
18	Northern Wintun	129	6.0	1.0	6.0	21.5	7.0	42	903	16,800	2,400	400	5.4
19	Central Wintun	82	6.0	1.0	6.0	13.7	6.3	39	518	8,030	1,274	206	6.4
20	Southern Wintun	139	6.0	1.0	6.0	23.5	6.3	39	876	14,030	2,227	360	6.2
21	Maidu	125	6.0	1.0	6.0	20.8	6.6	40	827	13,430	2,035	336	6.1
22	Sierra Miwok	123	6.0	1.0	6.0	20.5	5.4	32	664	14,150	2,620	442	4.5
23	Mono	125	5.1	1.0	5.1	24.5	3.6	18	454				
24	Yokuts, hill	131	6.0	1.0	6.0	21.8	3.8	23	498	11,720	3,048	510	4.2
25	Tubatulabal	75	6.0	1.0	6.0	12.5	3.7	22	278	33,100	8,949	1,505	0.8
26	Paiute, Mono Co.	110	6.0	1.0	6.0	18.3	2.5	15	275	40,350	16,140	2,690	0.7
27	Paiute, Inyo Co.	100	6.0	1.0	6.0	16.7	5.5	33	550	99,200	18,044	3,006	0.5
28	Sta. Rosa Island	356	6.0	1.25	7.5	47.5	11.6	87	4,130	25,100	2,164	288	16.4
29	Central Valley	1,130	6.0	3.0	18.0	62.8	20.0	360	22,600	41,400	2,070	115	54.6
30	Sta. Barb. Chan.	1,250	6.0	2.5	15.0	83.3	37.1	557	46,400	101,000	2,723	181	45.9

a very restricted territory, but also that the distributions of size are severely skewed by the presence of a few disproportionately large sites. This problem is similar to that encountered with the form of expression of the relationship between population and area in general. It was pointed out in the discussion of that problem that expressing all values as the logarithms reduces the skewing, normalizes the distribution, and minimizes the effect of the very extreme values on the general average. Thus, for the case at hand, we obtain for each region the average of the logarithms and convert this back into direct units of area (square feet). Each figure shown in Table 2, therefore, is the geometric mean rather than the arithmetic mean of the site or village areas. The geometric mean, if used consistently, gives a more faithful representation than the arithmetic mean of the ordinary style of sites in a cultural region.

The basic unit of habitation space is the floor area of the individual house. The corresponding population unit is the household, irrespective of blood or social relationship. However, in our experimental province, California, the mean house floor space varies widely from region to region, whereas the household number has been taken as a standard 6.0 in 18 out of 27 usable regions. Hence it is more instructive to study a derived magnitude—the *mean floor space per person* (Column V, Table 2). A priori there are three possible hypotheses which might be tested: (1) the floor space per person is unaffected, i.e., remains constant, regardless of the size of the dwelling; (2) the floor space per person increases; or (3) the floor space per person decreases as the dwelling size increases.

We first plot directly the values given in the table for floor space per person (Column V) against those for mean floor space per house (Column I) and compute the usual constants. The graph is shown in Fig. 2. The value of r is $+0.923$ and that of b is $+0.549$. It is immediately evident that the average floor space at the disposal of each person is dependent upon and increases with house size (*vide* hypothesis No. 2, *supra*). Otherwise r would have a value of no statistical significance, or b would be negative or zero. We still, however, do not know the function that relates the two magnitudes with the greatest degree of precision.

Inspection of Fig. 2 discloses two features. First, the trend of the points is on the whole linear, and might perhaps be expressed by the equation for a straight line. On the other hand, there is very perceptible scattering of the points, or deviation, from expected values. The degree of dispersion can be tested by means of the standard error of estimate. This factor has the value ± 7.71 square feet on a mean for y of 32.5 square feet. The standard deviation from the mean is ± 20.67 square feet, and the ratio of the standard error to the standard deviation is therefore 0.3732 or, multiplied by 100, 37.32.

The second feature is the apparent clustering of the 27 points into three groups, those indicated respectively by dots, crosses, and circles on the graph (Fig. 2). The second and third groups seem to be displaced horizontally to the right, as if each were in some measure independent of the others. Now, the dots represent those regions in which 6.0 persons were assigned to a single-family house; the crosses, those with single-family houses but

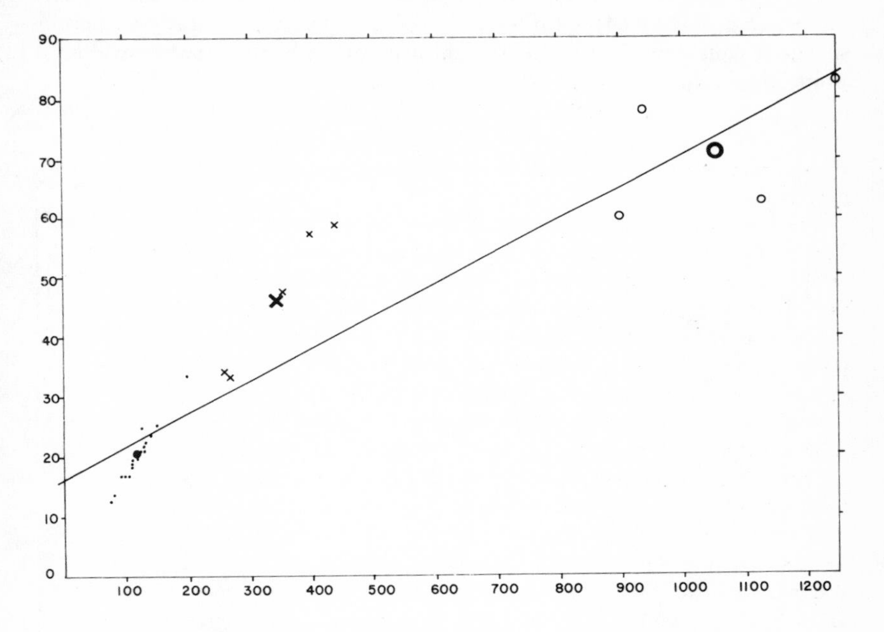

Fig. 2. Ordinate: floor space per person in square feet; means for 27 California regions. Abscissa: floor space per house; means as stated. Dots, crosses, and circles designate groups described in the text. Large symbols are general means for the three groups.

with 7.0, 7.5, and 8.0 persons per house; and the circles, those with multi-family houses, and 12, 15, or 18 persons. The positions of these three groups are emphasized on the graph by three heavy symbols placed respectively at the means for 18 sites (dot), 5 sites (cross), and 4 sites (circle). For the three points considered by themselves, r equals $+0.956$ which, for 2 degrees of freedom, is close to the 5 per cent level of probability (i.e., moderately significant). The value of b is $+0.499$. The standard error of estimate has little meaning with so few points; nevertheless the relative extent of dispersion can be estimated by eye from the graph.

The next step in the procedure is to plot points for the same factors but to compare this time the logarithm of the floor space per person with the logarithm of the house floor space. This is the exponential form and is expressed by the usual logarithmic equation. The result is shown in Fig. 3. From the graph it is evident that the points fall more closely on the regression line than in Fig. 2, an impression confirmed by the fact that *r* equals +0.972 (*b* equals+0.641). For the three points representing the regional group means, *r* equals +0.980, which is significant at about the 2 per cent level of probability.

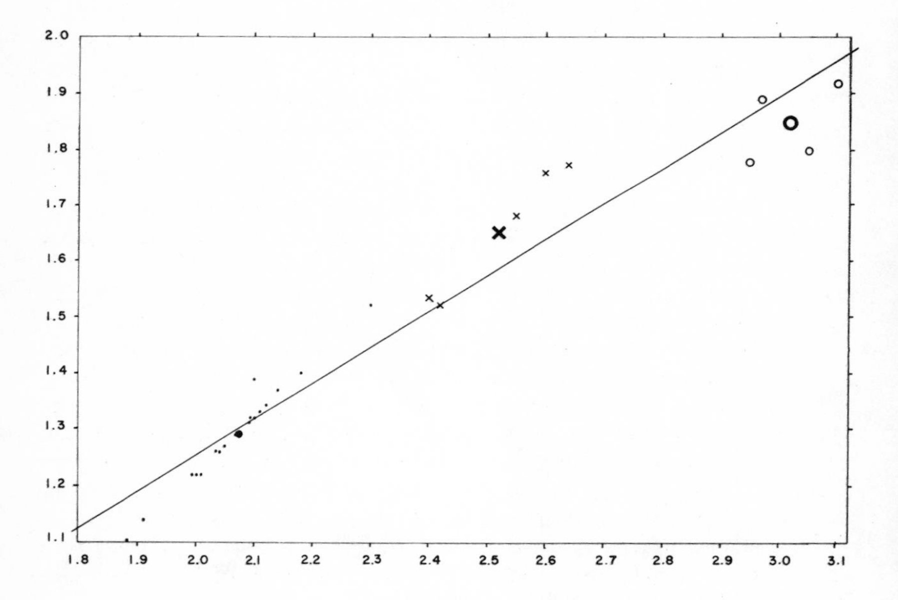

Fig. 3. Ordinate, abscissa, and symbols as in Fig. 2, except that the numerical values are the logarithms of the values plotted in Fig. 2.

The tentative conclusion to be drawn from these formulations is that as the mean floor space or house size increases, so does the mean floor space per person; that is to say, the average amount of floor space available for use to *each* resident. At the same time, since the exponent *b* is fractional, the *rate* of increase in floor space per person is less than that of domestic floor space as a whole.

At this point, it is desirable to reconsider the actual number of persons inhabiting the house. It was stated previously not to be feasible to derive constants for the 30 regions by plotting mean house area against number of persons because of the identity of values for so many regions. However, the problem may be approached, at least in part, in another way. We may consider the three *groups* of regions examined and represented in Figs. 2 and 3. To recapitulate briefly, these consist of (1) the 18 single-family house regions to which are assigned the conventional number of 6 occupants per house; (2) the 5 single-family house regions with 7.0, 7.5, and 8.0 occupants per house, or an average of 7.5; and (3) the 4 multifamily house regions with an average of 15 occupants. We may then plot the regional group means for house floor space against the corresponding group means for occupants per house. The result is that the plot with direct values approximates a straight line, with a value of b very close to 1.0. Using the logarithms produces a slightly better fit, but the difference between the two methods is insignificant. The relationship may therefore be regarded most simply as linear, with the number of persons per house directly proportional to the mean floor space per house. How may this fact be reconciled with the finding that the floor space per person increases with the increasing size of the house?

If we plot directly the mean house floor space against the mean number of persons per house for the three groups of regions and then extrapolate the regression backwards, the line crosses the x-axis (i.e., where y equals zero) at a value of 4.5 persons per house. This means hypothetically that no house could exist in native California with fewer than 4.5 occupants. In reality, the conventional family number of 6.0 represents the smallest *average* number of persons who ever did or could live in an ordinary house. Now the mean floor area of the houses with 6.0 residents (i.e., those in the 18 regions) was 120 square feet, or 20 square feet per person. Starting with this condition, if we allow the average number of occupants to increase, we find that each additional person will absorb 100 square feet (as shown by the data in Table 2) up to at least 12 to 18 persons. This process of allocating 100 square feet for each new individual, on a basis of 20 square feet for each of six original individuals, produces a straight line when the values are plotted logarithmically, but does not when they are plotted directly, for mean floor space per person against mean floor space per house. This, of course, is the result obtained from Columns I and V in Table 2, and is represented graphically in Figs. 2 and 3.

At this point we should emphasize that the technique utilized is not as arbitrary and abrupt as it may appear at first glance. The backward prolongation of the regression line to its intersection with the x axis at a value somewhere near 6 by no means implies that the sixth person in a family required 20 square feet of floor space whereas the seventh person required 100 square feet. It does indicate, however, that there are two intergrading but distinct types of relationship present, one governing space requirement when the family number is small, the other when it becomes larger. In brief, then, we have a minimal practical household of 6.0 persons, each with 20 square feet of floor space, and with the possibility of additional occupants so as to approach a value of 100 square feet per person. The social and cultural significance of this sudden augmentation of floor space is a matter for social anthropological inquiry. In the meantime, it is of interest to note a statement by Naroll (1961): "There is a suggestion that the population of a prehistoric settlement can be roughly estimated by archaeologists as one-tenth of the floor area in square meters occupied by its dwellings." Converting units, and equating to the individual, this means that in the community as a whole the floor space available per person would be of the order of 100 square feet.

Beyond the average *size* of a house, whether expressed in units of pure area such as square feet or in terms of area per person, the population of a settlement must be closely associated with the *number* of houses. If the houses of a single village, or a closely-knit group of villages, are all of approximately the same size, then the total population must be directly proportional to the number of houses, and because house size is constant, there is no relation between number and size of houses. However, it is conceivable that between regions or different cultures the number and size may vary mutually in some systematic manner. This possibility may be tested with the data in Table 2 by comparing for all regions the mean floor space per house (Column I) with the number of houses per village (Column VI).

When we again derive the values for constants, we obtain the results shown below, where x stands for mean floor space per house, y for mean number of houses per village, S.D. for standard deviation of y from the mean, and S.E.E. for standard error of estimate.

x	y	Mean y	S.D.	r	b	S.E.E.	S.E.E. x 100 / S.D.
direct	direct	8.40	6.98	0.910	1.853	3.07	44.00
log	log	0.838	0.254	0.926	0.644	0.119	46.76

From examination of this tabulation and of the derived constants shown above, it is clear that the mean house number per village increases with increasing floor space, or vice versa. The two factors are not algebraically independent as one would expect within a restricted province where the houses were substantially equal in size. From region to region in aboriginal California the larger settlements contained at the same time more houses and bigger houses than the smaller settlements. As to the nature of the relationship, the values for the standard error of estimate indicate a rather wide dispersion of the individual points although the strength of the association is attested by the high values of the correlation coefficients. For working purposes we may adhere to the logarithmic form of expression, and point out that the value of b is definitely less than unity.

We have by now encompassed one term in Naroll's equation, total floor space. This measure is, for a village, the product of house floor space and number of houses; and, for a region, the product of the mean house floor space and the mean number of houses per village. But it has been shown that these two parameters are mutually related, in California at least, and that the relationship is adequately and indeed preferably expressed as a logarithmic function. It follows, therefore, that total floor space in a single village is itself a complex entity, a compound of two other, and interdependent, magnitudes.

The other term incorporated in Naroll's equation is village or settlement population. This measure may be considered as the product of the average number of persons per house and the number of houses. If we relate population, as the mean number of persons per village per region, to the corresponding numbers of persons per house and of houses per village, respectively, and also utilize the data in both direct and logarithmic form, we derive the following results, which are summarized in the text rather than in a table. In lines I and II, x stands for mean number of persons per house; in lines III and IV, for mean number of houses per village. In all cases, y is the mean number of persons per village.

	x	y	Mean y	S.D.	r	b	S.E.E.	S.E.E. x 100 / S.D.
I	direct	direct	78.0	115.61	0.894	3.270	53.20	46.01
II	log	log	1.771	0.377	0.897	2.460	0.158	41.91
III	direct	direct	78.0	115.61	0.983	1.693	14.47	12.51
IV	log	log	1.771	0.377	0.956	1.468	0.071	18.83

When the number of persons per house is plotted against the number of persons per village, the dispersion of the individual points is seen to be great, and although the correlation coefficient is highly significant, the fit is not good in either the direct or the log-log plot. When, on the contrary, the number of houses per village is plotted against the number of persons per village, the values for r are extremely high, those for the standard error of estimate are very low, and even casual observation of the graphs demonstrates that the relationship is close. Moreover, as one would expect, the values for b are much greater than unity.

The quantitative expression of the relation between population and the first level of the spatial element, *floor* space, may now perhaps be put in the form of a few simple equations. It may also be repeated that the second order factors, or magnitudes, are the mean total floor space (which we shall designate S) and mean population, P. These are derived from the first order factors: mean floor space, or area per house q; mean number of persons per house, h; and mean number of houses per village, n.

According to Naroll's equation, total floor space, S, and population P, are related thus:

$$log\ P = log\ a + b\ log\ S$$

But we have shown that S is formed by the product of q and n, and P by the product of h and n. Then if the relationship is logarithmic,

$$log\ S = log\ q + log\ n \quad \text{and} \quad log\ P = log\ h + log\ n$$

We wish to eliminate the second order magnitudes and consider only the primary factors. Hence we substitute and transform to obtain:

$$log\ h + log\ n = log\ a + b\ (log\ q + log\ n)$$

$$\text{or} \quad log\ h = log\ a + b\ log\ q + (b\text{-}q)\ log\ n$$

$$\text{or} \quad h = a\ q^b\ n^{b-q}$$

A facile interpretation of these findings is not readily at hand in so far as the biology and sociology of primitive settlements is concerned. From the standpoint of operation and manipulation, it is evident that the three primary magnitudes–house area, house population, and number of houses per village–are both necessary and sufficient for the numerical expression of relationships. The fact that each pair of parameters is associated through a logarithmic function, or may reasonably be so associated, is not only of general significance to human ecology, as Naroll and Bertalanffy have pointed out, but is also of great value for investigation and study. If sufficient raw data can be secured, it should be possible to characterize a culture in terms of a set of constants, which would thereby form the basis for comparisons between cultures. The relationship of total floor space to total village population, although these are secondary derivatives, is then seen as a very convenient empirical formulation.

To conclude this discussion, and as an example of the similarities and differences that may be brought to light by the method just suggested, we may compare the data assembled by Naroll for 18 widely separated single settlements with those obtained as mean values from 27 California regions. As presented below, x represents mean population and y, mean total floor space per village or town. In each case the logarithms are employed.

Source	No. of cases	Mean x	Mean y	r	b	S.E.E.	S.E.E. x 100/ S.D.
Data from Naroll	18	2.954	2.855	0.879	0.858	0.411	49.05
California regions	27	1.771	1.131	0.978	1.536	0.128	21.24

The California villages are much smaller than those used by Naroll. For both sets of data the correlation coefficients are highly significant, but the values of b differ widely, one being smaller, the other greater, than unity. The standard error of estimate and its ratio to the standard deviation of y are both notably less for the California sample than for the world-wide sample. For the graph of the California regions, see Fig. 4.

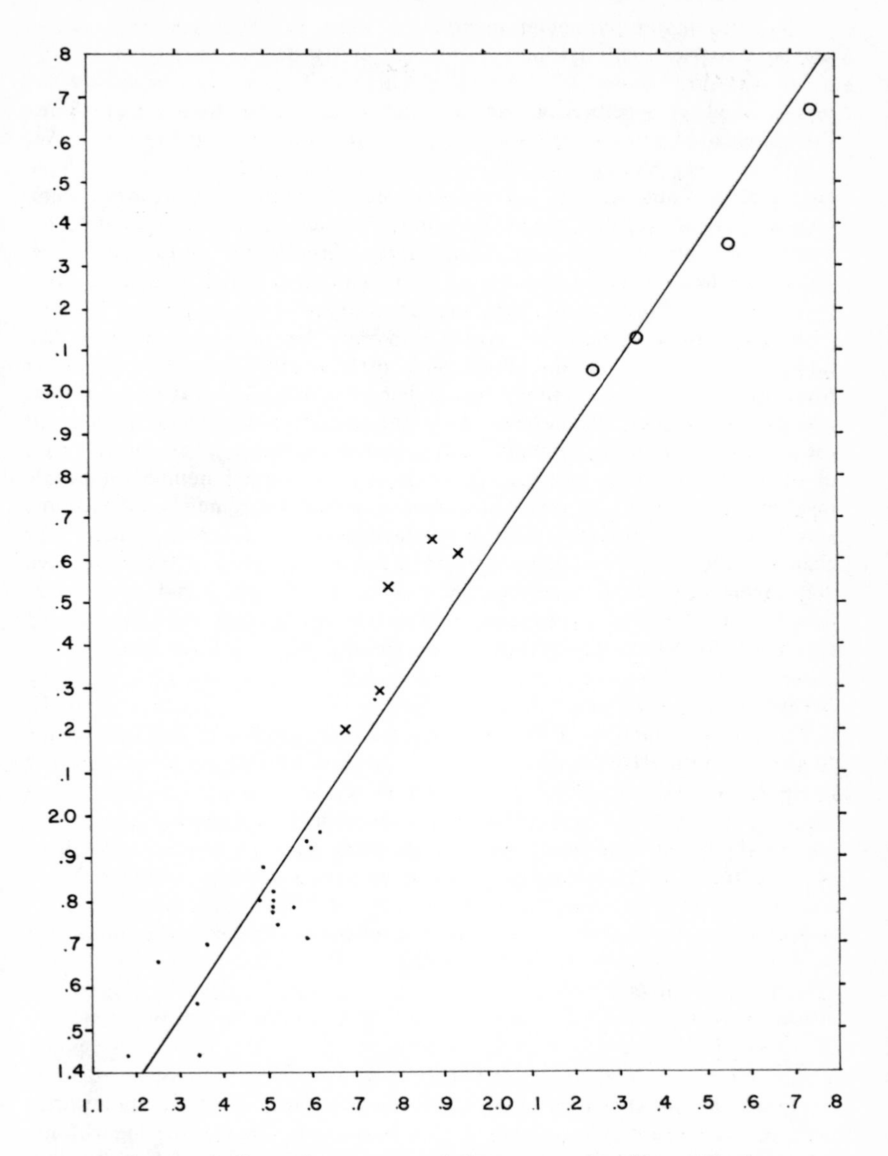

Fig. 4. Ordinate: log mean total floor space per village. Abscissa: log mean number of persons per village. Symbols and groups of regions as in Fig. 2.

The third major parameter mentioned earlier is village or site areas, or settlement space. This is not a compound entity derived through the interaction of other factors. It is the actual number of square feet or square meters covered by a settlement, and as such is analogous to the mean house floor area of the previous discussion rather than to the total floor area. We may ask as the primary question: is the site area related to population, logarithmically or otherwise, in a systematic manner comparable with that demonstrated by total floor space? The first approach to the question is to examine the data on a limited scale, and internally for certain localized, homogeneous regions. Within such a region, the house and household structure will be sufficiently uniform that in computing (or otherwise working with) population it becomes possible to consider house floor space and number of persons per household as constant, and consequently to refer total number of persons simply to number of houses. This rationale enables one merely to count the houses or, in the archaeological context, to count the house pits or other remains, and to use this number as an indicator of, or an *index* to, the population. Alternatively, the actual number of people may be utilized, but in this connection it should be remembered that the numerical factors of importance here, such as r and b, are not altered by changing the units when the logarithmic form is employed. We have been able recently to complete three studies of this type which have been published since the present manuscript was finished in late 1964 (Cook and Heizer, 1965). A summary of the principal findings will be presented here.

Seventeen Yurok Villages The first study, which may be taken as a model for purposes of demonstration, consists of a re-evaluation of the area on the Lower Klamath River inhabited by the Yurok. Our data for the region are taken from plans of 17 villages, drawn by T. T. Waterman (1920), which show the number and arrangement of existing and former houses. By various methods, all depending upon planimeter measurement, it has been possible to estimate the areas of these villages, and of course the house counts may be used to represent the relative population. For actual population, the house numbers have been multiplied by Kroeber's factor of 7.5 persons per household. When we equate the 17 values for area and total persons both directly and logarithmically, we obtain high correlation coefficients (r equals $+0.905$ and $+0.956$ respectively), indicating generally that there is a close correspondence between village area and village population. When the data are compared directly, the standard error of estimate is 43.58 per cent of the standard deviation of y; when the logarithmic form is used, the corresponding figure is 30.00 per cent. Clearly, the logarithmic form exhibits a better fit of points. Furthermore, the value of b when logarithms are used is $+1.585$, indicating that the exponent of x is much greater than unity.

The Yurok data afford an excellent opportunity to explore the effect on the derived constants of the method employed to compute the area of the settlements. On Waterman's maps there is no demarcation of the peripheral boundaries of the villages. Hence these and the areas must be estimated by the student. We developed six different methods of estimation, the details of which have been described in Cook and Heizer (1965). The first (No. 1) consisted of drawing a simple three or four sided figure so as just to include all the dwellings shown on any particular map. No. 2 embraced a figure, irregular in outline, but one which was drawn from one house to the next around the periphery of the group. The other four involved expanding method No. 2 in varying degrees so as to include more and more territory. The population, of course, was always the same for each village, the product obtained by multiplying the number of houses and house pits shown on the map by 7.5, the accepted mean household number. For each method of estimating size, therefore, the logarithms of the areas in hundreds of square feet, y, are equated to those of the population, x. Two results emerge very clearly from this procedure, the condensed figures for which are given below.

Method	x Mean log of no. of persons	y Mean log of area	r	b	Log of area for 7.5 persons
1	1.887	2.684	+ 0.901	+1.405	1.262
2	1.887	2.406	+ 0.956	+1.585	0.802
3	1.887	2.676	+ 0.913	+1.155	1.508
4	1.887	3.118	+ 0.907	+0.720	2.389
5	1.887	3.013	+ 0.840	+1.092	1.926
6	1.887	3.274	+ 0.812	+0.821	2.443

First, the value of the regression coefficient (or the exponent of x) symbolized by b, which is independent in the logarithmic form of the scale and the units employed to express the variables, is nevertheless seen to be highly sensitive to the type and nature of these variables. Population, the absolute number of individuals present, is a stable entity, but the extent of area used to represent village or settlement size is determined by some form of human judgment. Any factor modifying the manner in which this size is computed will thereby strongly alter the quantitative relationship between the size and the population.

Second, it is possible with the Yurok data to test the significance and value of the proportionality constant appearing in any exponential equation. When $\log y$ is plotted against $\log x$, and when the regression line is drawn so as to pass through the common mean of x and y, the point where the line, if extended backward, intersects the y axis determines the value of the coefficient a. The value of a is therefore identical with that taken by y when x is reduced to zero. In the present context this value could be interpreted literally as the area of the site or village when there were no houses or inhabitants; that is to say, the minimal limiting area which could support a village. However, a settlement with no occupants has no meaning in reality. The practical lower limit of x, as the population variable, would be one dwelling or one household. With the Yurok this implies an average of 7.5 persons. Consequently we calculate from the regression formula the area of the village that will just hold 7.5 people. The figures, in the logarithmic form, are given in the last column of the tabulation shown above. The range is wide and conforms closely to the mean area of the 17 villages, as computed by the six different methods ($r = +0.982$).

Settlements in Tierra del Fuego The second local region investigated in detail is far from California – in Tierra del Fuego. The bases for the estimates are the tables and maps given by S. K. Lothrop (1928). Like Waterman for the Yurok, Lothrop shows maps of sites formerly occupied by the Yaghan tribe on the shores of Beagle Channel in the vicinity of Harberton. By appropriate methods, which utilize the dissecting microscope and polar planimeter, the surface area of these sites can be measured from the maps. Lothrop also gives, in tabular form, the corresponding number of house pits for each site. Hence, by using house pits as an index to relative population, we can formulate the necessary equations.

There are three settlement groups, containing respectively 50, 10, and 5 sites. The corresponding values in the logarithmic form are: for r, +0.799, +0.652, and +0.755; and for b, +0.907, and +0.697, and +0.912. The correlation coefficient for the first group is highly significant; for the second group, moderately significant (near the 3 per cent level of probability); and for the third group, poor. The standard errors of estimate have been calculated: their values, expressed as per cent of the standard deviation of y, are 60.77, 80.47, and 81.79. All are high, and indicate a relatively high degree of dispersion of the points around the regression lines. Nevertheless, with all three of Lothrop's groups of sites, the linear trend is unmistakable when the data are plotted logarithmically. There can be little question that the logarithmic function is valid here, despite the obvious deficiencies in the raw data. Indeed it is surprising that the relationship can be demonstrated at all with this type of material.

Chumash Settlements The third study bearing upon the relation between village area and population was of the line of settlements occupied by the Chumash tribe, which was strung out along the shores of the Santa Barbara Channel in southern California. Here the procedure varied somewhat from that described above. A considerable number of late-culture village sites were examined and mapped by D. B. Rogers, and were later described in his book, *Prehistoric Man of the Santa Barbara Coast* (1929). His maps were carefully drawn on a scale sufficiently large so that no magnification is necessary for the measurement of area. For eight of these villages we have explicit statements concerning house numbers, made on the scene by the Spanish missionaries and explorers in the course of the expedition of 1769 (for more complete details we refer the reader to Cook and Heizer, 1965). These statements may be regarded as accurate to within perhaps ±10 per cent, and certainly to within ±20 per cent.

Equating the figures for area and house counts with the eight villages directly, we derive r equal to +0.721. Using logarithms, r is +0.762, b is +1.317, and the standard error of estimate is 69.90 per cent of the standard deviation of y. This showing, though not impressive, is sufficiently significant to support a conviction that the relationship may be expressed correctly in the logarithmic form.

The results obtained with the three widely separated regions reported above all support the same conclusion: there exists a close association between village area and population that can be suitably expressed in the logarithmic form, and that satisfies an equation where the exponent of x is either greater or less than unity. We shall now examine an aggregate of data derived in a quite different manner.

Eleven Geographic Regions In the files accumulated by the Archaeological Research Facility at Berkeley, there are records of several hundred sites for which both site area and number of house pits are given. Many of these sites have formed the basis for the data shown in Table 2, already extensively discussed. In Table 2, however, a factor of paramount importance is house size and floor space. Here we are interested primarily in house number (as shown by house pits) and total village population. Consequently, it is desirable to reorganize the territorial alignments and to establish a different set of regions on the basis of a geographic, rather than a tribal or ethnographic, segregation. This set consists of 11 regions, each of which contains more than 10 sites. The results are summarized in Table 3.

It must be admitted at the outset that there are serious deficiencies in the data. The site areas are, in some cases, little more than estimates. The house pits reported may or may not represent houses simultaneously occupied. The number of house pits seen may not be a true count of the houses in the village, due to the destruction or disappearance of other pits which originally existed. Nevertheless, the fact that any definite association whatever could be found between site area and number of house pits is testimony to the inherent tendency of site size to reflect the magnitude of the inhabiting population.

In equations and graphs, x is uniformly taken as the number of persons per village. This factor is the product of the number of houses (i.e., house pits) and the number of persons per household. The latter measure is 6.0, except for the Inland Pomo (15.0) and the prehistoric Santa Rosa Island Indians (7.5). The area is consistently expressed in units of 100 square feet.

TABLE 3

Population-Area Comparisons within Eleven California Regions

No.	Region	No. cases	x^*	y^{**}	r	b	Standard Error of Estimate as % of Standard Deviation of y
1	Northern Interior Rivers	74	1.461	2.155	0.515	0.910	90.22
2	Inland Yuki	170	1.408	1.621	0.611	0.782	81.14
3	Interior and Clear Lake Pomo	21	1.800	2.152	0.658	1.063	47.77
4	Coastal Pomo and Yuki	15	1.393	1.909	0.883	1.751	47.07
5	Hills of Lake and Napa counties	35	1.565	2.060	0.658	0.764	74.26
6	No. Central Tehama counties, on Sacramento River	15	1.668	2.119	0.813	1.496	58.22
7	Stony Creek Wintun	30	1.504	1.963	0.304	0.489	96.94
8	Sierra Foothills, Butte to Tulare counties	72	1.383	2.101	0.565	0.895	83.07
9	Santa Rosa Island	29	1.700	2.242	0.709	0.864	71.38
10	Paiute of Inyo and Mono counties	26	1.245	2.279	0.736	1.518	69.95
11	Paiute of Modoc and Lassen counties	11	1.214	2.195	0.752	1.808	69.34

* x: mean log of persons per village
**y: mean log of area of village in hundreds of square feet

The values of r vary considerably, but with one exception surpass the one per cent level of probability for the appropriate degree of freedom, and hence are highly significant. The exception is the region containing the Stony Creek Wintun, a small, compact area, for the failure of which to conform to the pattern of the other 10 regions there is no immediate explanation. The regression coefficient fluctuates widely, but is never very close to 1.0. Clearly, there are many factors that have not been controlled, or even taken into consideration, in the present formulation. The fact that the original data are unstandardized and include numerous sources of error is emphasized in the last column of the table, which gives for the standard error of estimate, expressed as per cent of the standard deviation of y, some very high values.

On the whole, however, the results with these 11 rather arbitrarily defined local regions in northern California support the conclusions previously set forth – that even when imperfect basic data are employed, a close association in the logarithmic form can be demonstrated between village area and number of inhabitants. It must be emphasized again, however, that this conclusion applies only to restricted territories or regions, within each of which the physical, biological, and social living conditions are relatively homogeneous and reasonably uniform.

General Relationships

The foregoing proviso now permits the extension of the study to approach the final problem: what is the relation of village area to population between one region and another? Is there any detectable quantitative, systematic, and universal association between the two parameters that overrides all geographic and ethnographic considerations? At least a partial answer may be afforded by the data shown in Table 2, which are based upon the 30 regions into which we first divided the state as a whole. Column VII of Table 2 presents the arithmetic means of persons per village for 30 regions in California, and Column IX shows the geometric means of village or site areas for 26 of these regions. The figures for the other four are unavailable. The two variables for the 26 regions may then be plotted both directly and logarithmically.

The effect of plotting the values directly is shown in Fig. 5. The most cursory inspection demonstrates a high degree of irregularity, with little indication of any consistent or regular relationship between site area and population. When the logarithms of both variables are plotted, the same general pattern persists, as is seen in Fig. 6. Although the individual points are shifted on the graphs, their relative positions are not materially altered. One aspect of the graph, however, is quite conspicuous. If we designate the entire 26 regions as the main group, we may segregate certain subordinate groups according to their placement in the scatter diagram. Thus we set apart as subgroup I the 17 regions in the coastal and hilly portions of northern California that contained only single-family houses, and we show the corresponding points in Figs. 5 and 6 as dots. The five desert areas with single-family houses are designated subgroup II, and are shown as crosses.

The coastal and hill areas, together with the Central Valley, which contained multifamily dwellings, are shown as circles and are designated subgroup III. The location on the graph and the arrangement of these points for the three subgroups are clearly distinct, one from another. This pattern is in sharp contrast to that seen in Fig. 4 where total floor space, rather than site area, is plotted against mean village population, and where the groups of points are distinguished solely on the basis of mean number of persons per household. To some extent, nevertheless, the two modes of segregation by subgroups overlap.

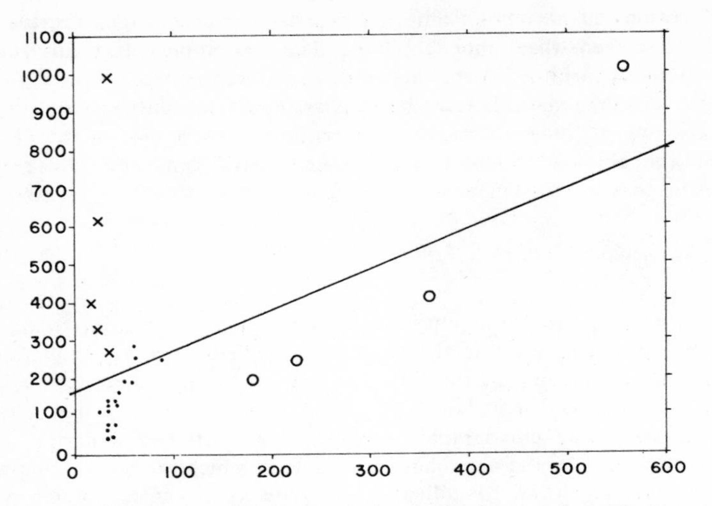

Fig. 5. Ordinate: mean site area in hundreds of square feet. Abscissa: mean number of persons per village. Dots, crosses, and circles designate subgroups of regions I, II, and III as described in text.

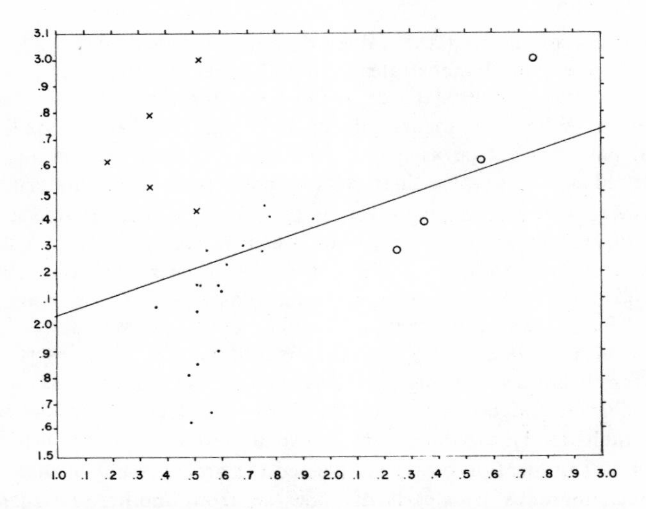

Fig. 6. Ordinate, abscissa, and symbols as in Fig. 5, except that the numerical values are the logarithms of the values plotted in Fig. 5.

The next step is to compute the values of *r*, *b*, and standard error of estimate for the main group and the three subgroups, using both the direct figures and the logarithms. The results are shown in Table 4.

When all 26 regions are included in the calculations and the direct values are used, the correlation coefficient is +0.524, which is beyond the one per cent level of probability and hence definitely significant. Yet, if one region is omitted from the calculation (the Central Valley, where large sites and multifamily houses abound), the remaining 25 regions give a coefficient of only +0.159, a completely nonsignificant value. Furthermore, for the 26 regions as a group, the standard error of estimate amounts to 272.73 per cent of the standard deviation of *y*, an enormous relative vertical dispersion of the points. When the figures for area and population are expressed as the logarithms, *r* is seen to have low significance, and the standard error of estimate is still very considerable. One cannot claim, therefore, that there is convincing evidence in favor of any systematic functional relationship between these two variables.

TABLE 4

Area and Population in Regional Groups in California

No.	Territory or regional group	Form of x*	Form of y**	No. cases	r	b	Standard Error of Estimate in units of y	S.E.E. as % of the Standard Deviation of y
	All 26 regions, from Table 2 (see text)	direct	direct	26	0.524	1.343	629	272.33
		log	log	26	0.372	0.351	0.338	94.68
I	Hill, river, coast areas; single-family houses	direct	direct	17	0.783	3.712	46	62.97
		log	log	17	0.656	1.159	0.195	78.00
II	Desert areas; single-family houses	direct	direct	5	0.392	15.095	311	106.14
		log	log	5	0.220	0.354	0.256	138.32
III	Hill, coast, Central Valley areas; multi-family houses	direct	direct	4	0.977	2.161	98	26.26
		log	log	4	0.982	1.388	0.073	23.17

*x: mean number of persons per village
**y: mean area per village or site in hundreds of square feet

When we use only the hill/river/coast single-family regions (subgroup I), r attains a significance beyond the one per cent level for both modes of expression. The standard error, or dispersion of points, is much less impressive but is, nevertheless, large. There is no strong evidence for preferring one type of function to the other.

The five desert regions (subgroup II) show very poor correlation coefficients and high standard errors of estimate. There is therefore no clear indication of any internal association between size and population. By contrast, the four multifamily regions (subgroup III) are strongly correlated with each other (r is above $+0.97$ for both modes of expression, hence at or beyond the one per cent level, even for three degrees of freedom), and the dispersion of points is much less than in any other group.

These data, though admittedly very approximate, would seem to warrant the conclusion that the mean site areas, from region to region, do not necessarily bear any fixed linear or logarithmic relation to the corresponding mean village populations. On the other hand, clearly defined functions linking site area and population within restricted groups or sets of regions may often be demonstrated. These functions do not appear to be predetermined with respect to type, but may be represented by linear or log-log plots, or both, in any particular case. Thus the *interregional* relationships differ profoundly from the *intraregional*, which are best expressed by a logarithmic function.

The idea that we are in fact dealing with at least three discrete entities (subgroups) when we examine the 26 regions just discussed is supported by a somewhat different line of approach. It is possible to subject the data to a simple test of the validity of the apparent group differences, using the values given in Column XI of Table 2 for the square feet of village surface per inhabitant. It is true that these values are derived empirically, by dividing the geometric mean site area (Column IX) for each region by the corresponding arithmetic mean number of persons per village. Nevertheless, for comparative purposes this magnitude is a fair index to the actual square footage available to each person. We may then segregate the figures for the three regional subgroups mentioned above: (1) hill/river/coast single-family regions; (2) desert single-family regions; and (3) hill/coast/Central Valley multifamily regions.

For this purpose, the subgroups contain, respectively, 16, 5, and 4 regions. Subjecting these figures to a direct analysis of variance, the value of F is found to be 43.5, where F is the standard variance ratio of Fisher, or Snedecor's (1955) F. With two degrees of freedom for the greater mean square and 23 for the lesser mean square, the number 43.5 is far beyond the one per cent level of probability. Hence there are solid distinctions between the three means of the three regional subgroups. As a secondary confirmation, it is possible to test the two groups that, from both the tabulations and the graphs, appear to be most similar, i.e. the hill/coast single-family and the hill/coast multifamily groups. The value of *t*, or the critical ratio of the two means, is found to be 6.65, in other words, highly significant.

One further test is available. It will be remembered that the total floor space in any village is the product of the mean house floor space and the mean number of persons per house. Moreover, this entity is related logarithmically to the mean total village population. Hence, mean total floor space (Column VIII, Table 2) ought to bear the same type of relationship to mean village or site space as does total population.

The appropriate data are plotted directly in Fig. 7. The presence of three distinct clusters of points, corresponding to the familiar three subgroups of regions, is quite apparent, and the pattern is duplicated if the data are plotted as the logarithms. Within each subgroup there is a tendency for mean total floor space and mean site area to increase in a parallel fashion, but this tendency, although clearly manifest in subgroup III (multifamily) is poorly expressed in subgroup I (hill/coast single-family), and scarcely apparent in subgroup II (desert). Indeed, one may doubt whether in the desert habitat there is any functional relationship at all between floor space and population on the one hand or between floor space and village area on the other. The suggestions prompted by the appearance of the graph in Fig. 7 are supported by an analysis of variance in the ratio of total floor space to mean

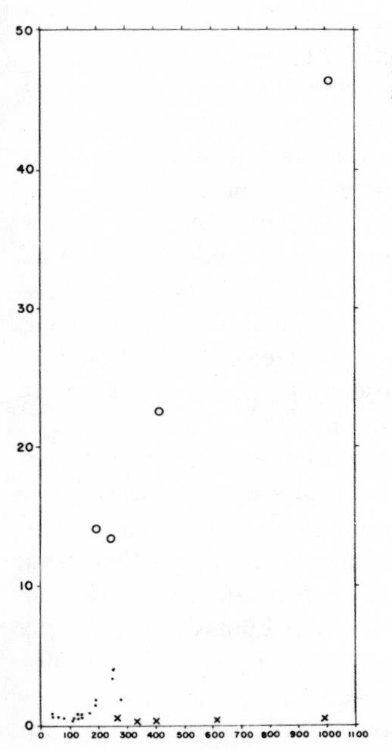

Fig. 7. Ordinate: mean total floor space per village, hundreds of square feet. Abscissa: mean site area, hundreds of square feet. Symbols as in Fig. 5.

total site area, for which an approach similar to that previously described is used. The value of F, which is 141.1, carries a very high degree of significance. When subgroup I is compared directly with subgroup II, the value of t is 18.64, which represents an extremely high level of probability.

We must conclude from these findings that village or site area and population in California may or may not be numerically associated. If they *are* associated and if the values are expressed as the logarithms, the exponent of the independent variable, x, may fall within a wide range, but seldom approaches unity. An association is seen most clearly in restricted regions where climate, living conditions, and social customs are relatively uniform. When we move to larger and larger areas, and diversity of all kinds begins to be accentuated, the association between village space and village population may weaken and may ultimately disappear. This trend should be contrasted with the relationship between house or total floor space and population, which evidently remains stable (and is best expressed in the logarithmic form) over a wide spectrum of peoples and environments. This distinction between the two kinds of space must be referable to a qualitative difference between those factors responsible for floor space and those which operate with total village or site space.

As one final item of evidence contributing to an understanding of the quantitative characteristics of village areas, we may look at this entity singly, i.e., without reference to populations, in the context of the California environment. From the files of the Archaeological Research Facility, it is possible to extract the dimensions, and hence the area, of several thousand archaeological sites, *irrespective of any information concerning houses or population*. Of these, 2,990 sites fall into regions sufficiently well delineated geographically to justify the calculation of mean site areas. Thus 25 such regions have been segregated and the geometric mean of the areas of the sites contained within each region has been computed. Again, we use the geometric mean, or the mean of the logarithms of the areas (in hundreds of square feet), because this method minimizes the effect of excessively large sites, the areas of which can readily distort the apparent average space at the disposal of the inhabitants. It should be emphasized strongly that this is a different constellation of regions from those that formed the basis of discussion regarding floor or site areas and population.

These figures are presented in Table 5. A key to the regional numbers used is given in Table 6. For each region the mean site area is given, first, as the mean logarithm itself and then as the number of square feet corresponding to the logarithm (i.e., the geometrical mean area), together with the standard deviation and the standard error of each mean. In addition to the 25 regions mentioned, the data for the Channel Chumash (region 26) have also been included, although their site areas have been separately derived by another method.

It is evident that a wide range in mean site area exists, extending roughly from 3,000 square feet to 100,000 square feet. The number of cases utilized is substantial and the differences among the means cannot, therefore, be referred to paucity of data. Nor can the differences be attributed to random fluctuation in site size within a particular region, even though these fluctuations are sometimes extreme. This conclusion is strongly supported by an analysis of variance performed with the figures shown in Table 5 (here the Chumash have been omitted). The value of F for 25 regions and 2,956 sites was 40.44. Specifically, the mean square for the 25 regional means was 13.808 and that for the sites within each region was 0.341. Since the one per cent level of probability for the existing degrees of freedom is at 1.80, and F exceeds this figure by a factor of close to 20, there can be no question concerning the reality of these regional differences.

In discussing the relation between site area and population, we mentioned that the regions as we had defined them appeared to fall into three primary groups: single-family house regions lying in the coast ranges; those in the desert area, all having single-family houses; and those in the coast ranges and Central Valley which had multifamily houses. If we consolidate the analogous three groups of regions as they are organized in Tables 5 and 6, we combine respectively, numbers II to X inclusive; numbers XVI to XIX inclusive; and numbers XX to XXV inclusive. The corresponding numbers of sites are 1,923, 193, and 646; the approximate estimates of area derived from the mean logarithms, expressed in square feet, are 8,400, 60,800, and 29,900. These figures closely simulate those derived from Table 2, in which the regional segregation was along tribal lines.

It is possible to draw even finer distinctions. Suppose we compare two hill or mountain territories, the first being the watersheds of the middle Klamath, the Trinity, the upper Sacramento, and the lower Pit rivers plus the line of Sierra foothills (regions II–IV of Table 5); the second comprising the north coast and northern coast ranges (regions V–X of Table 5) *excluding* the interior Pomo and the Wappo (regions XX and XXI of Table 5). The respective mean areas, in square feet, are 14,130 and 5,580. The significance of this difference may be estimated by a very approximate test for t. There are 672 sites in the first group, and 859 sites in the second. We know the mean logarithm for each group, and hence the difference between them. Since the standard errors of the means for all nine regions lie within a close range (from 0.024 to 0.083), we simply take the average and calculate the ratio of the difference between the two logarithms to the square root of twice the square of the average standard error. The result is 5.37. The true value of t must be even greater, and therefore the two regional groups of sites must differ significantly in mean area. It would be enlightening to know why these two territories, which are quite similar in climate and vegetation, should develop such a profound divergence in average size of living sites. Perhaps a more intensive study of local topography and ecology would point to a reason.

TABLE 5

Village Area in Relation to Habitat
(Each region represents a recognizable ecological province.
For description of regions see key to numbers)

Region No.	No. of sites	Mean log of area in 100's of square ft.	Area in sq. ft. corresponding to mean log	Standard Deviation of mean	Standard Error of mean
I	33	2.251	33,200	0.626	0.109
II	314	2.169	14,750	0.562	0.032
III	249	2.156	14,300	0.572	0.036
IV	109	2.069	11,700	0.653	0.063
V	107	1.501	3,180	0.673	0.065
VI	84	1.847	7,030	0.763	0.083
VII	414	1.664	4,610	0.479	0.024
VIII	77	2.070	11,750	0.387	0.044
IX	72	1.896	7,860	0.634	0.075
X	105	1.905	8,050	0.564	0.055
XI	184	1.966	9,240	0.533	0.039
XII	57	2.453	28,400	0.642	0.085
XIII	166	2.525	33,500	0.626	0.049
XIV	73	2.337	21,700	0.651	0.076
XV	73	2.512	32,500	0.805	0.095
XVI	76	2.789	61,500	0.715	0.082
XVII	18	2.530	33,900	0.555	0.131
XVIII	44	2.606	40,350	0.608	0.092
XIX	55	2.996	99,000	0.566	0.076
XX	191	2.357	22,750	0.580	0.042
XXI	100	2.276	18,850	0.502	0.050
XXII	99	2.443	27,700	0.560	0.056
XXIII	167	2.386	24,300	0.589	0.044
XXIV	53	2.431	27,000	0.476	0.065
XXV	36	2.473	29,700	0.526	0.088
XXVI	34	3.004	101,000	0.419	0.072

Two other matters of interest that emerge from the tabulation of site areas are the following:

First, the San Francisco Bay region is characterized as a whole by the presence of numerous shell mounds–sites at which the former residents deposited huge masses of molluscan shell together with the residues of other aquatic food, such as fish and bird bone. So far as we know, there was no material difference in food supply or other environmental determinant between the northern and southern ends of the bay. Yet the mean site area was three times as great to the south as to the north (the difference between the means of regions XI and XII shows a value of 5.20 for t). The line of demarcation followed the waterway through the Golden Gate. On the north shore,

TABLE 6

Key to Regional Numbers Used in Table 5

I	Coast of Del Norte and Humboldt counties; Yurok on lower Klamath River; Wiyot on Humboldt Bay.
II	Hill region south of Siskiyou Mountains and near Mt. Shasta; parts of Siskiyou, Trinity, and Shasta counties.
III	Sierra foothills from the valley floor to 3,000 feet elevation; from Tehama County south to Madera County.
IV	Sierra foothills from Fresno south to Kern County.
V	The coastal strip in Humboldt, Mendocino, and Sonoma counties from the mouth of the Eel to that of the Russian River; occupied by Mattole, Yuki, and Pomo.
VI	Coast of Marin County held by the Coast Miwok, from the mouth of the Russian River to the Golden Gate.
VII	The coast ranges of Mendocino and northern Lake counties held by the Yuki plus a few Kato and Wailaki
VIII	The inner coast ranges of Lake, Napa, Colusa, and Solano counties held by various tribes; all with single-family dwellings.
IX	The low hills, principally on the west side of the Sacramento River, in Tehama and Shasta counties, held by the Wintun.
X	The small area held by the Wintun on Stony Creek, in Tehama and Glenn counties.
XI	The northern part of San Francisco Bay, bordered by Solano, Napa, Sonoma, and Marin counties.
XII	The southern part of San Francisco Bay, bordered by San Francisco, San Mateo, Santa Clara, Alameda, and Contra Costa counties.
XIII	The coastal strip from San Mateo to San Luis Obispo counties.
XIV	The interior coast ranges from Alameda to San Luis Obispo counties occupied by Costanoans and Salinans.
XV	Santa Rosa Island, including all sites, irrespective of house type; the great majority are the single-family type.
XVI	The Modoc and Northern Paiute in the desert area of Modoc and Lassen counties.
XVII	The arid area held by the Tubatulabal on the upper Kern River, west of Walker Pass.
XVIII	The area held by the Paiute in Mono County, north of Bishop.
XIX	The area held by the Paiute in Inyo County, principally in Owens Valley.
XX	The Pomo of the interior valleys of Mendocino and Sonoma counties, together with the basin of Clear Lake; principally multifamily houses.
XXI	The Wappo of Napa and southern Lake counties; principally multifamily houses.
XXII	The Central Valley from Red Bluff south to the delta on the west and the northern boundary of Sacramento County to the east; includes flat land only; includes all recorded sites.
XXIII	The valley floor of Sacramento and San Joaquin counties, plus 7 sites in the delta region of Contra Costa County.
XXIV	The floor of the San Joaquin Valley from Stanislaus to Fresno counties, inclusive.
XXV	The valley floor of Kings, Tulare, and Kern counties; includes Tulare and Buenavista lakes.
XXVI	The Chumash of Santa Barbara Channel; the areas of sites were not taken from the primary records of the Archaeological Research Facility but were computed from the maps of D. B. Rogers (1929).

in Marin, Solano, Sonoma, and Napa counties, the mean size in square feet was 9,240; on the east and south shores, i.e., in San Francisco, San Mateo, Santa Clara, Alameda, and Contra Costa counties, it was 28,400 square feet.

There may be an ethnic, social, or tribal mediator involved here. It is noteworthy that to the north lived the Coast Miwok, Pomo, Wappo, and a few Patwin, whereas to the south there were only Costanoans, except for the Saclan, who were classed by Kroeber as Costanoan but are now known to have been Miwok. We may also look at the adjacent territories. On the north the bay peoples bordered on coastal tribes which, with the exception of the Pomo and Wappo, used single-family houses and small villages. On the south we find uniformly large sites (regions XIII and XIV), although we know nothing about the houses. The large site may thus have been a Costanoan cultural trait rather than the immediate effect of climate or food supply.

The second matter of interest is that all the sites given in Table 5 have been designated occupation or habitation sites, with the implication, if not the certainty, that they were lived on either continuously or for the major part of each year. By contrast, there are numerous other areas which the aboriginal inhabitants occupied only intermittently or occasionally; these areas were generally associated with food-gathering or the procurement of lithic materials. These are often denoted by such terms as "camp site," "fishing station," "bedrock mortar," "intermittent camp site," and "flint-chipping site."

It is worthwhile to inquire whether these industrially differentiated localities cover an area comparable to that characteristic of the permanent home. An opportunity to examine this question is presented by data from territory of several of the tribes inhabiting the Sierra Nevada and the desert to the eastward. Among these tribes are the Paiute in Mono County, to whom have been attributed, in the Archaeological Research Facility records, three kinds of sites. We have 44 permanent occupation sites (see region XVIII, Table 5) with a mean of 40,350 square feet area. There are 48 places labeled "temporary camp site" (not shown in Table 5) with a mean of 24,400 square feet; and 64 localities north and west of Bridgeport labeled "chipping stations," with a mean of 5,850 square feet. South and east of Bridgeport there are recorded 93 chipping stations, with a mean of 6,170 square feet. For the number of cases available, these differences among the three types of sites are very significant. The prospect is inviting for further investigation of the size differences with reference to the cultural and edaphic factors responsible.

Summary and Conclusions

In aboriginal California the floor space per individual house was based upon a minimum average of 6 persons, with 20 square feet available to each. Additional persons involved an increase of 100 square feet each, such that as the mean number of occupants increased, the floor space per person approached a limit of 100 square feet.

The relation between mean total floor space per village and mean population per village for any restricted habitat or region can best be expressed by a logarithmic equation. The exponent of the independent variable, x, which is usually population, or the regression coefficient, b, is rarely if ever 1.0, and may be utilized as an index of the nature of the relationship between floor space and population.

A close correlation between floor space and population can be demonstrated over a wide range of territory, irrespective of local variation. This relationship appears to be stable, generally valid, and applicable throughout the entire province.

Village or site area may be closely correlated with population, and related to it logarithmically within restricted and relatively uniform regions. On the other hand, as the territory embraced becomes more extensive, and more diverse in its characteristics, the association may break down and, indeed, disappear, the two variables tending to become completely independent. Floor space and site area, therefore, appear to be related to population through distinctly different mechanisms.

Mean site area, *per se*, and without regard to population, varies widely and significantly from region to region. The controlling factors appear to be derived from both the physical and the biotic environment, and from the cultural background of the people concerned.

References

BROWN, A. K.
1967 "The aboriginal population of the Santa Barbara Channel," *Archaeological Survey Report*, No. 69 (Berkeley: University of California Archaeological Research Facility).

COOK, S. F. and R. F. HEIZER
1965 "The quantitative approach to the relation between population and settlement size," *Archaeological Survey Report*, No. 64 (Berkeley: University of California Archaeological Research Facility).

COOK, S. F. and A. E. TREGANZA
1950 "The quantitative investigation of Indian mounds," *Publications in American Archaeology and Ethnology*, Vol. XL:223-62 (Berkeley: University of California Press).

HEIZER, R. F.
1966 *Languages, Territories and Names of California Indian Tribes* (Berkeley: University of California Press).

KROEBER, A. L.
1925 *Handbook of the Indians of California*, (Bureau of American Ethnology, Bulletin 78.)

LOTHROP, S. K.
1928 "The Indians of Tierra del Fuego," *Contributions of the Museum of the American Indian*, Vol. X.

NAROLL, RAOUL
1956 "A preliminary index of social development," *American Anthropologist*, Vol. LVIII:687-715.
1961 "Two solutions to Galton's problem," *Philosophy of Science*, Vol. XXVIII:15-39.
1962 "Floor area and settlement population," *American Antiquity*, Vol. XXVII, No. 4:587-89.

NAROLL, RAOUL AND LUDWIG VON BERTALANFFY
1956 "The principle of allometry in biology and the social sciences," *General Systems: Yearbook of the Society for the Advancement of General Systems Theory*, Vol. 1:76-89.

ROGERS, D. B.
1929 *Prehistoric Man of the Santa Barbara Coast* (Santa Barbara Museum of Natural History.)

SNEDECOR, G. W.
1955 *Statistical Methods*, 4th ed. (Ames, Iowa: Iowa State College Press).

WATERMAN, T. T.
1920 "Yurok geography," *Publications in American Archaeology and Ethnology*, Vol. XVI:177-314 (Berkeley: University of California Press).

VII

JOHN W. M. WHITING
and
BARBARA AYRES

Inferences from the Shape of Dwellings

In an important paper, Chang (1958) showed that inferences concerning the social structure of the culture of a given archaeological site could be justified by comparison with a sample of contemporary neolithic cultures. Using the same general procedure, we shall focus here upon the dwelling unit. Although the size and number of rooms will be considered, the shape of the floor plan and its associated architectural features will be our primary concerns. Given the shape of the floor plan of a dwelling, what can be said and with what degree of confidence concerning other features of the culture?

We have found in the course of our inquiry that certain practical and aesthetic considerations inherent in a given culture are related to the type of dwelling characteristically built in that society. Specifically, we have found that whether a culture is settled or nomadic, the form of its family and the presence or absence of status distinctions are related to its house type, and that house types can in turn be inferred from the floor plan. We assume that the sequence of causation is from culture to house type to floor plan. The floor plan is the dependent variable. For purposes of archaeological inference, however, the floor plan must be treated as the independent variable, and the cultural features must be predicted from it. That the chain of reasoning is thus reversed is important to bear in mind, since we shall seem at times to be arguing backwards.

Assembling the Sample

To test our hypotheses and to justify the inferences that can be made from floor plans, a sample of contemporary cultures is needed. To be of maximum use for archaeological interpretation, such a sample should be representative of prehistoric cultures. To draw a sample that exactly matches the distribution of known prehistoric cultures would be exceedingly difficult if not impossible. We have decided, therefore, to select a sample that is reasonably representative of contemporary cultures, and to rest our case on the assumption that any relationship observed in such a sample would hold true for prehistoric peoples.

There has been much concern lately about what has been called Galton's problem (Naroll, 1961; Naroll and D'Andrade, 1963). One is properly warned by these studies that some care should be taken that the cultures chosen for a sample be reasonably independent of one another. For this reason, the 700 cultures listed in the Ethnographic Atlas (*Ethnology,* Vols. 1-4) were rejected as an appropriate sample, since the list includes many clusters of closely related cultures.

A subsample of the *Ethnology* list was drawn by using the following criteria to minimize the probability that any two cultures were duplicates in the sense of having both been recent offshoots from a common origin or of having borrowed heavily from one another. First, we chose linguistic criteria to estimate the degree of separation of any two cultures from a common origin, and limited our sample to but one culture from each linguistic subfamily. The language code provided by the Atlas in *Ethnology* (Vol. 2, no. 2, col. 64), with certain modifications in Oceania based on Dyen's (Murdock, 1964) recent work, was used for this purpose. If lexicostatistical inference on the rate of linguistic drift is accepted, this implies that no two societies in our sample could have spoken an identical language for at least 1,000 years. Second, to minimize mutual borrowing, whenever two societies had contiguous boundaries, one was eliminated. It was presumed that if two societies are geographically separated and furthermore do not speak a mutually intelligible language, diffusion would be minimal. When two or more societies were considered to lack a sufficient degree of independence by these two criteria, the society with the best ethnographic coverage, if this could be determined, was chosen. If, however, two "duplicates" seemed equally well covered, the choice was made by tossing a coin. By using these criteria, a sample of 136 of the 700 societies listed in the Ethnographic Atlas was selected.

Certain judgments to be described below were made on a smaller subsample of 52 societies. This subsample was drawn from the larger one with

TABLE 1

Regional Distribution of the Sample

Region	Number of Societies
Africa	10
Circum-Mediterranean	16
East Eurasia	25
Insular Pacific	22
North America	38
South America	25

TABLE 2

Subsistence Levels of the Societies Composing the Sample, as Measured By Type and Intensity of Agriculture

Subsistence Level	Distribution*
Absence of agriculture	35
Casual agriculture	7
Horticulture	9
Extensive agriculture	38
Intensive agriculture with fertilizer	18
Intensive agriculture with irrigation	16

*From col. 28 of the Ethnographic Atlas, in *Ethnology*, Vol. 1, no. 2.

the rule that no two societies could be members of the same culture area, as defined in the Ethnographic Atlas (*Ethnology*, Vol. 1, no. 1).

The regional distribution of the larger sample is shown in Table 1. That North America may seem overrepresented and Africa underrepresented is a consequence of the relative linguistic diversity of the two regions. The sample is, we believe, reasonably similar to one that might have been drawn from a list of prehistoric cultures. As can be seen from Table 2, the largest group is the nonagricultural foragers and the next largest the extensive or "slash and burn" agriculturalists.

Code of Dwelling Features

Several years ago, judgments were made by Emily McFarlin at the Laboratory of Human Development on the floor plan, roof shape, number of rooms, etc., for dwellings in a large number of cultures, many of which appear in our present sample. Since then, a similar and somewhat more elaborate code has been developed by the editors of the Ethnographic Atlas (*Ethnology*, Vol. 2, no. 1, cols. 80 and 85), and most of the cultures in the Ethnographic Atlas sample have been classified according to this code. Although agreement between the Ethnographic Atlas and McFarlin ratings was high, some of the definitions differed slightly. Therefore, since we had decided to use the more elaborate Ethnographic Atlas ratings, we rated the cultures of the subsample described above in order to establish the reliability of the Ethnographic Atlas code on those features not rated by McFarlin. The obtained agreement of 85 per cent between the two sets of judgments was considered adequate, and with one correction (the Aranda from rectangular to circular) the Atlas ratings were accepted and will be used.

The code developed by the editors of the Ethnographic Atlas for describing the floor plan of a dwelling is presented in Table 3. In societies with two house types of nearly equal prevalence, both are coded; the more common house types are listed as the primary types and the less com-

TABLE 3

Distribution of Primary and Secondary House Types, as Defined by Floor Plans*

Floor Plan Type	Primary Use	Secondary Use
Circular	40	20
Elliptical or elongated with rounded ends	8	3
Polygonal	0	0
Quadrilateral around (or partially around) an inner court	6	4
Rectangular or square	82	21
Semicircular	0	3

* From cols. 80 (primary floor plan) and 85 (secondary floor plan) of the Ethnographic Atlas, in *Ethnology,* Vol. 2, no. 1.

mon as the secondary types. As shown in the table, more than one-third of the societies in the sample were judged to have a secondary type.

To simplify matters in subsequent analysis, the six house types distinguished in this code have been reduced to two: the semicircular cases have been combined with the circular to form a *curvilinear* type, and the rectangular and quadrilateral have been combined to form a *rectilinear* type; the elliptical form is essentially intermediate, but since in our analysis its associations were more similar to those of rectangular or quadrilateral houses, it was grouped with the rectilinear class.

TABLE 4

Relationship Between Shape of Floor Plan and Shape of Roof*

Roof Type	Primary House Type		Secondary House Type	
	Curvilinear	Rectilinear	Curvilinear	Rectilinear
Beehive	3	0	1	0
Conical	19	0	17	0
Dome	14	1	2	0
Semihemispherical	1	0	3	0
Flat	0	12	1	3
Rounded	0	4	0	1
Shed	0	3	0	1
Gabled	1	55	0	17
Hipped	1	15	0	5

* From cols. 80 and 83 and cols. 85 and 88 of the Ethnographic Atlas, in *Ethnology,* Vol. 2, no. 1.

ASSOCIATIONS BETWEEN FLOOR PLAN AND OTHER DWELLING FEATURES

Before attempting to relate other features of culture to floor-plan type, we shall undertake the more modest task of discovering associations between floor plan and other features of the house itself. To begin with, it might be asked whether there is a correspondence in shape between roof and floor. As Table 4 indicates, there is indeed such a correspondence: all but three of the 39 primary house types with curvilinear floor plans have either beehive, conical, or dome-shaped roofs, and all but five of the 90 primary house types with rectilinear floor plans have flat, gabled, hipped, or shed roofs. Thus, for primary house types, the shape of floor and roof correspond along the curvilinear-rectilinear dimension in more than 90 per cent of the sample. The correspondence for secondary house types is almost as strong.

The materials used for siding can also be determined to some degree by the shape of the floor plan. It would seem more practicable to use a plastic or pliable siding material for curvilinear house shapes, but for rectilinear house shapes either pliable or rigid materials such as wood, stone, or ice, would be suitable. As Table 5 indicates, rigid siding material is used in only three of the curvilinear houses but in more than one-third of the rectilinear houses.

TABLE 5

Relationship Between Siding Materials and Floor Plan*

Siding Materials	Primary House Type		Secondary House Type		Totals	
	Curvilinear	Rectilinear	Curvilinear	Rectilinear	Curvilinear	Rectilinear
Adobe, plaster	6	17	3	3	9	20
Bark	4	2	3	1	7	3
Felt, hides	3	3	3	3	6	6
Grass	18	16	6	6	24	22
Mats	2	11	4	1	6	12
Open	0	6	0	2	0	8
Earth	4	2	2	0	6	2
Ice	1	0	0	0	1	0
Stone	1	6	1	2	2	8
Wood	1	28	0	9	1	37

* Classification of siding materials is from cols. 82 and 87 of the Ethnographic Atlas, in *Ethnology*, Vol. 2, no. 1; siding materials for houses judged to have merged sides and roofs classified by reference to cols. 84 and 88.

The correspondence already observed between floor and roof shapes would suggest that flexible materials should also be utilized for the roof coverings of houses with curvilinear floor plans. As shown in Table 6, there is only one exception to this – the ice-block igloo of the Copper Eskimo.

The number of rooms in a house is another feature that can be predicted from a knowledge of floor shape. Of course, the number of rooms can often be determined directly from archaeological evidence, but in many construction schemes the interior partitions are made of relatively perishable

TABLE 6

Relationship Between Floor Plan and Roofing Materials*

Roofing Materials	Primary House Type		Secondary House Type		Totals	
	Curvi-linear	Recti-linear	Curvi-linear	Recti-linear	Curvi-linear	Recti-linear
Bark, felt	4	7	3	4	7	11
Earth	6	12	2	3	8	15
Grass	26	53	11	15	37	68
Hides	2	0	3	1	5	1
Mats	1	5	4	0	5	5
Stone	0	1	0	0	0	1
Ice	1	0	0	0	1	0
Tile	0	3	0	3	0	6
Wood	0	12	0	1	0	13

* Classification of roofing materials from cols. 84 and 89 of the Ethnographic Atlas, in *Ethnology*, Vol. 2, no. 1.

materials and will have vanished in the archaeological evidence. Multiple-roomed houses are constructed either by dividing a single-roomed house with partitions or by joining several single-roomed houses with a shared wall. In either case, the rectilinear house has the advantage. In the first place, it can be built larger, so that the partitioned rooms are of adequate size. The median size of the rectilinear houses in the subsample, estimated from floor-plan dimensions, is 300 square feet, whereas the median size of the curvilinear houses is but 100 square feet. In the second place, when multiple-roomed dwellings are made by addition rather than by division, the rectilinear form again has a clear advantage, since straight walls can be shared. Whatever the reason may be, rectilinear houses are more likely to be multiple-roomed than are curvilinear, as is shown in Table 7.

Certain deductions, then, can be made about a house from a knowledge of its floor plan. The shape of the roof, the materials used for roofing and siding, and the number of rooms are all in part influenced by the formal consideration of shape. The next step is to explore the relationship between floor shape and features of the culture that are not directly involved with the construction of a house. In other words, can anything be predicted about the nonmaterial or social culture of a society from a knowledge of the floor plan used for dwellings?

Associations between Floor Plan and Cultural Features

Why do some societies build large multiple-roomed houses while others are satisfied with small single-roomed dwellings? Two possible answers come to mind: large, multiple-roomed houses may be required (1) to house large extended families or (2) to mark the position of a family in the status

TABLE 7

Relationship Between Shape of Floor Plan and Number of Rooms*

Number of Rooms	Primary House Type: Rectilinear	Curvilinear
One	31	23
Two	12	1
Three	3	0
Four	4	0
Five	6	0
More	1	0

* Judgments of number of rooms made by Emily McFarlin at Laboratory of Human Development, for primary house type only; relationship between rectilinearity and multiple rooms, p = <.001.

hierarchy where such a hierarchy is present. The multiple-roomed dwelling occupied by an extended family, with separate rooms or apartments for each nuclear unit, is a familiar structure. Also familiar is the large ostentatious dwelling with servants' quarters and little-used parlors, to indicate the position of the family in societies with social class or wealth distinctions. As can be seen from Table 8, societies with multiple-roomed dwellings usually have extended families, status distinctions, or both. Only two of the 35 societies in our sample with multiple-roomed houses have neither of these features of social organization. It should be noted, though, that the converse of this statement does not hold: societies with single-roomed dwellings may or may not be based upon extended families, and they may or may not recognize status distinctions. Presumably a cluster of single-roomed dwellings in a compound may serve the same purpose as a multiple-roomed dwelling, but because no such distinctions were made in the classifications available, we were unable to test this hypothesis.

A similar prediction can be made for those cases in which division into

TABLE 8

Relationship Between Number of Rooms in Dwelling, Family Organization, and Status Distinctions*

	No Social Class or Wealth Distinction		Social Class or Wealth Distinctions *	
	Independent Families	Extended Families	Independent Families	Extended Families
More than one room	2	7	9	17
One room only	19	10	7	13

* Number of rooms coded at Laboratory of Human Development; classification of family organization and status distinctions from cols. 14 and 67 of the Ethnographic Atlas, in *Ethnology*, Vol. 1, no. 1, and Vol. 2, no. 1.

rooms cannot be determined from archaeological evidence, but the dimensions of the floor can be determined. Thus, 96 per cent of the societies using floor plans more than 200 square feet in area are characterized by either extended families or status distinctions or both. As we have seen, these large houses are usually rectilinear and multiple-roomed. Again, the implications of small houses are indeterminate.

The relative permanence of the dwelling suggests a second set of cultural features associated with the two floor-plan types. Permanence per se has not been coded, but it is reasonable to presume that houses with rectilinear floor plans are likely to be framed with much heavier timbers than are required for houses with curvilinear floor plans. The heavier roofing materials, as well as the long flat spans in rectilinear roofs require thick plates and rafters. In contrast, the cone and dome construction schemes associated with curvilinear floor plans require only the lightest and most flexible framing materials. These differences in weight of the materials used for framing the two types of buildings suggest that light, curvilinear houses might be preferred by nomads and the heavy, rectilinear houses by people with permanent settlements.

To test this hypothesis, both primary and secondary house types have been taken into account, since societies that wander in bands during certain seasons and settle down to a sedentary life during the rest of the year often construct both types of dwellings. As Table 9 indicates, predictions of settlement type can be made from rectilinear floor plans or from a combination of rectilinear and curvilinear floor plans, but not from curvilinear floor plans alone. Eighty per cent of the cultures with rectilinear floor plans are sedentary, and seventy-eight per cent of the societies with both curvilinear and rectilinear floor plans are seminomadic. In the latter instance, if a culture alternates between sedentary and nomadic seasons, the curvilinear house is more likely to be used in the nomadic phase. Although slightly

TABLE 9

Relationship Between House Shape and Type of Settlement*

Type of Settlement	Primary and Secondary House Types		
	Rectilinear	Both	Curvilinear
Nomadic (B)	8	0	7
Seminomadic (S and T)	7	15	12
Sedentary (H,N,V,W,X)	59	4	10

* As coded in col. 30 of the Ethnographic Atlas: seminomadic category combines seminomadic (S) and semisedentary (T) categories in atlas code; sedentary category includes hamlets (H), neighborhoods (N), nucleated villages (V), compact impermanent (W), and complex (X); nomadic includes only fully nomadic bands (B); difference between nomadic and sedentary societies, for rectilinear vs. curvilinear houses only, $p = < .005$.

more (65 per cent) of the houses with circular floor plans are found in nomadic societies, a substantial number are found among sedentary peoples, and no good prediction can be made about the permanence of settlements where curvilinear floor plans are in use.

It has already been shown that rectilinear houses are usually constructed of heavier building materials. Perhaps sedentary peoples living in an environment where trees are scarce are forced to build curvilinear houses. If so, one might be able to predict the type of settlement from a combined knowledge of the regional vegetation and the floor plan. Thus, curvilinear houses might predict nomadism only in forest and parkland areas, where both types of building materials are available.

To test this hypothesis, judgments were made of the natural vegetation of the area in which each society was situated. These judgments were made from a map of world vegetation (Goode, 1957, pp. 16-17). To check the reliability of this basis for judgment, ratings were made from ethnographic accounts of societies in the subsample. The obtained agreement between the two sets of judgments was 81 per cent. The judgments taken from the vegetation map were used in cases where data could not be obtained from the ethnography.

TABLE 10

Joint Relationship of Ecology and Settlement Type to House Types

Ecology and Settlement Type	Primary and Secondary House Types		
	Rectilinear Only	Both	Curvilinear Only
Forest and parkland			
Nomadic	6	0	4
Seminomadic	7	10	9
Sedentary	53	4	10
Grass, shrub, tundra			
Nomadic	2	0	3
Seminomadic	0	5	3
Sedentary	6	0	0

As can be seen in Table 10, contrary to expectation, all of the dwellings with curvilinear floor plans in treeless environments are the products of either nomadic or seminomadic peoples. Sedentary societies were predicted to construct curvilinear houses when heavy building materials were not available, but all of these societies, in fact, build rectilinear houses despite this difficulty. Equally surprising is the fact that all of the sedentary peoples who build curvilinear houses live in an environment where they could easily have built rectilinear dwellings. This analysis thus enables us to predict from the curvilinear form in grass and shrub environments only: all such cases involve nomadic or seminomadic peoples. Ecology does not influence the predictions that can be made about permanence of settlement for societies with rectilinear floor plans only or for those having both rectilinear and curvilinear houses.

Floor plan shape and size have thus been shown to predict certain features of the house itself and certain features of the social organization. It is noteworthy, however, that the curvilinear floor plan is usually the better predictor of the structure of the house itself; for example, with but one exception, people who build houses of this type use flexible materials for roofing and have but one room. By contrast, a great variety of materials is used for roofing houses with rectilinear floors, and the chances are about even that the house will have one room rather than several rooms.

For predicting from floor plan to social organization, the rectilinear floor plan is more effective. Given a society with large and/or multiple-roomed rectilinear houses, one can be fairly certain of finding either status distinctions, extended families, or both. Given a rectilinear house of any size or type, one can be reasonably certain that the society is sedentary. But given a society with curvilinear houses, one cannot tell whether there are status distinctions, extended families, or (unless it is one of the few societies with round houses in treeless environments) nomadism.

Associations between Floor Plan and Aesthetic Preferences

Since practical considerations underlie all of the relationships so far considered, it might be fruitful to turn now to aesthetic preferences. If curvilinear and rectilinear houses are equally practical to build, then perhaps the choice is determined by the builder's or the user's relative preference for straight or curved lines. Hopefully, this line of inquiry will yield some features of the social organization that can be predicted from the curvilinear form.

If aesthetic preference does in fact influence the form of a house, it might be asked whether there is any evidence of a form preference manifested elsewhere in the culture. For example, are societies that build curvilinear houses apt to arrange them in a circle and those that have rectilinear houses to arrange them in a line or a square? Table 11 suggests that the form of the settlement in most societies is determined by features of the terrain, such as streams, highways, paths, hills, and valleys, but in societies where such practical considerations do not prevail, there is a strong tendency for the form of the settlement to correspond to the form of the dwelling.

A more direct measure of an aesthetic preference for curvilinear rather than rectilinear forms is provided by a cross-cultural study of decorative art reported by Herbert Barry (1957). One of the subscales in this study – the relative preponderance of curved versus straight lines – is of particular

TABLE 11

Relationship Between Arrangement of Dwellings and Shape of Dwellings*

Arrangement of Dwellings	Primary and Secondary House Types		
	Rectilinear Only	Both	Curvilinear Only
In rectangle or square	2	1	0
In single or parallel lines**	7	0	1
In oval or ellipse	1	0	0
In circle	3	1	7
Scattered**	9	2	1

* Judgments of arrangement of dwellings made by Emily McFarlin at Laboratory of Human Development.
** Indicates settlement patterns presumably dictated by environmental features.

interest. If there is such an aesthetic preference in a culture one would expect it to be manifested both in house form and in decorative art. Since the Atlas ratings on floor plan were available for all of the societies in Barry's sample, it was possible to test this hypothesis. The results were disappointing indeed: there was no relation at all between curvilinear floor plans and the use of curved lines in decorative art.[1]

Because the preponderance of curved lines in decorative art may be a fortuitous consequence of the depiction of human or animal figures, rather than a preference for curvilinearity as an abstract form, Barry's curved-straight score may not be entirely valid for our purposes. A measure of purely abstract curvilinearity would be more appropriate. If the use of representational forms, as opposed to abstract forms, could be held constant, the curved-straight score would be more appropriate for our purposes. Unfortunately, Barry's representational vs. abstract score is not available, but a rating he labeled "simple-complex," which is highly correlated (+.72) with his abstract-representational score, can be used for this purpose. These scores were published by Fischer (1961). It may be assumed, then, that the use of curved lines in societies judged to produce relatively simple art would predict a similar preference in the shape of the dwelling.

As Table 12 shows, in those societies of the Barry sample judged to produce relatively simple and hence presumably abstract art, there is a reasonably strong positive association between the preponderance of curved lines in decorative art and the preference for the curvilinear form in house building. The correlation does not reach an acceptable level of statistical significance, but this may be due in part to the small size of the Barry sample. The

[1]Robbins (1966) reports a negative relation between house shape and art style at the .05 level of confidence. The difference between his results and ours is explained by the presence of three houses with elliptical floor plans which Robbins classed as curvilinear but which we have classed as rectilinear.

conclusions must remain tentative, but the association is strong enough to suggest that an abstract preference for curvilinearity or rectilinearity may be manifested both in dwelling shape and in decorative art.

Assuming, then, that there may indeed be a general aesthetic preference in a given society for either curvilinear or rectilinear forms, it may be asked whether any features of the culture may predispose the artist or architect to choose one or another. Fischer, in a recent article, addressed himself to this question. On the assumption, suggested by some recent psychological studies (Franck and Rosen, 1949; McElroy, 1954), that rectilinearity represents the male body image and curvilinearity the female, he argued that rectilinearity would be preferred in societies in which men have relatively high prestige. Taking patrilocal or avunculocal residence as an index of male solidarity and hence high male prestige, he found, to his surprise, a strong association in the opposite direction. The decorative art of eight out of nine societies with patrilocal or avunculocal residence was judged to have a preponderance of *curved* lines, whereas the decorative art of the majority of societies with other forms of residence was judged to have a preponderance of straight lines.

Fischer (1961, p. 85) offers the following *post hoc* explanation of this reversal in expectation:

> We may assume that when an adult individual is psychologically secure he will be extroverted and look for pleasure by seeking out members of the opposite sex. In fantasy a man will be creating women and vice versa. When, on the other hand, one sex is relatively insecure psychologically, members will be introverted and more concerned in fantasy with improving their own body image and seeking successful models of their own sex to imitate.

But most psychological theories would suggest that the content of fantasy is better predicted from conflict and anxiety than, as Fischer suggests, from security. Anxiety resulting from severe child-rearing practices, for example, was shown by Whiting and Child (1953), in a cross-cultural study, to predict the content of the explanations for illness. The securities presumed to be induced by child rearing, on the other hand, were not predictive. Thus, in contrast to Fischer's explanation, we would expect the more frustrated and anxious males to be preoccupied with the female body image and hence to prefer curvilinear shapes. Moreover, we would predict that anxiety in the domain of heterosexual behavior should be particularly relevant. Specifically, this hypothesis, if it is to account for Fischer's findings, would predict greater sexual conflict in patrilocal and avunculocal societies than in those with other forms of residence.

Judgments concerning degree of restrictions on premarital sex, available in the Ethnographic Atlas, permit a test of this hypothesis. Using our subsample of societies as their basis, Goethals and Whiting (Ms) found that patrilocal and avunculocal societies are significantly more restrictive in

TABLE 12

Relationship Between Rectilinearity and Curvilinearity In Floor Plan and Decorative Art*

Preponderance of Straight vs. Curved Lines in Decorative Art		Complexity of Decorative Art/Primary House Type: High Complexity		Low Complexity	
		Curvilinear	Rectilinear	Curvilinear	Rectilinear
Straight	10	1	1	0	1
	9	0	0	2	1
	8	0	0	0	**3**
	7	0	1	1	1
	6	0	1	1	1
	5	0	**3**	**0**	0
	4	0	0	3	0
	3	**2**	0	1	0
	2	0	3	0	0
Curved	1	1	2	0	0

* Complexity factor partialed out; median cases are in boldface type.

their rules governing premarital sex than are societies with other forms of residence. A similar association is reported by Murdock (1964), who found societies with patrilineal descent to be the more restrictive.

Finally, the relation between restrictions on premarital sex and the use of curved vs. straight lines, based on the 18 cases of the Barry sample on which appropriate scores are available, is in the direction opposite to Fischer's *post hoc* explanation. Three of the four societies requiring virginity use more curved lines, and nine of the fourteen societies with no restrictions on premarital sex use more straight lines in their decorative art. Perhaps men who are sexually inhibited are more likely to be more preoccupied with the female body image and hence to prefer the curvilinear form.

In any case, and whatever the correct interpretation may be, the relationship between residence and dwelling shape should be explored. Column 17 of the Ethnographic Atlas provides scores on marital residence. The relationship between these scores and the shape of the primary house was negligible. Seventy-three per cent of the societies with rectilinear houses have either patrilocal, virilocal, or avunculocal residence, whereas 67 per cent of the societies with curvilinear houses had other residence patterns. This association, though slightly in the direction reported by Fischer, is far from significant statistically.

Fischer also reported that monogamous societies were more likely to use a preponderance of straight lines in their decorative art than societies with nonsororal polygyny. The same security hypothesis interpretation was used to explain these results, but several recent studies (Whiting, Kluckhohn, and

Anthony, 1958; Burton and Whiting, 1961; D'Andrade, 1962; Kuckenberg, 1963; Munroe, 1964) suggest an alternative interpretation that seems to us more plausible. These studies all indicate that the relative salience of the mother and father during infancy has an influence on the cognitive style of the individual that persists into adulthood. One of the most powerful predictors in this regard was shown to be the intimate and exclusive relationship between mother and infant that is associated with polygyny. In such societies, the mother and infant usually sleep in the same bed during the nursing period, which lasts from two and one-half to three years. The father generally sleeps in a different bed, usually in a different room. Furthermore, the mother and father usually do not eat together in polygynous societies. Under such circumstances, it is hypothesized, the child in his early formative years perceives his mother to be much more important than would his counterpart in a monogamous family, where the father is more salient. In polygynous societies, it is the mother who is seen to control all the goods and resources that are important to the child. It is she who occupies the position of highest prestige in his eyes. Furthermore, when he is eventually weaned, his preoccupation with his mother and hence with the female body image should be maximal. In monogamous societies, on the other hand, where men and women are more equally important to the child during his early years, the preoccupation with the female body image should, according to this hypothesis, be less intense.

The ratings on polygyny given in the Ethnographic Atlas (col. 14) are based on the proportion of polygynously married men in the society. For the purpose of testing our hypothesis, the proportion of polygynously married women is more appropriate, since it is a more direct estimate of the number of children in the society brought up in the manner described above. Such ratings were available for the majority of the sample from Whiting (1964). Ratings were made on as many of the remainder of the sample as the ethnographic evidence permitted. Because either males or females may be used as a basis for judging a society to be monogamous, the Ethnographic Atlas (col. 14) classification of this category was accepted.

The association between percentage of polygynously married females and floor plan shape is presented in Table 13. As can be seen from the table, there is a strong and statistically significant relationship in the direction reported by Fischer for decorative art. Societies with curvilinear houses tend to be polygynous, and those with rectilinear houses to be monogamous.

We seem, then, to have uncovered a feature of social organization that can be predicted from the presence of a curvilinear floor plan: the chances are three to one that the society practices a polygynous form of marriage. It is further presumed that this relationship is a consequence of an aesthetic preference developed by differences in child-rearing practices in polygynous and monogamous societies. Thus it seems that aesthetic as well as practical considerations determine the choice between curvilinear and rectilinear dwelling types.

TABLE 13
Relationship Between Shape of Dwelling and Form of Marriage*

Form of Marriage	Primary House Type		
	Curvilinear	Both	Rectilinear
Monogamous	6	2	27
Polygynous	19	12	40

* Societies in which less than 10 per cent of females of marriageable age are polygynously married were classified as monogamous; difference between monogamous and polygynous societies, in terms of presence or absence of curvilinear houses, p = .025.

SUMMARY AND CONCLUSIONS

In summarizing our findings, it may be useful to divide our sample into cases from the Old and New Worlds, to discover whether the relationships obtain with equal force in each instance. To subdivide the sample further would reduce the sample size unduly, and would not, therefore, be expected to produce reliable estimates. The percentages thus obtained are given in Table 14, for each dependent variable together with confidence limits calculated at the 95 per cent level.

As will be seen from the table, an inference based upon the total sample can be confidently made for each of the relationships listed; in no instance does the lower confidence limit fall below 50 per cent and the upper limits are all above 80 per cent. Furthermore, a confident prediction can be made for each relationship in either the New World or the Old World but never

TABLE 14

Obtained Percentage and 95 Per Cent Confidence Limits for Predictions Indicated*

	New World	Old World	Total Sub sample
Multiple-roomed houses by extended family	**100**% (69–100)	65% (43–84)	**76**% (57–89)
Multiple-roomed houses by status distinctions	50% (19–81)	**83**% (63–95)	**65**% (64–81)
Rectilinear houses by sedentary settlement	64% (47–79)	**80**% (66–90)	**72**% (65–84)
Both rectilinear and curvilinear houses by seminomadic settlement	**90**% (59–99)	50% (12–88)	**80**% (52–94)
Curvilinear houses by polygyny	70% (39–91)	**84**% (55–98)	**77**% (56–91)

* Statistically significant predictions, i.e., those where lower confidence limit is greater than 50 per cent, are in boldface type.

in both. This is in part due to the reduction in sample size and in part to the unequal distribution of one or another of the variables involved. In any case, we believe we have demonstrated some useful inferences that can be made from a knowledge of the basic floor plan of the dwellings in any given site.

References

BARRY, HERBERT III
1957 "Relationship between child training and the pictorial arts," *Journal of Abnormal and Social Psychology*, Vol. 54:380-83.

BURTON, R. V., and J. W. M. WHITING
1961 "The absent father and cross-sex identity," *Merrill-Palmer Quarterly*, Vol. 7:85-95.

CHANG, K. C.
1958 "Study of the Neolithic social groupings: Examples from the New World," *American Anthropologist*, Vol. LX, No. 2:298-334.

D'ANDRADE, R. G.
1962 "Father absence and cross-sex identification," unpublished Ph.D. thesis, Harvard University.

"Ethnographic Atlas," *Ethnology*, Vols. 1-4.

FISCHER, J. L.
1961 "Art styles as cultural cognitive maps," *American Anthropologist*, Vol. LXIII, No. 1:79-93.

FRANCK, K., and E. ROSEN
1949 "A projective test of masculinity-femininity," *Journal of Consulting Psychology*, Vol. 13:247-56.

GOODE, J. P.
1957 *Goode's World Atlas*, E. G. Espenshade, Jr., editor (Chicago: Rand McNally and Company).

GOETHALS, G., and J. W. M. WHITING
n.d. "A cross-cultural study of premarital sex," Research in progress, William James Hall, Harvard University

KUCKENBERG, KAROLYN GAI
1963 "Effect of early father absence on scholastic aptitude," unpublished Ph.D. thesis, Harvard University.

MCELROY, W.
1954 "A sex difference in preference for shapes," *British Journal of Psychology*. Vol. 45:209-216.

MUNROE, R. L.
1964 "Couvade practices of the black Caribbean: A psychological study," unpublished Ph.D. thesis, Harvard University.

MURDOCK, G. P.
1964 "Cultural correlates of the regulation of premarital sex behavior," *Process and Pattern in Culture: Essays in Honor of Julian Steward*, Robert A. Manners, editor (Chicago: Aldine Press):399-410.

NAROLL, RAOUL
1961 "Two solutions to Galton's Problem," *Philosophy of Science*, Vol. XXVIII, No. 1:15-39.

NAROLL, RAOUL, and R. G. D'ANDRADE
1963 "Two further solutions to Galton's Problem" *American Anthropologist*, Vol. LXV, No. 5:1053-67.

ROBBINS, M. C.
1966 "Material culture and cognition," American Anthropologist, Vol. 68, No. 3:745-48.

WHITING, J. W. M.
1964 "Effects of climate on certain cultural practices," *Explorations in Cultural Anthropology*, Ward Goodenough, editor (New York: McGraw-Hill Book Company):511-44.

WHITING, J. W. M., and I. L. CHILD
1953 *Child Training and Personality* (New Haven: Yale University Press).

WHITING, J. W. M., RICHARD KLUCKHOHN, and ALBERT ANTHONY
1958 "The function of male initiation ceremonies at puberty," *Readings in Social Psychology*, Eleanor Maccoby, T. M. Newcomb, and E. L. Hartley, editors (New York: Henry Holt and Company):359-70.

VIII

WILLIAM SEARS

The State and Settlement Patterns in the New World[1]

This paper suggests that analysis of settlement patterns may be combined with suitably analyzed data of other sorts that are archaeologically obtainable to permit some degree of reconstruction of prehistoric states. It is, in effect, an extension of an earlier effort of mine in this direction (Sears, 1962).

A set of models is developed, from available data, that appears reasonably representative of reality. These models are then tested against actual situations from areas where we have sufficient settlement pattern and other information to make such testing practicable.

Basic Premises

It appears in this study, as in most studies of cultural phenomena, that we are dealing with continua. That part of the continuum of cultural development that is of interest to us – that part representative of at least semisedentary cultures – is allocated to three segments: the village community, the priest state, and the militaristic state. A larger or smaller number of segments could in theory be possible; those selected, or their cut-off points, seem to relate to the same thresholds in cultural development that have been used for cultural classifications based on other criteria. There is here an obvious bias toward cultural evolution, for which no apologies are offered.

Definition of the State Hoebel's definition of the state continues to be useful. The state is " . . . the organized association of men (the group) for whom a specialized sub-organization functions to transmit state policy into social action " (Hoebel, 1949, p. 377). The definition does, however, omit

[1] This paper owes a great deal to several studies, to which it has not always been possible or convenient to give specific credit. These are: Willey and Phillips (1958); Gearing (1962); Adams (1956); and, especially, Beardsley *et al*. (1956). My use of their facts, interpretations, and hypotheses is of course my own responsibility.

territoriality, which is of particular importance in this study. The importance of territory is implied by Gearing (1962, p. 7), who also contributes to clarification of other areas of confusion in stating that " . . . and societies which draw into a sovereign political unit several or many face-to-face communities must have centralized mechanisms for exerting coercion over communities, kin groups, and individual members." Further elucidation of the political mechanisms may be found in another statement of Gearing 's: "All students seem to agree that, when a population, acting as a single organized group, by orderly procedure binds itself to one course of action among alternative possible courses, it acts politically " (Gearing, 1962, p. 70).

To identify a prehistoric state then, we need to:

(1) Identify, archaeologically, the *group* which is presumed to be composed of a number of communities.

(2) Define the territory of the group, which is essentially equivalent to defining the group itself.

(3) Identify a specialized suborganization that could (and hypothetically did!) transmit state policy into social action.

The Areal Community Pattern The identification of the group is accomplished to a considerable extent through identification of an "Areal Community Pattern – complex patterning of a definite culture complex within the definable culture area; the macrocosmic aspect of community patterning." (Sears, 1961, p. 226.) Defining the culture area by using culture complexes can be something of a problem. A rapid survey of the literature indicates that "culture complexes" vary widely in their composition. In some instances in North, South, and Middle America, a simple style, expressed in ceramics or architecture, and occurring with widely varying materials from site to site, is used in comparisons and analyses almost as if it constituted a culture. A good example, in Southeastern United States, is the Weeden Island culture from the west coast of Florida, sometimes considered to have existed in any site in which Weeden Island ceramics are found. But since the pottery occurs almost entirely in two kinds of burial mounds that are relics of communities whose utilitarian ceramic complexes vary greatly, it is quite clear that "Weeden Island" includes a number of readily distinguishable cultures. Because so much work in South and Middle America appears to have been based on architectural or art styles, the same problems occur there. Ford points this out specifically with respect to the Gallinazo, Mochica, and Tiahuanaco styles in the Viru Valley, which are rare in midden collections but common in the cemeteries (Ford and Willey, 1949, p. 41). We shall return to this problem further on, using specific instances for illustration.

Generally, I think, the current state of archaeological techniques is such as to allow identification of the group and its territory by the location of sites possessing a specific ceramic complex – specific, that is, in terms of types, styles, modes, or any combination of these, and their relative proportions, as well as the identification of ceremonial and trade wares. Gradual shifts in time pose no problems, of course; they simply demonstrate continuity of the group. Once time control has been established, gradual shifts in space, and therefore boundaries, must be committed to arbitrary decisions, just as is necessary in the delineation of any culture area.

Another problem, already alluded to, is the differential distribution of ceremonial ceramics. This may raise a question of the nature of the relationship between groups that are ceramically, and hence culturally, discrete in midden ware, but related at the ceremonial level and, perhaps, the political level. Multicultural states are one answer; states politically discrete but sharing a common religion are another. Again, if the real, not the inferred, distribution is studied, problems can be solved.

In any event, in an area determined by ceramic distribution, where limits in time and space have been controlled, the archaeologist is in a position to study settlement patterns at the level of areal community patterns. If his interest is study and interpretation, as exemplified by the Viru study (Willey, 1953), and not simply description of the available variety of settlement patterns, as is so often the case, he must first establish this control. Only then can he work meaningfully and analytically both within the framework of a culture and in comparisons of specific cultural types and settlement patterns.

Full study of an areal community pattern quite obviously requires study of its constituent site community patterns. In each of these site patterns, some estimation of the probable type and number of dwelling units is necessary, and the pattern of their relationships to ceremonial and other nonresidential units must be worked out. This step accomplished, the study of areal community patterning can proceed. At this level, recognition of the ceremonial or political centers of a culture becomes a possibility. Again, we shall return to this point after discussing some concrete examples—as concrete, at least, as we appear to have at present.

The Suborganization One last matter requiring some preliminary discussion is the "suborganization" or, indeed, the political organization of any sort that may be archaeologically visible. Three points can be made. First, I feel we must accept the premise that the "state" will exist only in those societies in which kinship is not the major structuring agency for social relations–that is, with stable economic bases (generally agriculture) and a sizable population. The lengthy discussions and references possible here are obviously outside the scope of this paper. The full transition from "folk" to "urban" need not have been made, but the societies we are here concerned with will certainly be well along on this route.

Second, a matter of observation rather than of theoretical elaboration: a type of class structure will be visible in a society possessing a state; distinguishable groups of people operated the "association" and the "suborganization."

Finally, it seems inevitably true, on the basis of observation and theory, that religion was intimately involved in the structure of the states we are concerned with – that the upper classes were in fact, the priesthood, or if derived from it, continued in a particularly intimate relationship with the supernatural. As Adams (1956, p. 228) points out, secular organizations per se, and conquest states, do arise from priest-controlled states. Then "the transfer from sacred to secular was probably accomplished by a gradual shifting in the nature of the power exercised by the leaders." (Willey and Phillips 1958, p. 12.)

These points are important, though perhaps not more important than others that may be adduced, because they can, demonstrably, be observed archaeologically.

Village Communities

Village communities are present in the formative or early formative stage (Willey and Phillips, 1958, p. 155), and are partially equivalent to the semi-permanent sedentary community pattern of Beardsley *et al.* (1956, p. 140). The relationship to other stage and period concepts will be apparent. The state is not present in this form of organization and settlement patterning, although individual communities are of course elements of the states to be discussed below.

Territorial Organization and the Group Territorial organization and the group, in this instance, may be defined by the areal dispersion of sites with specific ceramic complexes, with temporal limits under control. We should here expect gradually changing continua in time and space, since each community is discrete politically. Community interaction would have existed, of course, based on the bonds of kinship and, often, the needs of seasonal ceremonialism. Nevertheless, each economically and socially self-contained community interprets the basic culture patterns somewhat differently. This is reflected in artifact complexes, particularly ceramics, and accounts for the "looseness" of some types and complexes. In spite of this difficulty, the definition of culture areas and the consequent definition of the territory and the group are quite possible, but cannot be as precise as comparable definitions in the culturally more rigid and more formal priest and militaristic states.

Suborganization No suborganization above the individual village level exists, by definition.

Settlement Pattern The individual community, in which great variation is possible and present, represents the settlement pattern here. The significant factor in this study is the areal community pattern, not the individual site

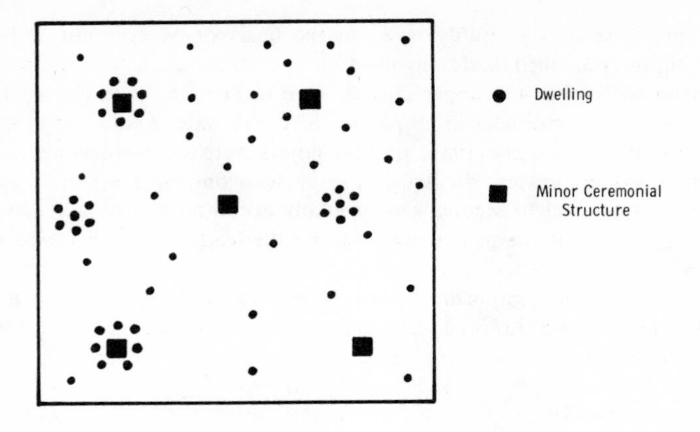

Fig. 1. VILLAGE COMMUNITY PATTERN

patterns. Since we are here concerned only with sedentary village life, reasonably compact villages are part of our definition, although sites produced by individual scattered houses, farms, etc., may exist. If so, they will relate to specific villages, of which they are functionally a part. New villages would have formed by splitting off from old ones, and might be quite small. Ceremonial structures, such as kivas, compounds, small temple platforms, and council houses, are present in some, perhaps many, of the villages of a particular village culture. If there are villages of different sizes, or ceremonial structures present in some and not in others, these will be represented by numbers in each class. A single village much larger than others, or a ceremonial center, that is clearly physically distinctive, is indicative of the priest or militaristic states.

A point perhaps in need of emphasis is that here, and in the more complicated communities making up complex states, ceremonial structures and the ceremonialism that is practiced may be but the local representation of a widespread manifestation. This does not, in itself, indicate the presence of a widespread political organization. Many horizon styles, such as Hopewell, are of this nature, a nature that may, as the representation of a religious cult, be utilized in state formation in some areas but simply represent the religion practiced in others. I suspect that Chavin is another example.

VILLAGE COMMUNITY EXAMPLES: SOUTHEASTERN UNITED STATES

We face here the usual problem with the Southeast in archaeology – that of knowing more about potsherd distribution than about settlement patterns, architecture, ceremonialism, or anything else. However, part of this confusion may arise directly from the primary characteristics of village communities – the social, and to a degree cultural, distinctness of each.

A problem of some consequence is that, until we have reasonably full control of the total settlement pattern of a specific culture, the portion we do have some feeling for may be completely misunderstood. For example, a series of villages in one modern state or one river valley may be part of a complex state with its center in another state or another valley. A good illustration is the Weeden Island–Kolomoki culture of the northwest Florida coast; the coastal sites of this culture have been known since 1902, but its single ceremonial center 100 miles inland was not recognized until forty years later. The single politico-religious center of the priest state, discussed in the next section, causes the greatest confusion. This suggests that we must know the total distribution of a ceramic complex, and the settlement patterns of the sites on which it is found, before we can deal with data sufficiently valid for this kind of study. A culture settlement pattern must be demonstrably such if we are to engage in much more than guesswork.

However, there are complexes that appear, from the information available, to represent cultures whose largest units are roughly equivalent to villages.

Deptford Sites The sites occupied in the early part of Deptford development, along the Atlantic and northern Gulf coasts from South Carolina to Pensacola Bay, and across northern Florida and southern Georgia below and above the Okefenokee Swamp, seem to be a good example of this kind of culture, the village community. The shell mound sites, both coastal and riverine, all fall in a narrowly constrained size range, with an obvious upper limit, and are usually spread out along banks or old beach ridges. No structures are known. The implied pattern is a simple shorewise alignment of lightly built dwelling units, dispersed only to the extent needed to give each unit convenient access to the water. Inland sites are not as well known, but do exist, probably in large numbers, on rivers and smaller streams. No alignment of structures is probable, since middens are simple, vaguely round patches. Agriculture was probably pursued, since there is some evidence for it in the next period; in any case, it should have started at this earlier level, a period of great cultural spread.

Miller Culture Sites The Miller Culture of the Tombigbee River drainage in Alabama and Mississippi, known in part from Jenning's work (1941) and in part from my own unpublished survey, is quite possibly a better example. Again, generally formless middens are typical, and are spread out only with respect to river terraces, implying again no real patterning of structures with respect to each other or to anything else. Some of these sites are quite large, however – one lower Tombigbee site, occupied in both Miller I and Miller II periods, averages 100 yards in width and is three quarters of a mile long. Miller-complex sites, except for the smallest, usually have burial mounds adjacent to, sometimes in, the village. On the lower Tombigbee, these occur in clusters of as many as thirty small mounds. Clusters upstream are of fewer mounds. These mound clusters occur in many apparently contemporary sites, indicating duplication of a common pattern. Differences, if any, appear to be between the northern and southern communities. Although some class structure is probably involved, with mound burial reserved for specific classes, there is no evidence for a single ceremonial center for the culture, nor for centers for parts of the culture. If, on Fig. 1, these burial-mound clusters are symbolized by the minor-ceremonial-structure symbol, the Miller-culture settlement pattern fits the diagram very well.

Other Sites A list of other cultures that might be included would be very lengthy indeed. A few examples are the early St. Johns I period in peninsular Florida, with burial mounds at least in the St. Johns Valley (Goggin, 1952); the Napier of north Georgia (Wauchope, 1948; Sears, 1952); the Tchefuncte of the lower Mississippi Valley (Ford and Quimby, 1945); and the culture represented by the Tchula period in the central Mississippi Valley (Phillips, Ford, and Griffin, 1951). The pattern of occasional small ceremonial structures, dispersed among scattered, generally formless midden units, obtains here as elsewhere.

THE PRIEST STATE

The priest state is present in the Formative and Classic (Willey and Phillips, 1958) periods, and is apparently the only type for the state in the simple, nuclear-centered community pattern (Beardsley *et al.*, 1956, p. 141).

Definition This type of state has the most uniform culture pattern of the three types of organization being considered. It is composed of a number of communities all very similar in size and composition, but includes a single, physically distinct community–the ceremonial center, the "trademark" of this type of state.

Uniformity of culture is produced by a common, rigidly interpreted religion and its ceremonialism. The ceremonialism reaches its quantitative and qualitative peaks at the ceremonial center and with the priesthood there, the latter forming the larger part of the upper class or caste for the total culture. Representatives of this class are present in the larger villages, where, as the local leaders of the religion, or state cult, they control ritual and culture patterns, in keeping with the standards of the state cult. This cult, then, with the top levels of its hierarchy at the ceremonial center and its representatives in lesser communities, constitutes the suborganization of our definition.

Territorial Organization and the Group Definition by ceramic-complex distribution is perhaps simplest and most practicable in this instance, since we may expect pottery to be one of the aspects of culture that is permeated by and standardized by the centralized religious cult. Specialized ceramics, usually found in mortuary association, are particularly prominent. Careful investigation usually reveals that these ceramics are found in mortuary context, with a relatively limited number of persons out of the total populace, indicating that the ceramics are associated with the ceremonialism of the state cult. The persons with whom the pots are found are then presumed to be members of the upper class or caste, members of the politico-religious organization that exercises functional rule of the society. Artifacts other than pottery may be involved, as is suggested in some of the examples that follow.

Again, care must be taken to avoid including too many cultures in the state, since horizon styles and widespread cults, reinterpreted in specific states for local consumption, appear often to be involved. Utilitarian ceramic complexes, reasonably uniform from site to site in a specific culture, serve as a guide here.

Suborganization Effectively, the suborganization is the state cult, as the definition above makes clear. For a culture to be identified as a priest state, the state cult, with its ceremonial center and village-community representatives, must be identified.

Settlement Pattern Fig. 2 is representative of the ideal settlement pattern for the priest state, in some of its variants. The component parts are the cer-

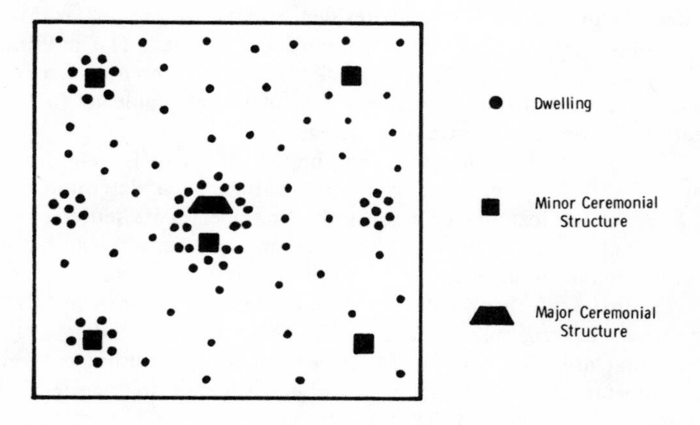

Fig. 2. PRIEST STATE PATTERN

emonial center, the village communities, and the areal community pattern.

Ceremonial Center. The ceremonial center is composed of public structures spatially organized for the participation, mostly on the participant-observer level, of very large numbers of people. This usually involves one major platform mound and a plaza or courtyard arrangement. Other platform mounds and other structures for specialized ceremonial purposes, such as ball-courts, slave posts, and council houses, are to be expected. Dwelling units are certainly part of ceremonial centers, and may be sufficiently numerous to house large populations. However, the midden representation of dwelling areas, usually surrounding the public area in part, may be sparse, and therefore indicative of a small resident population.

The location of the ceremonial center in the culture area might be expected, ideally, to be central. In two of the Southeastern United States examples that follow, however, the ceremonial centers are on the periphery of the culture area. Presumably, this dislocation is the result of historical accident.

Village Communities. Village communities here do not differ greatly from their counterparts in the village-community kind of organization. A number of communities that are very similar in size and plan are to be expected, each with its own minor ceremonial or politico-religious structure. The patterns of these communities are expected to be quite similar with respect to the spatial relationships of ceremonial and residence units. These communities will be of fair size, often with substantially larger populations than the ceremonial center. Their size derives in part from their providing economic support to the state-cult structure, local and central.

Hamlets, farms, and other small residence units are present in this structure, satellites spatially and functionally of the villages. The patterning of these units would be determined primarily by such economic factors as the distribution of land that is fertile in terms of the available technology and the location of rivers used for transportation.

Areal Community Pattern. This is the important factor in determining the existence of this form of state. With the culture area determined (which means in effect the location of a substantial number of its settlements of all kinds), a single, readily distinguishable ceremonial center will be visible. In an area around or adjacent to it will be a number of villages of roughly equal size, many of them with ceremonial units of their own. Clustered around these, in turn, may be the small, nonpatterned hamlets and single residences that are often part of a culture with an agricultural economy. In some circumstances, though not to my knowledge in southeastern United States, the single center may serve as the focus of an areal community pattern consisting only of hamlets or isolated dwellings. Generally, I would expect such a pattern to indicate that the observed unit is a minor center, that this was a dispersed village pattern in effect, related as a whole to a ceremonial center for the total state not yet located or recognized as such.

PRIEST STATE EXAMPLES: SOUTHEASTERN UNITED STATES

Etowah A state with the Etowah site as its political and ceremonial center has been suggested, and the supporting data have been outlined (Sears, 1962, p. 114). We may review and supplement this suggestion in certain respects, so that we may use it as a test for the priest-state concept.

Culture Area. Most sites are in the Etowah valley, the upper Chattahoochee drainage, the upper parts of the Tugalo and Savannah Rivers, and in adjacent parts of north Georgia, northwestern South Carolina, and northwestern North Carolina. Ceramic determinants for the culture are the Etowah and sequent Wilbanks complexes. A further determinant is the Southern Cult, indicated by characteristic symbols and artifacts of various kinds. All sites were not occupied throughout these ceramic periods, which dated perhaps 1300–1600 A.D., but the ceramic sequence has been subdivided into periods which appear quite uniform throughout the Etowah culture area. Since the period subdivisions are but convenient segments of a continuum, even greater accuracy in establishing contemporaneity of two or more specific excavated complexes is quite possible.

Suborganization. The Southern Cult would seem to be the chief suborganization here. The association of quantities of cult artifacts with a very limited number of persons, and the burial of these persons in locations or circumstances indicative of particular, upper-social position, give rise to the possibility that a religion and a very formal and rigid ceremonialism are involved. That this religion and ceremonialism were of great social significance is demonstrated by their association with monumental public structures. A few functionaries of this cult, identified by the regalia associated with a few burials, were present in the individual villages, each of which often possessed a single public structure–typically, a small platform or an earth lodge-council house.

Partly from this internal evidence, and partly from analogies with historic nations, such as the Natchez or the lesser known sixteenth-century societies (e.g., the Alibamu and the Timucua), it appears that this religion was the basis for political structure. The upper social class was composed of religious functionaries, who operated the political system. This class, having supplemented kinship to a degree (although class membership probably remained hereditary, as it tends to do in most societies), was the chief structuring agency for social and intercommunity relationships (the latter a necessity for an effective state). This agency operated through the cult structure, which was as much political as religious in function, and was represented throughout the nation, very probably in a graded hierarchy with all of the highest positions at Etowah.

Settlement Pattern. Etowah was the state's major ceremonial center. This site has one very large temple mound with a facing plaza. A smaller platform mound erected above, and in connection with, older ceremonial structures has cult functionaries buried in all levels and construction phases. There is another mound of uncertain use, other plazas of various sizes, and a number of large buildings possibly for public use. Apparently there were many residents on the site in all periods.

The Wilbanks site (Sears, 1958) is representative of the village sites. Wilbanks has a large council house, a few cult symbols in a few graves, and a house arrangement apparently around the council house and along the river. The earlier levels of such historic Cherokee sites as Nacoochee (Heye, Hodge, and Pepper, 1918; Chauga, Kelly, and Neitzel, 1961) and Tugalo appear most similar, as do many other unnamed sites having pottery of the Etowah–Wilbanks complexes and small mounds that were once small platforms or collapsed earth lodges.

Kolomoki In the postulated Kolomoki state, only the presumptive ceremonial center, the Kolomoki site itself, has been excavated in such a fashion as to produce data of the sort useful here. Recent excavations at Tucker, a northwest Florida coastal site, have provided some useful information (Sears, 1963). On the basis of the Kolomoki and Tucker data, and the publications and field notes of Clarence B. Moore (Moore, 1902), certain reasonably accurate inferences can be drawn concerning the many sites Moore excavated. We can, I think, propose that a state did exist on the Gulf coastal plain, with Kolomoki as the ceremonial, or politico-religious, center for its state cult.

Culture Area. Kolomoki appears to be the northernmost site of any consequence of the culture. Other sites, recognizable mostly from the work of Moore (1901; 1902; 1903a; 1903b; 1907), are along the Chattahoochee, Flint, and Apalachicola Rivers south of Kolomoki, and spread out along the Gulf Coast on the lower courses of other rivers and on bays and inlets from the Aucilla River west to Pensacola Bay. The state did not include west-coast Florida communities south of the Aucilla River.

The diagnostic ceramic complex has two significant components, the Weeden Island and the complicated stamped series, which have quite different origins and independent distributions. For this state, the Weeden Island series, Kolomoki Complicated Stamped, other complicated stamped types of the Swift Creek genre, and some representations of Wakulla Check Stamped are, in several complexes, diagnostic in midden or village occurrence. The same series, typologically, occurs in compact deposits on one side of burial mounds. However, the Weeden Island types are apt to be highly specialized, particularly in the rather common effigy forms. Specimens of the other series are usually particularly well made, and often show, by such features as decorative perforation and kill holes cut through before firing, that they were manufactured specifically for ceremonial purposes. The time-space permutations of these complexes, somewhat different at every site, are not well understood. Even the temporal relationship of the two major complexes in middens at Kolomoki, one with only Kolomoki Complicated Stamped and a plain ware, the other with the Weeden Island series and variants of Swift Creek Complicated Stamped (Sears, 1951), has not been demonstrated stratigraphically.

Suborganization. Kolomoki Complicated Stamped does occur in burial mounds that are extremely similar in plan, structural sequence, and content throughout the area described, even though the pottery in associated middens may vary greatly. These burial mounds are the same ones in which, in the same deposits, effigy vessels and decoratively perforated vessels are common.

There is some reason to believe that in all these burial mounds, most of which were excavated by C. B. Moore, there is evidence of many kinds for class stratification. The specialized pottery was ceremonial, not simply grave offerings, and there is real reason to associate the upper class and the culture-wide uniform ceremonialism.

This upper class, associated with such specific insignia as copper ornaments and conch-shell beads, appears to have served cultural purposes very similar to those suggested for the Southern Cult functionaries at the Etowah site. The top levels of the hierarchy appear to have been present at Kolomoki, where there are earthworks representing the labor of far more people than ever lived there. But functionaries of the same sort, practicing the same ceremonies and buried in exactly the same way, were present in the villages. Again, because of the implied rigidity and uniformity of ceremonial structure, a state cult appears to have been present. There is no evidence for any other class of persons with specific powers. The priest state, with a state cult as the basis for its organization, seems the most probable hypothesis to account for the observed phenomena.

Settlement Pattern. Kolomoki, the center for this state, has a settlement pattern completely different from that of any other site in the culture area. It is unique in that only it, of hundreds of sites, has a temple mound and a plaza. Other structures, such as burial mounds, dwelling areas, and less readily classifiable features, are placed so as to facilitate public participation in or observation of the ceremonies. These ceremonies would appear to have served, individually or collectively, religious and political ends.

Villages appear generally unstructured. Coastal shell midden sites tend to spread out along the shorelines. Inland sites may be on river banks, with some shell debris, or on smaller streams, with little or no shell refuse. All communities of any size at all had a burial mound nearby, usually directly adjacent to the village. Early mounds, related to the earlier occupation of some of these sites (Sears, 1963, p. 5) tend to be a bit farther away. However, the presence of ceremonial pottery vessels in caches in these mounds, and the burial of religious functionaries in a manner interpreted as representing rigid mortuary ceremonialism, suggests that there was a public structure in each village, a temple or shrine in some part of which the ceremonial equipment was kept and used. Adequate excavation of some of the smaller sites should produce evidence of these structures. There are, as Moore noted, small, sterile mounds at some sites, in addition to the burial mounds, which may have constituted platforms for the public structures.

To me, the most impressive feature in all of this—and I have visited and collected from most of these sites—is the uniformity of these communities, each community with its acre or so of midden and its adjacent five- to ten-foot-high burial mound. This sort of gross physical uniformity, in conjunction with the tremendous internal similarity of the burial mounds, in everything from artifact complexes to the location of artifacts, implies great cultural uniformity, a uniformity representative of an advanced and populous society. One cannot but infer some sort of culture-wide control system.

Other Southeastern Priest States A few other possible priest states may be suggested. Quite possibly, from survey data filed at various institutions, these hypothetical states could be demonstrated to have at least as high a probability of existence as the Etowah and Kolomoki States—or, from the same data, rendered less probable.

The Marksville area, with its ceremonial center shifting around the immediate neighborhood and its culture area shifting and expanding through the Marksville-Troyville-Coles Creek period, is one possibility. Several other fairly obvious ones may be noted in the Caddoan area. Centers would be the Spiro site, with the cult as political mechanism; the Harlan site, with the little-understood religious cult imported from the Davis site area; and the Davis site itself. Here, I am informed, the smaller villages are becoming known through intensive survey activities recently and currently in progress.

Farther east, an early, pre-Kolomoki state at the late Hopewell level appears to have the Mandeville site (Kellar, Kelly, and McMichael, 1962) as its center. Villages occupy the same area as those in the Kolomoki state, and are in fact often the same villages. With its Hopewellian cult, this state represents perhaps a stage in the development of the Kolomoki State. A last possibility, persisting from the Hopewellian period to a time well along in the period of Weeden Island development, is Crystal River (Moore, 1903a). Survey work here is only beginning, but a very definitely circumscribed area with a very distinctive and limited utilitarian ceramic complex is known, with sites on many Key and shoreline sites.

Many other states and state centers could be suggested, on the theory that a major site, with earthworks, unique in an area, probably represents the seat of power for such a state. Those listed are at least sufficient for our purposes here.

The Militaristic State

The militaristic state is equivalent to the advanced, nuclear-centered, supra-nuclear integrated state of Beardsley *et al.* (1956), and to the Classic and Post-Classic of Willey and Phillips (1958).

Definition The militaristic state is an integrated community, consisting of numbers of villages, each perhaps with satellite hamlets and farmsteads, all members of one organization that expands by conquest. There seem to be two distinguishable kinds of such states.

Conquest and Incorporation. In this case—certainly the most familiar in history and in theory—other states, such as priest states, individual communities, and other cultures generally, are brought into the state by conquest and may, for some time at least, retain some of their individual cultural characteristics.

Conquest and Replacement. In this instance, nothing seems desired by the conquerors except the land of the conquered. The states, communities, and cultures thus conquered disappear from the historical-archaeological record in the area. The record from that point on is of only one culture, that of the conquering state.

After trying to fit what I felt quite strongly were conquest states of the late protohistoric and early historic Southeastern United into my definition of the conquest state, these two variants were recognized. The Southeastern States—and indeed, I think, most North American states—fit the second type most closely. Parallels with the westward expansion of our own states, and the consequent replacement of Indian cultures, become obvious, and the thought then loses its novelty.

Territorial Organization and the Group Without such aids as roads or irrigation systems, the incorporating type of conquest state is difficult to recognize archaeologically. Such a state, developed through conquest, may include a number of distinct cultures and their ceremonial centers; at another stage, their urban political centers. Single traditions expressed in art or architecture may help, but these are present at the village-culture level. Until a center of centers is located, truly urban and truly distinct from other centers in a geographic area, the definition and study of such a state is difficult.

The replacement conquest state, which we appear to be dealing with in the Southeast, is far simpler to work with because of its relatively uniform culture. Urban centers for sacred and secular control are present, as well as the residences of the specialists who can be supported by the same expanding economy that permits, and perhaps causes, conquest and expansion. Similarly, there are other centers, at a distance from the capital, that serve these same functions in the provinces. At the frontiers, there are small, scattered communities and a few large, fortified settlements. Farms at any distance can be little more than that because of the need for defense. In any event, there is little difficulty defining the territory, and the group that occupied it, by ceramic and other artifact assemblages representing the single culture

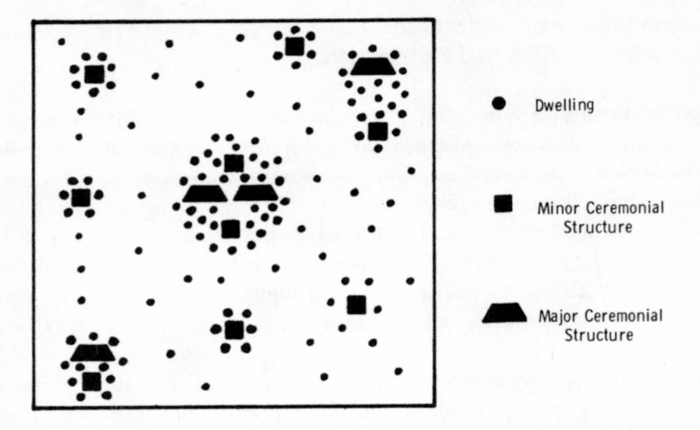

Fig. 3. MILITARISTIC STATE PATTERN

involved. Accurate time control is a necessity, because rapid change is part of the picture; some excavation, therefore, is generally called for.

Suborganization A warrior class is present, and would appear to be closely affiliated with the state cult. Full-time warriors, excepting possibly a limited number of leaders, are not expected. A divine king, high priest, or supreme lord of some kind may be drawn from either the warrior or priestly classes, very likely combining attributes of both. Or, both may be represented, and may function according to the needs of the moment. In either instance, class membership was probably hereditary; and in either case, functional political leadership was able to employ both sacred and secular sanctions.

Settlement Pattern The two types of militaristic states might be very similar, perhaps even indistinguishable, on the basis of settlement patterns alone. Effectively, in either instance, the settlement pattern is that of the priest state, or of a number of priest states, with two additional features:

(1) An urban ceremonial center, physically readily distinguishable from other ceremonial centers within the boundaries of the state because of its greater size and complexity and possibly greater population.

(2) Fortifications: particularly of the urban center, with the incorporating variant; of the frontier towns or cities, with the replacing type.

MILITARISTIC STATE EXAMPLES: SOUTHEASTERN UNITED STATES

Middle Missisipppi Culture In recent years, it has become increasingly apparent, in many instances at least, that when late Middle Mississippi cultures appeared in an area, they replaced resident cultures. Since the Middle Mississippi cultures were quite uniform over wide areas, and since the cultures replaced varied greatly, it is becoming increasingly difficult to accept the many simultaneous overnight conversions to Middle Mississippianism, conversions including architecture, pottery, and site-location traits. Further, more and more Middle Mississippi sites were fortified, with the sophisticated type of palisade, often plastered with corner and wall bastions and towers. Moreover, many Middle Mississippi towns were large, with many building platforms and residents. Estimates for the DeSoto period of many thousands of residents in some towns do not seem to me at all exaggerated.

In the comparatively short period of time during which some Middle Mississippi sites were occupied, a period measured in years rather than in centuries, many feet of midden accumulated. The middens are a solid mass of postholes and fireplaces from structures, burial pits, refuse pits, and so on. In some sites, the midden, apparently accumulated inside a palisade, eventually assumed the proportions of a large platform mound.

Since no study has been directed toward political entities of this size as such, a few comments pertinent to particular sites, cultures, and areas are all we can offer now.

Moundville

Culture Area. The upper drainage of the Alabama River, including of course the Black Warrior River, where Moundville itself is located, constitutes the Moundville culture area.

Definition is on the distribution of sites, often with temple mounds, most of them of considerable size, that have a classic Middle Mississippian ceramic assemblage. This assemblage is very close to the Tennessee Cumberland ceramic complex, as displayed at Kincaid, Wycliffe, and many other huge sites. Only the well-advertised engraved bottles and cult ceremonial equipment are distinctive, and are limited almost entirely to Moundville, as De Jarnette (1952, p. 283) and others have noted.

Somewhat later, as indicated by the distribution of sites with the Pensacola Complex (Willey, 1949) in several variants (Trickey, 1958) the area extends down the valley of the Alabama and Mobile Rivers to the coast, and along the coast westward to the Mississippi Delta and eastward to Pensacola. Few temple mounds were built in this period, although burial mounds such as Bear Point (Willey, 1949) and certain burial urn sites (De Jarnette, 1952, p. 283) are known. Expansion of this state by conquest seems rather obvious. De Jarnette (1952, p. 280) states that Middle Mississippi culture in Alabama does not appear to have developed from any of the precedent complexes. In-place development of the pre-Mississippi complexes, over very long periods, is quite clear. My own survey work has led me to the same conclusion for the southern part of the state. In all instances, the invasion seems to have been from the north, the Tennessee–Cumberland area. Except for a few features of ceramic decoration, there are no connections with preceding cultures. These features of ceramics could very well have been acquired by Middle Mississippians before they invaded, through normal intercultural diffusion.

Suborganization. Perhaps the Southern Cult, or a variety of it, represents a suborganization of the postulated Moundville militaristic state. Suborganization is certainly present at Moundville, and a few cult artifacts or, in the later period, objects such as spatulate "spuds" have shown up in lesser sites and may be expected at others. In the later period particularly, and in other Middle Mississippi states where the cult artifacts are scarce or lacking, a different sort of organization must have been present. It seems probable, of course, that this organization emphasized warfare and secular or political leadership, rather than religious leadership. As such, it may well have derived from the cult, and continued to utilize some of the same ceremonialism and sanctions. The DeSoto accounts describe populous societies and large towns in south or south-central Alabama, which must be represented by this ceramic complex. The fortified town of Mabila is a case in point: powerful chiefs, who with their associates formed a distinct upper class; special costumes, litters, and insignia; and subject or vassal towns and provinces are described. The organization is obviously there; its structure remains to be determined. The sixteenth–seventeenth century "decline" so often mentioned, certainly a major social change, eliminated this form of social organization before many accounts were written, so that archaeology will have to suffice as the major source for its elucidation. However, more work will probably reveal remnants of the militaristic state in historic Muskhogean organization, and perhaps more than remnants in such areas marginal to Middle Mississippi culture as South Georgia and South Carolina.

Settlement Pattern. That part of the settlement pattern at Moundville represented by platform mounds is well known, as are some of the grave contents. There is, I think, little doubt that there were a great many houses, organized according to some rather rigid plan, and that the site was fortified. Its location on a river bank allowed the river to serve as a highway, and placed the site in an area of fertile bottom lands.

Areal Community Pattern. Most of the sites are relatively large, of several acres at least, and often considerably larger. Temple mounds may or may not be present. Middens have rather well-defined boundaries, indicative of community planning and probably of palisades. The few small sites known are near larger sites. All of the sites are on river banks or terraces. The function of the rivers for transportation, as described by the DeSoto chroniclers on the Mississippi, and the importance of the broad, fertile bottoms, more distinctively a location for Middle Mississippi sites than for any earlier cultures in the area, cannot be overstressed.

Other Examples Beyond these observations, we must become even more hypothetical–although careful analysis of the available data, both published and filed, would permit testing these hypotheses much further than there is time or space for in this paper. A large number of classic Middle Mississippi foci or phases, almost all of them in the drainage of the Mississippi itself, possess some of the features indicative of conquest states. Perhaps it would be simpler to list these outstanding features, and then comment on a few of these foci, as appropriate.

(1) Replacement of earlier cultures that, although individually varying, seem in each instance to have developed over long periods in their area.

(2) Large, urban or at least populous centers, with large public structures.

(3) Many large communities.

(4) Fortifications.

(5) Location on rivers, which served as routes for conquest and provided the soil for productive agriculture–which in turn fostered and supported the population boom that apparently produced the need for conquest.

Cahokia. This focus was one of the sources of Middle Mississippi culture. Consequently, replacement of earlier cultures is lacking around the urban center itself, but is probably present in the outer limits of the area. Aztalan, with the same culture, appears to represent the founding of a new state by conquest.

The Tennessee–Cumberland Aspect–Kincaid and Wycliff. Available information suggests that there was only one state in this very uniform (at any one time) culture area. There were many large urban centers. Which of these might have been the principal center is uncertain.

New Madrid Focus. This focus was closely related to the Tennessee–Cumberland culture. All specifications seem to be met.

Parkin Focus. The Parkin site or the Rose site was probably the center; excavation, with special attention to overall community pattern, would probably determine this.

This listing could be extended almost indefinitely, particularly by extending it to areas where even less work has been done, and where, as a result, less knowledge is available. The Fort Walton complex, with a center somewhere on the Chattahoochee or Apalachicola Rivers, and the "Lamar" complex of Louisiana and Mississippi are examples. There seems to be little reason to follow such a procedure now.

Conclusions

The concepts of the priest state and, in two fairly obvious variants, the militaristic state, seem, on testing, to have sufficient validity to warrant further investigation. Certainly there are two distinguishable kinds of areal community patterns: one is the single-major-ceremonial-center type; the other has multiple centers, with large populations, and at least one very large, complex, and truly urban ceremonial and population center. The two patterns do seem, in an overall view of Southeastern prehistory, to conform, respectively, to distinguishable and successive emphases on religion, on the one hand, and to conquest and secularization, on the other. They seem also to have followed trends of population increase and attendant improvement in agricultural production.

References

ADAMS, R. M.
1956 "Some hypotheses on the development of early civilizations," *American Antiquity,* Vol. XXI, No. 3: 227-32.

BEARDSLEY, R. K., *et al.*
1956 "Functional and evolutionary implications of community patterning," *Society for American Archaeology Memoir No. 11,* Robert Wauchope, editor.

DE JARNETTE, D. J.
1952 "Alabama archaeology: A summary," *Archaeology of the Eastern United States*, J. B. Griffin, editor (Chicago: University of Chicago Press): 272-84.

FORD, J. A., and G. I. QUIMBY, JR.
1945 "The Tchefuncte Culture, an early occupation of the lower Mississippi Valley," *Society for American Archaeology Memoir No. 2.*

FORD, J. A., and G. R. WILLEY
1949 "Surface survey of the Viru Valley, Peru," *The American Museum of Natural History Anthropological Papers* , Vol. XLIII, Part 1.

GEARING, FRED
1962 "Priests and warriors. Social structures for Cherokee politics in the 18th century," *American Anthropological Association, Memoir* No. *93.*

GOGGIN, J. M.
1952 "Space and time perspective in northern St. Johns archeology, Florida," *Yale University Publications in Anthropology, No. 47.* (New Haven: Yale University Press).

HEYE, G. G., F. W. HODGE, and G. H. PEPPER
1918 "The Nacoochee Mound in Georgia," *Contributions from the Museum of the American Indian*, Heye Foundation, Vol. IV., No. 3.

HOEBEL, E. A.
1949 *Man in the Primitive World.* (New York: McGraw-Hill Book Company).

JENNINGS, J. D.
1941 "Chickasaw and earlier Indian cultures of northeast Mississippi," *The Journal of Mississippi History,* Vol. III: 135-226.

KELLAR, J. H., A. R. KELLY, and E. V. MCMICHAEL
1962 "The Mandeville site in southwest Georgia," *American Antiquity,* Vol. XXVII: 336-55.

KELLY, A. R., and R. S. NEITZEL
1961 "The Chauga site in Oconee County, South Carolina," *Laboratory of Archaeology Series,* University of Georgia, Report No. 3.

MOORE, C. B.
1901 "Certain aboriginal remains of the Northwest Florida coast, I," *Journal of the Academy of Natural Sciences of Philadelphia,* Vol. XI, Part 4.

1902 "Certain aboriginal remains of the Northwest Florida coast, II," *Journal of the Academy of Natural Sciences of Philadelphia*, Vol. XII, Part 2.

1903a "Certain aboriginal remains of the central Florida west coast," *Journal of the Academy of Natural Sciences of Philadelphia*, Vol. XII, Part 3.

1903b "Certain aboriginal mounds of the Apalachicola River," *Journal of the Academy of Natural Sciences of Philadelphia*, Vol. XII: 440-92.

1907 "Mounds of the lower Chattahoochee and lower Flint Rivers," *Journal of the Academy of Natural Sciences of Philadelphia*, Vol. XIII.

PHILLIPS, PHILIP, J. A. FORD, and J. B. GRIFFIN

1951 "Archaeological survey in the lower Mississippi Alluvial Valley, 1940-1947," *Papers of the Peabody Museum of American Archaeology and Ethnology*, Harvard University, Vol. XXV.

SEARS, W. H.

1951 "Excavations at Kolomoki," *University of Georgia Series in Anthropology*, No. 2.

1952 "Ceramic development in the South Appalachian Porvince," *American Antiquity*, Vol. XVIII, No. 2.

1958 "The Wilbanks site (9CK-5) Georgia," *River Basin Surveys Papers*, No. 12, Bureau of American Ethnology Bulletin 169:129-94.

1961 "The study of social and religious systems in North American archaeology," *Current Anthropology*, Vol. II: 223-46.

1962 "The state in certain areas and periods of the prehistoric southeastern United States," *Ethnohistory*, Vol. IX: 109-25.

1963 "The Tucker Site on Alligator Harbor, Franklin County, Florida," *Contributions of the Florida State Museum*, Social Sciences, No. 9.

TRICKEY, E. B.

1958 "A chronological framework for the Mobile Bay region," *American Antiquity*, Vol. XXIII: 388-96.

WAUCHOPE, ROBERT

1948 "The ceramic sequence in the Etowah drainage, northwest Georgia," *American Antiquity*, Vol. XIV, No. 1: 201-9.

WILLEY, G. R.

1949 *Archaeology of the Florida Gulf Coast*, Smithsonian Miscellaneous Collections, Vol. CXIII, Washington, D. C.

1953 *Prehistoric settlement patterns in the Viru Valley, Peru*, Smithsonian Institution, Washington, D.C.

WILLEY, G. R., and PHILIP PHILLIPS

1958 *Method and Theory in American Archaeology* (Chicago: University of Chicago Press).

IX

EVON Z. VOGT

Some Aspects of Zinacantan Settlement Patterns and Ceremonial Organization[1]

In this paper I shall describe some aspects of the settlement patterns of Zinacantan, trace the relationships of these settlement patterns to ceremonial organization, suggest how rhythmic ceremonial movements have important integrative functions, and discuss the possible implications of these data for our understanding of ancient Maya society. The data should be taken as preliminary, since my ten-year field study in Chiapas with the cooperation of the Instituto Nacional Indigenista of Mexico is still in progress.

Zinacantan Settlement Patterns

Elsewhere (Vogt, 1956), I have defined settlement patterns as "the patterned manner in which household and community units are arranged spatially over the landscape." With the aid of schematic figures, let us examine how the species Zinacanteco is distributed over the landscape.

Consider Fig. 1. Zinacantan is one of several municipios of Tzotzil Indians located in the pine-covered, limestone and volcanic mountains of Chiapas. Tzotzil is a Mayan language; hence Zinacantan is located near the western border of Mayan distribution.

[1]Reprinted in revised and expanded form by permission of the publishers from Evon Z. Vogt, "Some Aspects of Zinacantan Settlement Patterns and Ceremonial Organization," *Estudios de Cultura Maya* (Seminario de Cultura Maya, Universidad Nacional Autónoma de México) Vol. I: 131-46. Mexico: 1961.

An earlier version of this paper was presented at the 58th Annual Meetings of the American Anthropological Association, Mexico, 1959. The field research in Chiapas is supported by a ten-year grant (No. M-2100) from the National Institute of Mental Health and sponsored by the Laboratory of Social Relations and Peabody Museum at Harvard University. I am grateful to my colleagues and students—especially Nicholas Acheson, Susan Carey, Benjamin Colby, Lore Colby, Frank Cancian, Francesca Cancian, George Collier, Jane Fishburne Collier, Mathew Edel, Robert Laughlin, Mimi Laughlin, Jack Stauder, Susan Tax, Allen Young, and Manuel Zabala Cubillos—who have done field work in Zinacantan and who have contributed importantly to my understanding of Zinacanteco culture. The paper has benefited from comments by Gordon R. Willey and Frank Cancian.

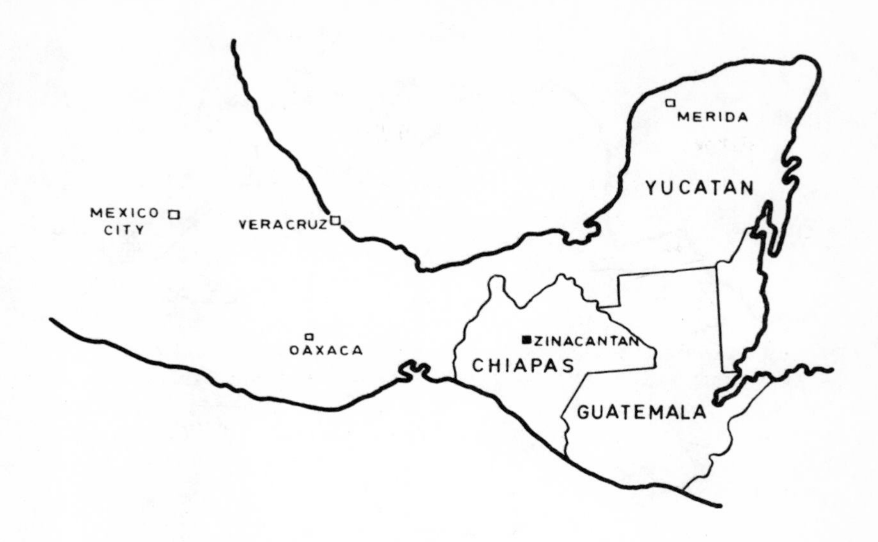

Fig. 1. GENERAL LOCATION OF ZINACANTAN

Fig. 2 shows the location of Zinacantan in relation to the Ladino town of San Cristobal Las Casas, located in a mountain valley at 7,000 feet.[2] Note that the municipio of Zinacantan, covering an area of 117 square kilometers and containing a total population of 7,611 Indians (1960 census) lies just to the west of San Cristobal along both sides of the Pan American Highway.

Zinacantan constitutes an example of what has been described by Sol Tax (1937) as a "vacant-town," or by Borhegyi (1956) as a "concourse" type of settlement pattern. The *cabecera,* or ceremonial and political center, located near the northern boundary of the municipio, contains the two central Catholic churches, with saints that command religious allegiance throughout the municipio; the *cabildo,* where the political officials have their headquarters; and a plaza, where important markets are held for the brisk exchange of goods during fiestas. In and around this ceremonial center is located a series of sacred waterholes and sacred mountains – which figure importantly in the ceremonial life of the whole municipio.

Approximately 800 people live in the densely settled valley in which the ceremonial center is located. Of this figure, only 51 are Ladinos; these run small stores in the center, teach school, and serve in the office of the town secretary. The others are Zinacantecos. The bulk of the population (approx-

[2]See Colby and Van den Berghe (1961) for a description of Indian-Ladino relationships in Highland Chiapas.

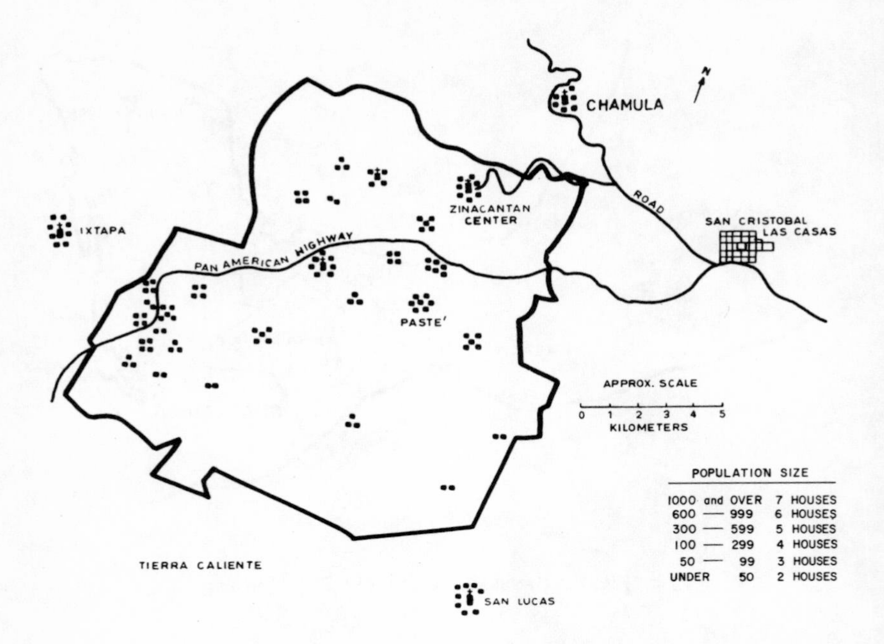

Fig. 2. MUNICIPIO OF ZINACANTAN

imately 6,800) lives in eleven scattered hamlets (or *parajes*, as these are called in Chiapas) distributed throughout the northern and western parts of the municipio. There is a steep escarpment just south of Paste' where the land drops off precipitously from about 7,000 feet down toward the Tierra Caliente – a physiographic fact accounting for the low density of settlement in the southern part of the municipio.

The sizes of these hamlets range from small settlements of under 150 people up to large settlements of more than 1,200. Relative size is schematically represented by numbers of houses. Two of the parajes have small Catholic chapels – a fact to which I shall return later.[3]

Finally, note the locations of Ixtapa and San Lucas, two towns lying beyond the borders of the municipio, which also figure importantly in the ceremonial life of Zinacantan.

Fig. 3 shows some aspects of the settlement pattern of the paraje of Paste' (1960 population: 1,276), where my field headquarters is located and where

[3] In 1962, a small Catholic chapel was established for the first time in a third outlying paraje.

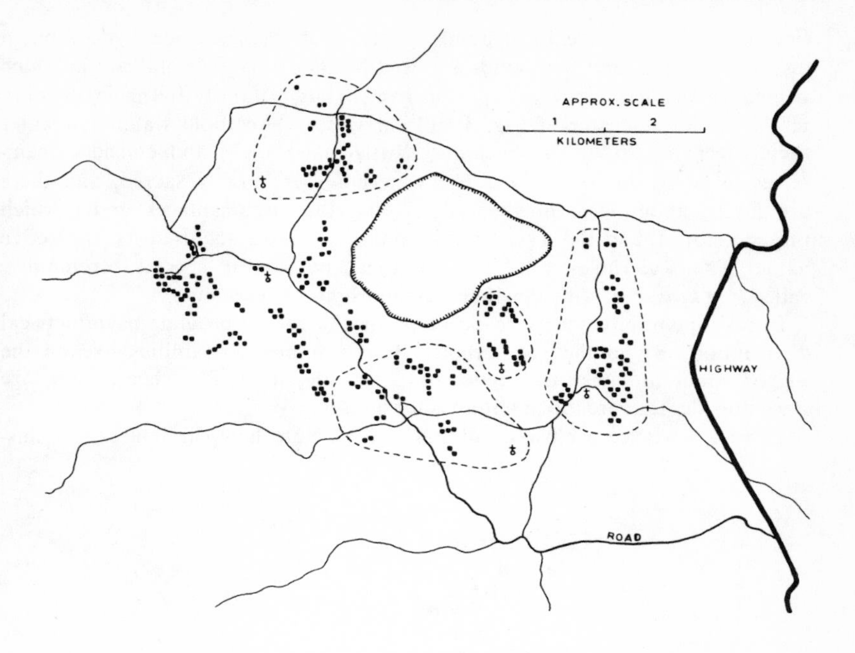

Fig. 3. PARAJE OF PASTE'

I am doing intensive field work. These data are based on an aerial photograph taken in 1954 and brought up to date by field work in the summer of 1959. Note first the pattern of roads and main trails. The road leading in from the Pan American Highway connects the Institute school and our field house with the outside world by jeep or Landrover. The trails leading off to the right connect Paste' with Zinacantan Center (some two hours away if you can walk as fast as a Zinacanteco, longer if you cannot!). The trails leading off to the left connect Paste' with Tierra Caliente, some seven or more hours away on foot, where most of the maize feeding the population is grown. At the bottom of the map a trail leads into San Cristobal about three hours away. Other trails connect the various parts of the paraje.

Note that the houses are neither compactly located nor distributed evenly over the 4 by 5 km land area of the paraje. Rather, the population is clustered around five important waterholes, indicated by circles with crosses.[4] These

[4] There are three additional small waterholes from which a few families belonging to the paraje of Paste' carry their water; the other families in these waterhole groups belong to the parajes of Nachih and Elamvo'. The fact that waterhole groups cut across paraje lines indicates to me that waterhole groups may be older and more fundamental in the social organization than parajes.

five waterholes are the focal points for each of the settlements–each has a distinctive name, and the names are used by the Indians to indicate in which neighborhood of the paraje a person lives. Thus, a family living in the cluster in the lower center of Fig. 3 will carry their household water and water their sheep at *Bik'it Vo'* (meaning "little waterhole") and consider themselves as living in *Bik'it Vo'*. The waterholes are highly sacred, and there are myths about each of them describing the circumstances under which the ancestors found the water and how the waterhole acquired its distinctive name. The waterholes are also the focal points for special ceremonies, called *k'in krus*, performed by their neighborhood settlements.

Local topography seems to account for the rather peculiar asymmetrical distribution around these waterholes. For example, no families live on the rugged mountain near the upper center of the map. Elsewhere, there are steep hillsides that are too precipitous for houses.

In Fig. 4 we see a close-up of *Bik'it Vo'*. Note how the houses are clus-

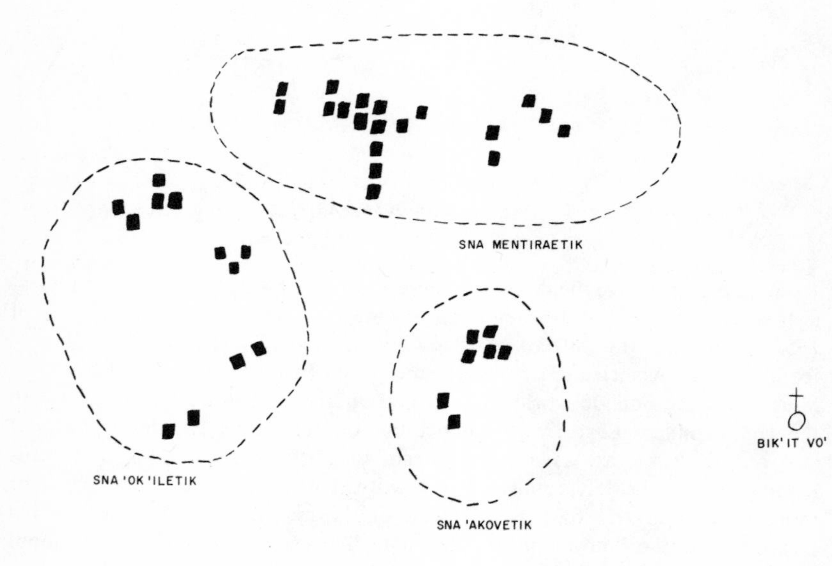

Fig. 4. WATERHOLE GROUP OF BIK'IT VO'

tered in units of two, three, four, or five within the neighborhood. These are, for the most part, the house groups of patrilocal extended families.

These patrilocal extended families in turn live in larger units which I shall call *snas*. The term *sna* means literally "the houses of," and it is the term the Zinacantecos themselves use to refer to these residential units composed of one or more localized patrilineages. The *sna* takes its name from these lineages. In cases where the unit contains only one lineage, there is no problem; the unit is simply called, for example, *sna 'akovetik*, or "the houses of the wasp nests." In larger *snas* containing two or more lineages, the unit takes its name from the predominant lineage.[5] Thus, *sna 'ok'iletik*, or "the houses of the coyotes," contains the coyote lineage, but also contains two smaller lineages that have settled next to the coyotes and intermarried with them. *Sna mentiraetik*, or "the houses of the liars," is also of this type.[6]

I do not have to depend merely upon informants' statements and my mapping procedures to describe the boundaries and composition of these *snas*. An observational measure of who's who in the world of the *snas* is available in the *k'in krus* ceremonies performed by each *sna* twice a year for their *totilme'iletik* (meaning "fathers-mothers"), who function as ancestral deities, and for *yahval balamil* (the "earth-owner"). These ceremonies normally follow by a few days the *k'in krus* ceremonies performed by the waterhole groups as a whole. Although these *k'in krus* ceremonies occur near the time of Santa Cruz in May, they occur also at the end of the rainy season in October, and appear to have little to do with the Christian concept of the cross. Christ and the crucifixion are not mentioned, despite the use of the word *kalvaryo* (derived from the Spanish word "calvario" or "calvary") to designate ancestral shrines. Rather, it appears that the ceremonies are symbolic means of expressing (1) the rights of the members of the *sna* in the lands they now use, which they have inherited from their patrilineal ancestors, and (2) the rights of the members of the waterhole group to draw water from their waterhole, and their obligations to care for the waterhole properly.

Moving to even larger scale in Fig. 5, note the principal settlement features of one patrilocal extended family *sitio,* as the house compounds are called in Chiapas. The sitio is usually surrounded by a pole and brush fence. Inside are the houses (in this case, of a father and two of his married sons), the granary, the sweat house, and, in the center, the patio crosses, which constitute the household shrine. Just outside the fence is located the small milpa and the sheep corral. In a very important sense, the Zinacanteco lives in a milpa and looks out at the world from between the stalks of corn.

Relationship of Settlement Patterns to Ceremonial Organization

One of the critical problems for a cultural unit with this type of dispersed settlement pattern is how the unit is to be structurally integrated and coor-

[5] Our data indicate that the predominant lineage was the first to settle on the land now controlled by the *sna*, and that this fact accounts for its preeminent position.

[6] A fuller description of the complexities of the social structure may be found in Vogt (1964b).

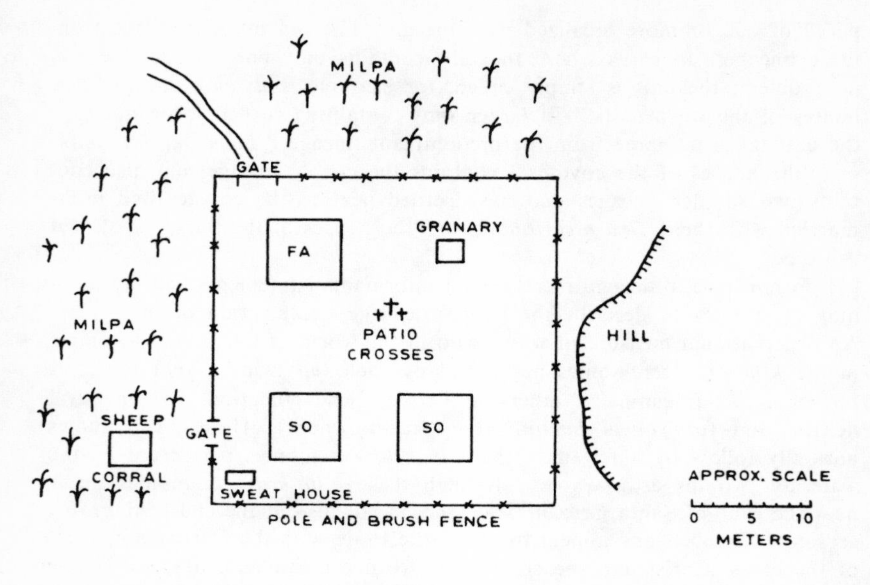

Fig. 5. SITIO IN PASTE'

dinated. There are many aspects to this problem, but let me concentrate on one of these: the rhythmic ceremonial movements that occur in the daily and annual flow of Zinacantan life.

I shall begin with the simpler rituals. Fig. 6 shows the movement of people from houses to the patio crosses[7] for prayers and offerings, and from patio crosses to sweat house. All of this movement takes place within the sitio and has deep ceremonial significance not only in curing ceremonies but at various other points in the ceremonial cycle. No ritual entrance into or departure from a Zinacanteco house is ever made without prayers being said at the patio crosses. The sweat house is used by patients after they have gone through major curing ceremonies, and more especially by women after they have given birth.

Fig. 7 shows a typical ceremonial circuit that occurs during a *k'in krus* ceremony for a *sna*, in this case for *sna 'akovetik*. Note that the movement is counterclockwise, and that the ceremonial group visits patio crosses, a cave to pray to the "earth owner," and ancestral shrines *(kalvaryos)* on hills to pray to the ancestors from whom they inherited the land. In the course

[7]I use the plural, for although there is usually only *one* wooden cross in the patio, the shrine is ritually and conceptually made into *three* crosses by the addition of two pine boughs on each side of the wooden cross for all ceremonial occasions. See Laughlin (1962) for more detail on religious symbolism in the ritual life of Zinacantan.

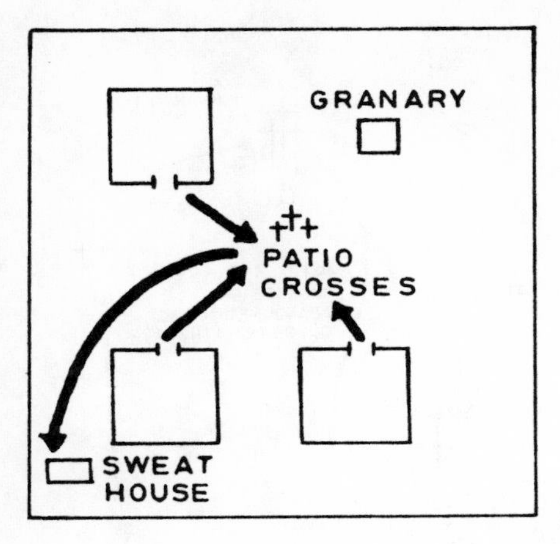

Fig. 6. CEREMONIAL MOVEMENT IN SITIO

of this circuit to nine sets of crosses they also ritually draw an approximate boundary around their lands.

Fig. 8 shows the movement of people within a waterhole group to the sacred waterhole representing the focus for the *k'in krus* ceremony for the waterhole group. Again, this ceremony is of crucial structural importance for the families living within the waterhole group; it is the only time when they cooperate significantly as a group.

In Fig. 9, I show the ceremonial movement that must occur in a major curing ceremony from the sitio of the patient to the ceremonial center. The curing group consists of the patient, the *h-'ilol* (curer), and a group of assistants, the number depending upon the type of ceremony. The group visits, in fixed order, four sacred mountains located around the ceremonial center. At the first three mountains, prayers are said and offerings are left at crosses located at the foot and/or on the summit of each of the mountains. The fourth mountain is *kalvaryo*, where the ancestral gods are believed to conduct their council meetings.[8] Special rituals, including the sacrifice of a black chicken, take place here, and the curing group then returns to the sitio of the patient to continue with the ceremony. The important point here is that no other mountains close to one's paraje can be visited for this ceremony. Regardless of how far one lives from the ceremonial center, this ceremonial pilgrimage must ordinarily be made to the proper mountains, which are all located around the central ceremonial center.

Fig. 10 brings us to more complex and more geographically distant ceremonial movements involving larger groups of people. First, let me point out the continual movement that occurs between highlands and lowlands, as men from Paste' travel to Tierra Caliente to make milpas. Most of this

[8]The ancestral gods and other key concepts in the religious system are discussed in Vogt (1964a; 1964b; 1964c).

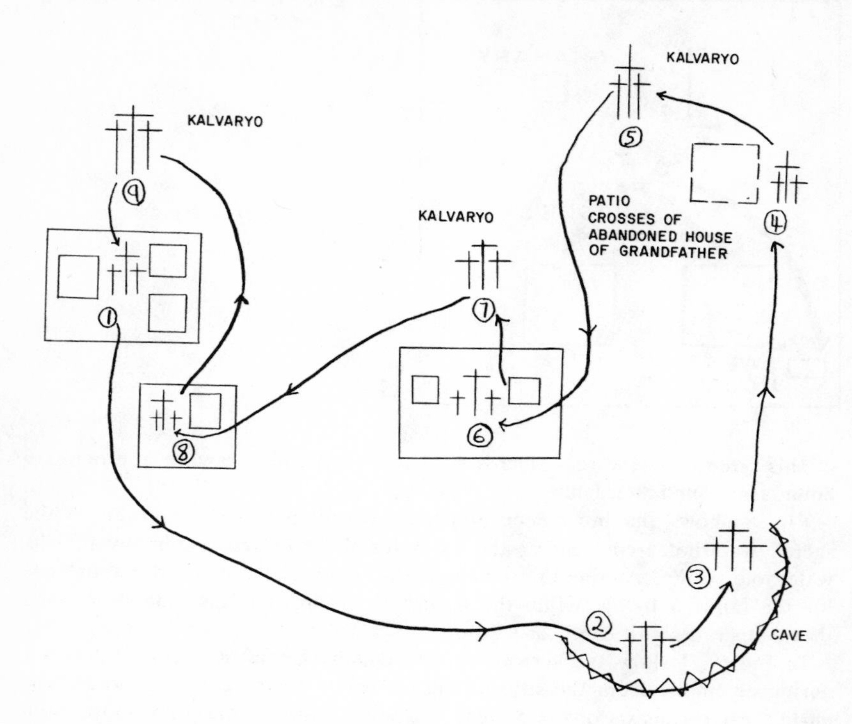

Fig. 7. CEREMONIAL CIRCUIT FOR K'IN OF SNA 'AKOVETIK

movement is, of course, wholly economic in character. But it is not without its ceremonial aspects, since milpa ceremonies must also be performed in the fields in Tierra Caliente.

Let us examine, now, these major ceremonial movements. The cult of the saints focuses upon the Catholic churches and the religious hierarchy in Zinacantan center. The fiestas for these saints involve three kinds of important ceremonial movements: (1) the bringing of candles, incense, rockets, aguardiente, and the Catholic priest out from the Ladino town of San Cristobal; (2) the ceremonial visits of saints from the two parajes that have small chapels and saints of their own, and from two neighboring towns; (3) the movement of ceremonial personnel from parajes to the ceremonial center to fill *cargo* positions in the religious hierarchy of Zinacantan.

The two parajes with chapels and saints of their own are Navenchauk and Salinas; the two neighboring towns are San Lucas and Ixtapa, located to the

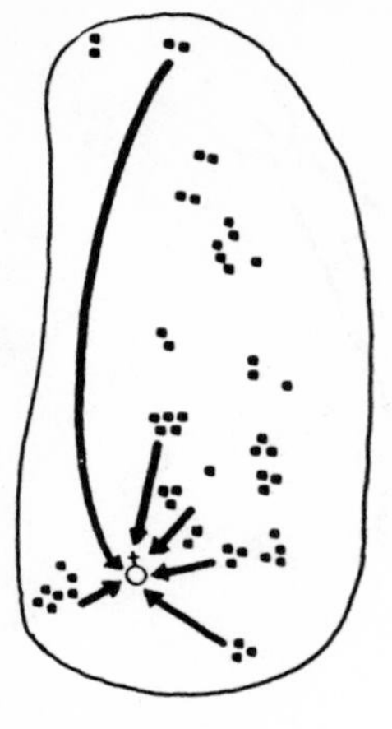

Fig. 8. CEREMONIAL MOVEMENT FOR K'IN KRUZ CEREMONY

south and west, respectively, of the municipio of Zinacantan. The visits from these parajes and towns are full-scale pilgrimages involving many people – not only the caretakers of the visiting saints, but also a brass band that usually comes from San Lucas, and many others who come along to trade lowland products or simply to celebrate, during the fiesta. At first, I thought the visits of these saints could be interpreted almost purely in economic terms, especially inasmuch as San Lucas, Ixtapa, and Salinas are all located in lower ecological zones, and I interpreted the movement as having a basic relationship to an exchange of highland and lowland products. But I now believe there is an important dimension of social integration involved in these movements, for I find that San Lucas is a town that was settled by Zinacantecos within the past one hundred years. Ixtapa is a highly acculturated town whose Indian population probably derived from Zinacantan, or that was at least closely related culturally and linguistically with Zinacantan in the past. By these visits Zinacantan center is not only commanding ceremonial and political allegiance from the parajes with chapels and saints of their own (like Navenchauk, which is threatening to split off from Zinacantan), but it is also continuing to reach beyond the borders of its municipio to retain important ceremonial links with towns that historically are likely to have been offshoots from Zinacantan.

There is finally the structurally very strategic movement of ceremonial personnel from parajes to the ceremonial center, to fill cargo positions in the all-important religious hierarchy of Zinacantan. This hierarchy consists of a ranked series of four levels of priestly officials.[9] To pass through this ceremonial ladder,

[9] See Cancian (1962) for additional details on this religious hierarchy.

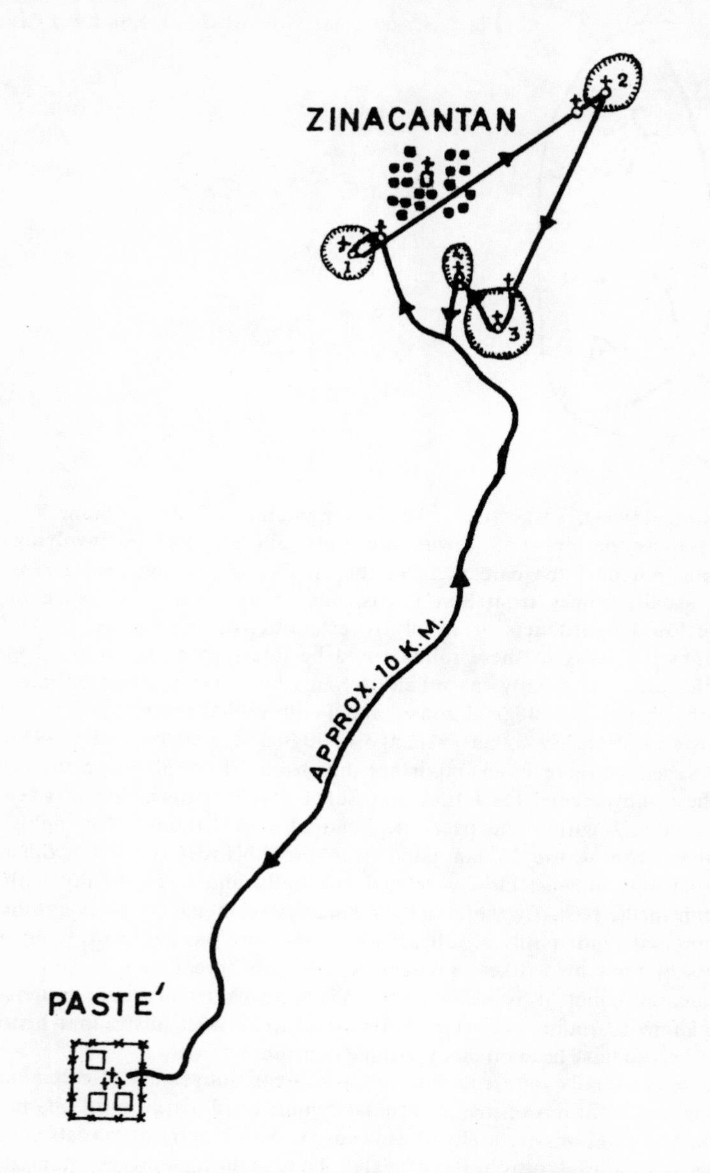

Fig. 9. CEREMONIAL MOVEMENT TO FOUR SACRED MOUNTAINS IN CURING CEREMONY

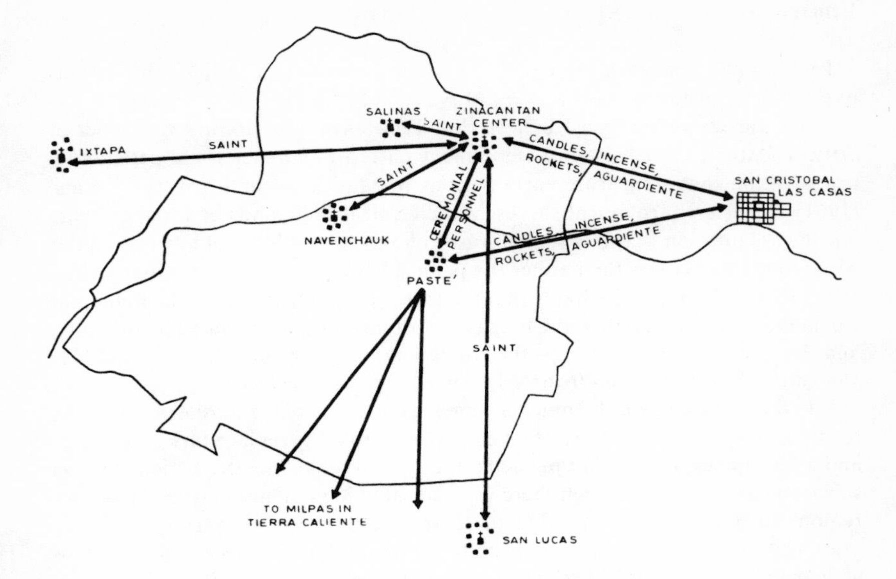

Fig. 10. CEREMONIAL MOVEMENTS IN ZINACANTAN

a man must serve a year at each level, and during the time he holds a cargo he is expected to move into the ceremonial center and engage in a complex annual round of ceremonies. The ceremonies are expensive, costing as much as 14,000 pesos for some cargos, and time-consuming. But while he fills the role he enjoys special prestige and wears special costumes for ritual occasions. At the end of the year he turns the office over to the next incumbent, and moves back to the paraje to become once again a corn-farmer. Some years must elapse before he can work himself out of debt and accumulate enough wealth to ask for the cargo position at the next higher level – and so on until he passes through the ceremonial ladder and becomes an honored "*pasado.*"

I am impressed by how efficiently this system handles a very complex ceremonial life and by how well it transmits quite complicated ceremonial knowledge, without benefit of permanent administrators. It is purely a system of personnel rotation – from corn-farming in the parajes, to ceremonial positions in the ceremonial center, and back again to corn-farming. I shall return to this point in a moment.

We have not examined all the details of ceremonial movements in Zinacantan. But I have said enough to indicate how these rhythmic ceremonial movements of people and ceremonial paraphernalia link Zinacantan center not only with its far-flung parajes but also with offshoots beyond its municipio borders.

IMPLICATIONS FOR THE STUDY OF ANCIENT MAYA SOCIETY

I wish now to advance some hypotheses concerning the possible implications of these data for the study of ancient Maya society.

For a variety of reasons I believe that Zinacantan exemplifies a number of critical features of subsistence, settlement pattern, and social and ceremonial organization that stem from early periods in Mayan cultural history. Adams' (1961) recent archaeological survey of the Central Highlands of Chiapas bears out the assumption that this region was probably less influenced by oth[illegible] Mesoamerican centers than either the peninsula of Yucatan or the Gu[illegible] Highlands. I think it quite likely that the three contiguous areas of the [illegible] Cuchumatanes, and Highland Chiapas are importantly interrelated his[illegible] and that they constitute perhaps the crucial region for the understandi[illegible] yan culture in *relatively undisturbed form* at various time levels.

I doubt that there will be much argument about the basic subsistenc[illegible] for take away machetes, axes, chickens (which probably replace turke[illegible] and a few horses, mules, and pigs, and the system looks like the ancie[illegible] subsistence pattern. Although there are nucleated Maya communities [illegible] regions today, I would guess that these are the results of (1) very spe[illegible] graphical circumstances (Lake Atitlán, for example), (2) successful programs of change by the Central Mexican invasion of Mayan lands in about 1,000 A.D. and reactions to this invasion, or (3) policies of *reducción* by the Spanish conquerors. In other words, I take the basic type of settlement pattern to be one of ceremonial center surrounded by dispersed hamlets in a way approaching that of modern Zinacantan. This conclusion is in line with our best settlement pattern data – from Gordon Willey's project in the Belize (Willey, 1956a) and from the survey work of William R. Bullard (1960) in the Petén. In fact, I would tend to make the following equations between Zinacantan and the settlement pattern units described by Bullard for the northeastern Petén:

Zinacantan	*Classic Maya in the Petén*
Sitio (patrilocal extended family)	House group
Sna	Cluster
Waterhole group	Cluster group
Paraje	Hamlet with minor ceremonial center
Cabecera (of the municipio)	Major ceremonial center

I would like also to suggest that just as the settlement pattern appears to take the form of an aggregate of aggregates, so the social structure and the ceremonial organization appear to manifest some orderly replications of increasing structural scale, from the simple household ceremonies involving only the extended family to the complex ceremonies in the ceremonial center involving the whole tribal unit.

As I suggested at the Paris meetings in 1960 (Vogt, 1964a) and in two more recent papers (Vogt, 1964b; 1964c), there is probably an important historical and structural relationship between (1) the sacred mountains around the ceremonial center in Zinacantan and the steep-sided pyramids in the ceremonial centers of the Maya Classic – in each case, what is represented may be the dwelling places of ancestral gods worshipped by certain lineages or other types of social units in Mayan society; and (2) the ritual performed at cross shrines at the foot and on top of sacred mountains in Zinacantan and the ritual performed at the round altars in front of stelae at the foot of Classic Maya pyramids and in the temples atop the pyramids. These two hypotheses have recently received some confirmation from Holland (1961), who finds similar concepts and symbols in the religious system of San Andrés Larrainzar.

Further, I hypothesize that the ceremonial circuits performed for *snas*, waterhole groups, and the ceremonial center in Zinacantan may have had their counterpart in Classic Maya ceremonial procedure. A comparable kind of counterclockwise ceremonial circuit is described by Landa for the so-called *Uayeb*, or "New Year," ceremony (Tozzer, 1941, pp. 144-48). Landa states that the purpose of this ceremony was to ritually establish boundaries and to ritually purify the area and people enclosed by the circuit – an interpretation that would not be out of line for the Zinacantan ceremonial circuits. From a Zinacanteco point of view, all of the ceremonies performed by the *h-'iloletik* (the shamans) have the purpose of ritually purifying Zinacantecos by asking pardon from the *totilme'iletik* (the gods) for their clients, whether they be individual patients in curing ceremonies or all of Zinacantan in the large ceremonies held in the ceremonial center for "the new year," "the middle of the year," and "the end of the year."

Taking the argument one step further, I would suggest also that the early Maya may have also organized at least some orders in their priestly hierarchies in the ceremonial centers by means of some kind of system of rotation in office, with men from certain lineages coming in from the outlying hamlets to serve a year in cargo positions and then returning to corn-farming while they awaited service in the next higher position in a system of graded ranks. If such a system prevailed, we would have some answers to the mystery of structural integration of dispersed Maya settlements – to the question, How did the supposed priestly class manage to induce the peasants not only to bring food into the ceremonial center, but to provide labor for their support and for the construction and maintenance of their centers? It would mean that there was less of a gulf between the peasants farming corn in the hinterland and the priests in the ceremonial center than has been supposed. Rather, men would rotate between the roles of peasant farmer and priest within a system that still prevails in basic type in Zinacantan today.

Several immediate objections to this hypothesis can be predicted. What about the Spanish reports of aristocracies in Yucatan and in highland Guatemala? I would remind Maya scholars that these systems had clearly been under the influence, if not outright conquest, of Central Mexico for over 500 years by the time the Spanish arrived, and we know that Central Mexico did have strongly aristocractic systems. How could a series of rotating offices have provided the leisure to develop a complex Maya calendar, Maya writing that we cannot yet wholly decipher, and notable achievements in art, mathematics, and astronomy? I think it possible that were we to look at these intellectual and artistic achievements from the inside rather than from the outside, they would not seem so complex. If we were Maya priests in the Classic, for example, we would *know* what all the glyphs meant and would not be aware of the celebrated argument going on between Thompson and Knorozov. I think it questionable whether the ancient Maya carried along *vastly* more knowledge than the contemporary Zinacantan ritual specialists regularly carry in their heads concerning the details of ceremonial life.

We may ask whether there is any evidence that the present religious hierarchy in Zinacantan is wholly of Spanish origin. It is clear that certain features are—the names of the offices are Spanish, and many of the cargos are attached to Catholic saints. But if the saints are in fact descendants of Mayan idols, and the old Mayan names for cargos have been replaced by Spanish names, these Spanish elements would already be largely accounted for. Otherwise, I have found little evidence that the basic system exists in Spain (see also Carrasco, 1961; Zabala Cubillos, 1961).

We may also ask whether there is any archaeological or ethnohistorical evidence for the pre-Conquest existence of the system? Again, Gordon Willey's (1956b) data from the Belize Valley suggests that ". . . the relationship between rural village and ceremonial center may have been considerably more tight-knit than the conventional picture would have it." He adds that " . . . it is likely that the ceremonial centers recruited artisans, retainers, and even some levels of the priesthood from peasant groups." More recently, Coe (1965) has published a brilliant analysis of the probable structure of pre-Conquest Maya Lowland communities. Basing his interpretation on the Uayeb rites described by Landa and others, Coe presents a model that involves the shifting of ritual power among quadripartite divisions through a cyle of four years, and " . . . the holding of this power by a different *principal* each year" (1965, p. 103).

There of course exists the possibility of a core of permanent priests in the ceremonial center—especially by the time of the late Classic, when we find elaborate tombs for special personages in the temples of the ceremonial centers (see Coe, 1956)—and that these permanent priests carried the major responsibility, while the lower ranks were filled by rotation in a graded series.

Still another possibility has been suggested by Cancian (1964), who observes that in Zinacantan today we have (1) the prestigious cargo positions filled by men from the outlying hamlets who have been able to accumulate enough of a surplus from corn-farming activities to devote an expensive series of years to the offices, and (2) a number of more permanent ritual specialists serving the hierarchy of priestly cargo-holders. These ritual specialists are the *sacristanes,* who know special prayers for certain crucial rituals associated with the care of the images of the saints, which the *mayordomos* (who occupy cargo positions in the first level of the religious hierarchy) themselves do not normally know when they enter their cargos; the *musicians,* who play for the *alfereces* (the alfereces hold positions in the second level of the religious hierarchy) and are given lifetime tenure, and hence accumulate specialized knowledge of the alfereces' ritual duties; and the *escribanos,* who know how to read and write, and are charged with keeping the sacred books containing the lists of Zinacantecos who are scheduled to assume cargo positions at given years in the future. To this list I can add certain ritual specialists living in the outlying parajes, who own and control sacred ceremonial paraphernalia that is brought into the ceremonial center for fiestas. For example, the lineage in Elamvo', which owns a small sacred drum, called the *t'ent'en*, always brings this drum into the ceremonial center for the Fiesta of San Sebastian in January. The men in this lineage control much specialized knowledge about the proper rituals to be performed by the cargo-holders for and with this drum during the Fiesta.

None of these ritual specialists have much formal power as compared to the cargo-holders, but by virtue of their serving in the same ritual roles year after year, they have exclusive control of a great deal of specialized ritual knowledge, and we have observed them briefing the cargo-holders on the details of complex ceremonial procedure. Further, it is significant that in return for their assistance and counsel at the various ceremonies during the course of the year, the cargo-holders furnish them with food and liquor at their own expense. These patterns suggest the interesting possibility that Classic Maya centers contained permanent ritual specialists and artisans, but that rather than holding the dominant positions in a hierarchy, they served and were supported by men who came in from the outlying hamlets to serve in rotating ceremonial positions – and, in the process, to expend their economic surpluses in ceremonial activity. How these men who might have held such priestly cargo positions were selected raises a further intriguing question, especially if they were lineage heads or somehow represented lineages who would have assisted them in meeting the expenses of their periodic ceremonial duties. And, whether it might have been the ritual specialists or the heads of important lineages who were buried with ceremonial pomp in the pyramids (perhaps thereby becoming the ancestral deities) is still another unsolved problem in this line of speculation.

These hypotheses of course run counter to prevailing thought on Mayan priests and rulers and to current theories of a revolt of the peasants against priestly rule as a possible explanation of the decline of the Classic. But I submit they are hypotheses that should be explored. It is clear that we need to study the Maya in terms of Mayan data–archaeological, linguistic, ethnohistorical, and ethnological–and not simply extrapolate to the Maya what we know of more highly organized aristocratic systems in central Mexico, or impose upon the Maya a set of Western European models of political authority and social class that have little validity for either the ancient or the contemporary Maya.

Since the first publication of this paper, my hypotheses have been challenged by Ruz (1964) who repeats the orthodox position that the ancient Maya had an aristocratic ruling class, but provides no significant new data to support this position. More recently, Haviland (1966) also has argued that the ancient Maya must have been ruled by a dynastic aristocracy, and has based his argument upon new data from Tikal. He makes two fundamental points: (1) that settlement-pattern data from Tikal and its sustaining area indicate a minimum population of 20,000 to 22,000 and that this population was too large to manage with a rotating cargo system; and (2) that the principal individuals buried in the "tombs" at Tikal were taller and probably lived longer than the rest of the male population, and hence (by inference) were well cared for in life and were hereditary rulers or priests. Haviland's first point can be answered by calling attention to the municipio of Chamula (located just north of Zinacantan), which now has a population of nearly 40,000 Indians and which functions with a rotating cargo system that is similar to the one described for Zinacantan. His second point is difficult to assess in the absence of more precise data than is yet available on the range of variation found in the skeletal materials from Tikal. In the meantime, I would only comment that I know a number of tall, well-fed ritual specialists in Zinacantan who one day will become more impressive skeletons than the cargo-holders they served.

Implications for the Study of Settlement Patterns

These Mayan data suggest some important implications about the relationship of settlement pattern to social and ceremonial organization. In the contemporary Maya communities, with their dispersed hamlets in a sustaining area around ceremonial centers, rhythmic ritual movements of personnel and paraphernalia from hamlet to center are one of the most important structural mechanisms for social and political integration. Certainly the picture is vastly different from that of a culture with compact settlement patterns, such as the Pueblo culture of the Southwest. Over time, these contrasting types of systems develop markedly different patterns of social organization. That they evolve down these separate paths raises the interesting question of the extent to which change in social organization accompanies or resists change in settlement pattern. I recall two very perceptive comments by two of my colleagues, concerning the relationship of settlement pattern to social organization. John M. Roberts (personal communication, 1962) remarked, about the social organization of the Zuni farming village of Pescado (which has by now achieved perhaps more dispersion than an outlying hamlet of Zinacantan), that the Zunis in this outlying village still behave as if they were living in a very compact settlement: the patterns of close cooperation among large groups of Zunis in such pursuits as agriculture and house-building were persisting even though the actual conditions of dispersed settlement would seem to make other forms of social organization more appropriate. On the other hand, Sol Tax (personal communication, 1962) observed that although the Maya village of Panajachel on Lake Atitlan is now very compact, the people in the village behave as if they are still living in small, dispersed hamlets: there is relatively little close cooperation in agricultural activities or other such enterprises beyond the level of the family, and even though the families now live within short distances of one another, they continue to act as if each were living in an isolated family compound somewhere in the mountains. These observations underscore the fact that peoples like the Zuni are basically compact-town-dwellers, and have over the centuries developed patterns of social organization and world view that are geared to town-dwelling. On the other hand, the Maya seem to be basically small-hamlet-dwellers, and have over the centuries developed patterns of social organization and world view appropriate to hamlet-dwelling, periodic ceremonial and economic activities bring them into their ceremonial centers, but at the end of the fiesta or the year of ceremonial duty, they welcome the return to their small hamlets, where they feel at home in their dispersed thatched huts and milpas in the mountains or the bush.

References

ADAMS R. M.
1961 "Changing patterns of territorial organization in the central highlands of Chiapas, Mexico," *American Antiquity,* Vol. XXVI, No. 3: 341-60.
DE BORHEGYI, S. F.
1956 "Settlement patterns in the Guatemalan highlands: Past and present," *Prehistoric Settlement Patterns in the New World,* G. R. Willey, editor, Viking Fund Publications in Anthropology, No. 23: 101-6.
BULLARD, W. R., JR.
1960 "A survey of ancient Maya settlement patterns in the Petén, Guatemala." *American Antiquity,* Vol. XXV, No. 3: 355-72.

CANCIAN, FRANK
1964 "Some aspects of the social and religious organization of a Maya society," *Actas y Memorias del XXXV Congreso Internacional de Americanistas* (Mexico) 1962, Vol.I:335-43.
1965 *Economics and Prestige in a Maya Community: A Study of the Religious Cargo System in Zinacantan, Chiapas, Mexico.* (Stanford: Stanford University Press.)

CARRASCO, PEDRO
1961 "The civil-religious hierarchy in Mesoamerican communities: Pre-Spanish background and colonial development," *American Anthropologist,* Vol. LXIII: 483-97.

COE, M. D.
1956 "The funerary temple among the Classic Maya." *Southwestern Journal of Anthropology,* Vol. XII, No. 4: 387-94.
1965 "A model of ancient community structure in the Maya lowlands,", *Southwestern Journal of Anthropology,* Vol. 21, No. 2:97-114.

COLBY, B. N., and PIERRE VAN DEN BERGHE
1961 "Ethnic relations in southeastern Mexico," *American Anthropologist,* Vol. LXIII, No. 4: 772-92.

HAVILAND, W. A.
1966 "Social integration and the Classic Maya" *American Antiquity*, Vol. 31, No. 5, Pt. 1:625-31.

HOLLAND, W. R.
1961 "Relaciones entre la religion Tzotzil contemporánea y la Maya antigua," *Anales, Instituto Nacional de Antropología e Historia* (Mexico), Vol. XIII: 113-32.

LAUGHLIN, R. M.
1962 "El símbolo de la flor en la religion de Zinacantan," *Estudios de Cultura Maya* (Seminario de Cultura Maya, Universidad Nacional Autónoma de México,) Vol. II:123-39.

RUZ LHUILLIER, ALBERTO
1964 "¿Aristocracia o democracia entre los antiguos Mayas?" *Anales de Antropología,* Universidad Nacional Autónoma de México, Vol. 1: 63-75.

TAX, SOL
1937 "The municipios of the midwestern highlands of Guatemala," *American Anthropologist,* Vol. XXXIX, No. 3: 423-44.

TOZZER, A. M.
1941 *Landa's relación de las cosas de Yucatán*, Papers of the Peabody Museum of American Archaeology and Ethnology, Harvard University, Vol. VIII.

VOGT, E. Z.
1956 "An appraisal of 'Prehistoric settlement patterns in the New World,' " *Prehistoric Settlement Patterns in the New World,* G. R. Willey, editor, Viking Fund Publications in Anthropology, No. 23:173-82.
1964a "Ancient Maya concepts in contemporary Zinacantan religion" (VIe Congrès International des Sciences Anthropologiques et Ethnologiques, Paris, 1960), Tome II, Musée de l'Homme, pp. 407-502.
1964b "Some implications of Zinacantan social structure for the study of the ancient Maya," *Actas y Memorias del XXXV Congreso International de Americanistas* (Mexico) 1962, Vol.I:307-19.
1964c "The genetic model and Maya cultural development," *Desarrollo Cultural de los Mayas,* E. Z. Vogt, and Alberto Ruz Lhuillier, editors, Universidad Autónoma de México, pp. 9-48.

WILLEY, G. R.

1956a "Problems concerning prehistoric settlement patterns in the Maya lowlands," *Prehistoric Settlement Patterns in the New World,* G. R. Willey, editor, Viking Fund Publications in Anthropology, No. 23: pp. 107-14.

1956b "The structure of ancient Maya society: Evidence from the southern lowlands," *American Anthropologist,* Vol. LVIII, No. 5: 777-82.

ZABALA CUBILLOS, MANUEL

1961 "Instituciones politicas y religiosas de Zinacantan," *Estudios de Cultura Maya,* (Seminario de Cultura Maya, Universidad Nacional Autónoma de México) Vol. I:147-59.

X

WILLIAM Y. ADAMS

Settlement Pattern in Microcosm: The Changing Aspect of a Nubian Village during Twelve Centuries

In archaeology, the study of settlement pattern usually focuses on the distribution and character of habitation remains over wide geographical areas. From the regularities that are observed, it is possible to infer the presence of cultural and natural determinants that served to shape the relationship between man and environment. If there is time depth in the archaeological record, it is also possible to plot changes in the relationship of man and environment, as reflected in changing settlement patterns.

Settlement pattern has a microcosmic aspect as well – the occupation and exploitation of land within the confines of a single community. Within this narrower context the variables presenting themselves for interpretation are such factors as village size, village plan, architectural norms, and land tenure. In the continuity and change they exhibit, it is possible to observe the influence of many of the same environmental determinants that are deduced from the study of settlement patterns over much more extended areas.

What follows is an attempt to define the changing relationship of man and environment in ancient Nubia, as evidenced by changes that took place in a single small village over a period of 1,200 years. The site in question, Meinarti, is situated on an island in the Nile immediately within the northern frontier of the modern Republic of the Sudan. Before excavation, it was a mound of fallen brick and accumulated debris about 200 meters long, 80 meters wide, and 12 meters high at its summit, surrounded on all sides by level floodplain. Because of the unparalleled opportunity to study the evolution of settlement pattern, it was decided to confine the excavation to a single contiguous area (the southern half of the mound), rather than to excavate a series of disconnected trenches and squares. This procedure made it possible to "strip" the mound completely, level by level, down to the floodplain itself, assuring maximum stratigraphic control.

The excavation revealed some 20 well-defined occupation levels within the mound. All but the uppermost of these levels represented for all practical purposes a continuum of occupation, beginning probably about 200 A.D. and ending some twelve centuries later.[1]

Such, then, is the sample upon which the succeeding analysis is based: an area less than 100 meters square, which might at most have contained 250 inhabitants.[2] Before we proceed to a detailed consideration of the developments that took place within these confines, it will be necessary to describe briefly the historical and cultural milieu of the village of Meinarti.

THE PROVINCE OF NUBIA

In the popular imagination, the River Nile has two paradoxical images. One is the land of Pharaohs and pyramids, the cradle of civilization, and by all odds the most celebrated river of the ancient world. The other is the home of pygmies and Nilotic giants, the river of mystery whose source was discovered within the lifetime of men still living.

The two images derive, of course, from regions many thousands of miles apart. One belongs, geographically and historically, to the Mediterranean Basin, the other to Black Africa. Between them, and connecting them, lies an enormous tract that is hardly known to the popular imagination even today. This "Middle Nile" belongs wholly neither to the Mediterranean nor to the African world; it is the one permanent corridor between the two. Its cultures are an interweaving of Mediterranean and African elements, and its peoples a stable blend of Caucasian and Negroid strains. The region has been conquered and overrun again and again by outsiders, but has never lost its special racial and cultural identity. It has been known through history under a variety of names: *Kush* to the ancient Egyptians and Hebrews, *Aethiopia*[3] to the Classical world, *Nubia* to medieval and modern scholars.

[1]The excavation of Meinarti was undertaken by the Sudan Government Antiquities Service, as part of the general Nubian salvage campaign necessitated by the building of the Aswan High Dam. The work was carried out between February 1963 and June 1964 by a force of 250 laborers, under the writer's direction. Preliminary accounts of the excavations are contained in Adams (1964; 1965b).

[2]The southern, or excavated, half of the Meinarti mound was considerably higher than the northern half, chiefly because in the early centuries the settlement was largely confined to this area. The excavated portion therefore does not constitute a uniform 50 per cent sample of the village as a whole; it varies from perhaps 75 per cent of the earliest levels to 50 per cent of the latest. However, it was not possible in any case to ascertain the full extent of the settlement, for peripheral flooding during and after occupation had destroyed the outermost rooms at every level. Thus it was never possible to define the ultimate limits of the village.

[3]The term *Aethiopia,* occurring in Classical and Biblical texts, refers in general to the region now called Nubia. The Ethiopia of today, formerly Abyssinia, lay outside the known world of ancient times.

The lower limit of Nubia has remained fixed for 5,000 years at the First Cataract of the Nile (modern Aswan). From here northward, the river is open to the sea, and the floodplain is broad and fertile. South of Aswan, the Nile Valley assumes more the form of a canyon confined between granite and sandstone bluffs, and navigation is impeded periodically by cataracts.

The upper limit of Nubia is much less sharply defined. Nubian-speaking peoples, who have given the region its modern name, today occupy the Nile Valley between the First and Fourth Cataracts.[4] However, in the historic past there has been a general continuity of society and culture extending southward as far as the confluence of the Niles (modern Khartoum), and this point may conveniently be taken to mark the southern limit of Nubia.

The physiographic environment throughout this region is by no means uniform. Lower Nubia, between the First and Second Cataracts, is only slightly less productive than the adjoining portion of Egypt, and has usually supported a considerable population. Clearly, it has been more subject to Egyptian influence than the more southerly regions of Nubia, and most of it is subsumed politically by Egypt today.[5]

Between the Second and Third Cataracts lies the formidable *batn el hajar* (Belly of Rock), the most inhospitable part of the Nile Valley. Here the river meanders across a lunar landscape, arable land is confined to vestigial pockets in protected coves, and navigation is rendered all but impossible by a long series of cataracts. Beyond the Third Cataract begins the much more fertile province of Upper Nubia. The region between the Third and Fourth Cataracts, often called the Dongola Reach, is especially productive and has been the seat of many important Nubian kingdoms in the past. The valley is broken above the Fourth Cataract by occasional rocky zones, but is generally broad and fertile as far south as the junction of the Blue and White Niles.

From the Fourth Cataract northward, the Nubian environment has one common characteristic that has profoundly affected its human history. Throughout this region the Nile is an exotic stream flowing through a rainless desert; the only life, and the only possibility of life, is found along its banks. Nubia is thus an attenuated corridor with only two entrances, at the north and south ends. This condition has prevailed for at least 5,000 years.

Nubia is not one of those storied regions in which the Nile annually over-

[4] The Nubians are among the relatively few "arabized" tribes of the Sudan who retain their original languages, which are usually assigned to the Eastern Sudanic family. With minor exceptions, they are today confined to the Nile Valley between the First and Fourth Cataracts. Most modern Nubians also speak Arabic.

[5] The present frontier between Egypt and the Republic of the Sudan is fixed at 22° N. Lat., a short distance north of the Second Cataract. Hence the whole of Upper Nubia lies in the Sudan, whereas most of Lower Nubia is in Egypt. There is no ethnic division corresponding to the international frontier.

flows its channel. On the contrary, through most of this region the river flows between steep mud banks, and irrigation is possible only where water can be raised by artificial means. Floods, when they do occur, are an unmitigated disaster, for they not only destroy houses and fields, but often carry away a large part of the alluvium at various points, thus greatly reducing the land available there for cultivation.

Peoples and Cultures in Nubian History[6]

In Nubia, it is not possible to make a clear distinction between prehistory and history. The region, lying as it does upon the frontiers of the civilized world, has been repeatedly washed by the high tides of history, but they have just as regularly receded. In effect, therefore, we have an alternation of historic and "nonhistoric" periods–the most recent of which ended in 1821. Even for the best documented periods, the written records of Nubian history are poor and fragmentary; such illumination as we possess comes chiefly from the archaeological record. Thanks to the building of three successive dams at Aswan,[7] that record is probably more complete than for any comparable area in the world.

Nubian "history" begins about 4,000 years ago, when Lower Nubia was

[6]There is as yet no good general source book on Nubian history and archaeology. The best overall coverage is provided by Arkell (1955), Emery (1965), and Trigger (1965). For the individual phases of Nubian history, the principal sources are: pre-Pharaonic (Firth, 1912, pp. 5-21; 1927, pp. 13-15; Reisner, 1910, pp. 314-42; Steindorff, 1935, vol. I); Pharaonic (Säve-Söderbergh, 1941; Steindorff, 1935, vol. II); Napatan and Meroitic (Reisner, 1919; 1922; 1923); X-Group (Emery, 1938, vol. I, pp. 5-24; Kirwan, 1939, pp. 39-48, and Monneret de Villard, 1938, pp. 24-52); Christian (Crowfoot, 1927; Monneret de Villard, 1938); post-Christian (Macmichael, 1922). To a considerable extent, however, all sources on Nubian history are now out of date as a result of the enormous accumulation of new data from the recent excavations.

[7]The Aswan Low Dam or "barrage" was built during the first decade of the present century, and led to the original Archaeological Survey of Nubia, from Aswan to Wadi es-Sebua. The "survey," actually an intensive excavation program, was the first systematic archaeological salvage project ever undertaken, and in many ways set the pattern for those that have followed. The height of the dam was increased in the 1920's, necessitating the extension of the survey as far south as the Sudanese frontier.

In 1957, construction began on the still-uncompleted Aswan High Dam, which will back up the waters of the Nile for another 200 km beyond the head of the previous reservoir. Because the archaeological and conservation problems engendered by the new project were beyond the resources of the two nations involved, their governments asked Unesco to launch an international appeal for expeditions to work in Nubia. As a result, more than thirty expeditions, representing almost as many countries, took part in the salvage campaign in Egypt and the Sudan between 1958 and 1964.

conquered for the first of many times by Egyptian armies. The region had already had for many centuries a considerable sedentary farming population, whose advance beyond the Neolithic level is suggested chiefly by their acquisition of odds and ends of Egyptian trade goods. The first Egyptian occupation was merely a military holding operation designed to protect Egypt's southern frontier, and had little cultural effect upon the native population. After a couple of centuries the garrisons were withdrawn, and Nubian squatters took possession of the abandoned fortresses.

The Egyptians returned in force shortly after 1600 B.C., not only to conquer but to colonize the country, as far south as the Fourth Cataract. The occupation was once again short-lived, but it brought about a considerable acculturation of the native population, and from this time onward Egyptian influence was never absent from Nubian culture. In time, a declining level of the Nile forced a total abandonment of Lower Nubian and the *batn el hajar,* and the inhabitants withdrew in opposite directions—the Egyptians to Egypt, and the Nubians to the more productive Dongola Reach.

There is no archaeological or historical record of the next 300 years. In the ninth century B.C., however, there arose in the vicinity of the Fourth Cataract a well-developed royal state closely modeled on the Egyptian pattern. At the height of their power, the Napatan kings, as they are called, conquered the whole of Egypt and reigned as the Pharaohs of the 25th Dynasty, known to history as the Ethiopian Dynasty.[8] Paradoxically, the whole of Lower Nubia seems to have remained uninhabited while the Nubian kings ruled the lands to the north and south of it.

The Nubians were soon driven out of Egypt, but they maintained for another century or two the semblance of a Pharaonic court in Upper Nubia. They built temples and pyramids at numerous points, and commemorated their exploits in hieroglyphic texts. How far the Egyptian veneer ever extended beyond the court and priesthood is problematical; it would probably be a mistake to view the Napatan "state" as anything more than an exceptionally powerful tribal kingdom, with a lot of borrowed finery.

The Napatan kingdom and culture rapidly declined after about 500 B.C., but there was a marked renaissance in the last century B.C., and a new period of prosperity that lasted for two or three centuries. The royal seat had now been shifted southward to Meroe,[9] in the region of the Sixth Cataract. The culture of this period, known as the Meroitic, is obviously related to

[8] The last of their number, Taharqa or Tirhaka, has achieved immortality of a sort as the "bruised reed" upon whom the Assyrian envoy warned the King of Judah not to lean (II Kings 18:21).

[9] The name of this ancient city has come down from classical antiquity; it was known to Herodotus in 455 B.C. (Book II, p. 29; Book III, p. 18). For translations, see Godley (1948, vol. I, pp. 307-9; vol. II, p. 25).

the contemporary Ptolemaic revival of Egypt, and exhibits a blend of Egyptian survivals and Graeco-Roman influences.

During the Meroitic period the whole of Lower Nubia was finally reoccupied, after a lapse of nearly 1,000 years. This development was apparently made possible by the introduction of the *saqia,* or "Egyptian"[10] water wheel, which for the first time freed irrigation from its dependence upon a comparatively high level of flow in the Nile. It seems probable, in fact, that the Nile continued at a low level during most of the Meroitic period. Nevertheless, the cultural "center of gravity" shifted back to Lower Nubia at this time, and remained there for the next 1,000 years.

The second and third centuries A.D. were a period of social upheaval and migration in the Central Sudan, in the course of which the Meroitic power in Upper Nubia was ultimately submerged. Whether immigrant peoples played a similar role in the history of Lower Nubia is questionable. In the post-Meroitic population of Lower Nubia (termed the "X-Group" people), some experts profess to recognize a marked new Negroid admixture, but the X-Group culture is almost purely a blend of Meroitic and Byzantine influences, and does not manifest a sharp break with previous tradition.

The Meroitic was the last of the great tribal kingdoms that was able to dominate the whole of Nubia. After its demise, political authority was apparently divided among a scattering of local kingdoms and subtribes, the most powerful of which had its capital at Ballana, in Lower Nubia. The "X-Group period," lasting from the final decay of the Meroitic culture until the coming of Christianity, is conspicuous for the absence of any suggestion of uniform religious practice. Nubia seems to have shared in the general religious uncertainty which characterized the Mediterranean world at that time.

Christianity was introduced to Nubia in the middle of the sixth century, and was rapidly adopted throughout the region, as far south as the confluence of the Blue and White Niles.[11] This development marks the apogee of Egyptian influence in post-Pharaonic Nubia, since the churches were subject to ecclesiastical control from Alexandria. But after the Arab conquest and the Islamization of Egypt (640 A.D.), the church became a focus of Nubian independence, and the clergy often played a dominant role in secular affairs. There arose at least three independent Christian Nubian

[10] Actually, a Roman introduction in the Nile Valley.

[11] Christianity thus became, for about one century, the established religion over the whole of northeastern Africa, from the Abyssinian highlands to the mouth of the Nile. It was supplanted by Islam in Egypt in 640 A.D., and in the Sudan about eight centuries later, leaving Abyssinia the only surviving Christian kingdom in Africa. In the early centuries there was competition between the Orthodox Byzantine and the heretical Monophysite (Coptic) sects, but the latter prevailed after the seventh century.

kingdoms, which at one time were powerful enough to send an embassy to the Caliph in Baghdad and to intervene in Egyptian affairs.

The heyday of Christian Nubia, which occurred between the eighth and eleventh centuries, marks the last important period of Nubian cultural and political autonomy. From this time on a new influence began to be felt: the rise of pastoral nomadism in the southern Sahara. In consequence, the settled farmers of the Nile Valley were exposed to new and vigorous enemies on their southern flanks, a development that undoubtedly quickened the decay of their culture and society. Intermittent wars with Egypt, which began after the eleventh century, were greatly intensified when the Mamelukes conquered Egypt in 1250. The combination of wars in the north, raids in the south, dynastic feuds, and the disintegration of the Nubian church seems to have culminated in a general depopulation of Lower Nubia during the fifteenth century. From this time on, nothing is known of the history of the region, either archaeological or documentary, until it was penetrated for the first time by European travelers in the nineteenth century. It is recorded that Christianity survived in Upper Nubia until 1504, when the southernmost of the medieval kingdoms was attacked and destroyed by a Moslem confederation.

Through all the vicissitudes of Nubian cultural history it is possible to recognize certain constant and unchanging factors. The most important is the overall environment. The desiccation of the Sahara was already complete thousands of years before the first Egyptian penetration of Nubia, and from that time to the present the river and its banks have offered man his only subsistence.

The river itself, on the other hand, has been notoriously unstable. Not only is there an enormous annual variation in flow between the high and low seasons, there has also been highly irregular fluctuation from year to year, resulting sometimes in crop failures and sometimes in disastrous floods. There have even been whole centuries of exceptionally high and exceptionally low Niles, responding to climatic fluctuations in the East African highlands, which have had a profound effect upon the course of human history.

A second constant in Nubian history has been the basic subsistence complex. For the most part, the same crops (primarily wheat, millet, beans, a few vegetables, and dates) have been grown in Nubia, and the same animals (cattle, sheep, goats, donkeys) raised, since the dawn of history. The later additions of the horse and the camel have improved transport without significantly altering the subsistence pattern.

Third, there has been only one important technological advance: the introduction of the *saqia* (water wheel). Otherwise, the tools and methods of farming, of animal husbandry, of architecture, and of the domestic arts changed scarcely at all, from Pharaonic times until the beginning of the twentieth century.

Finally, Nubian society itself has remained essentially peasant in character. Kings, priests, and tax collectors represented a veneer of Mediterranean–Near Eastern culture that overlaid but did not supplant the older social order. Their authority was probably acknowledged, when it could not be avoided, much as modern Nubians acknowledge the fiat of the Egyptian and Sudanese Governments–as a foreign imposition not of their own choosing.

The Island and Village of Meinarti

The Second Cataract, like the other cataracts of the Nile, is not a waterfall or cascade but a succession of sharp rapids, about 12 km in length. Here the river divides into an intricate network of narrow, swift channels interspersed with scores of rocky islets, most of which are far too small and barren to support human habitation. At the foot of the cataract, however, there is a considerably larger island, Meinarti, which is formed entirely of level alluvium. It is about 1 km long and half as wide, and is one of the very few islands in this region that bears both a modern settlement and important archaeological remains. The site has a certain strategic importance as the head of navigation on this stretch of the Nile, and also because it commands a panoramic view over the Second Cataract, but there is no evidence that it was ever in fact occupied or fortified for this reason.[12] In land-short Nubia, the appeal of Meinarti from the beginning seems to have been simply the expanse of low-lying arable land that it offered.

Lower Nubia was probably recolonized in the first century B.C., but the village of Meinarti was not founded until considerably later. In the interval, the land may have been cultivated by farmers living on the mainland. The first structures were built on the island near the close of the Meroitic period, probably about 200 A.D., at a spot near its southern end. Thereafter, the same site continued to be occupied, with only minor interruptions, until Lower Nubia was again depopulated twelve centuries later, at the close of the Christian period.

The original buildings occupied the top of a low sand dune, which probably afforded the only elevated ground on the island at that time. Its summit was little more than a meter above the average level of the surrounding alluvial flat. Twelve hundred years later, after innumerable rebuildings and the steady accumulation of wind-blown sand, the top of the last structure built at Meinarti was more than 10 meters above this original level. Between these two stratigraphic extremities were nearly a score of intermediate occupation levels.

Although the occupation of Meinarti village was for all practical pur-

[12] Except in the time of the Dervish Wars (1885-98), when the Anglo-Egyptian garrison of Wadi Halfa built a small gun emplacement on top of the ruins of Meinarti village. The remains of this structure constituted Strat. Level 1.

poses continuous, there were occasional brief evacuations brought about by floods or attacking armies. These evacuations were usually followed by extensive rebuilding. There were also, apparently, instances of widespread restoration resulting from nothing more than contagious zeal, inspired by the example of a single energetic individual or family–the sort of thing that can often be observed in modern communities. The result, in any case, was a series of eighteen reasonably well-marked occupation horizons at Meinarti from the time of its original founding to its final abandonment. Most of these horizons obviously involve comparatively little change in the aspect of the village–merely minor alterations and routine repairs, plus a general raising of floor levels through the steady accumulation of debris. There were also, however, some half dozen "macrostrata," representing occasions when the village was very largely rebuilt, often on a plan quite different from that which preceded. The differences between these levels, major and minor, are the basis for the present analysis of changing settlement pattern at Meinarti.

In the history of Meinarti village, as in Nubia generally, there were certain factors that remained constant throughout. One of these was the ethnic composition of the population. Although the village was founded in the Meroitic period and endured through the X-Group and Christian periods, at no point is there evidence of social or cultural upheaval such as might mark the appearance of a new group of settlers, or the displacement of a former group. On the contrary, the record points to an orderly and uninterrupted process of development, from beginning to end. The growth and decay of the community can therefore be considered as the life of a single social organism, and can be analyzed in terms of its own individual mutations rather than with reference to the general phase designations "Meroitic," "X-Group," and "Christian."

Another constant at Meinarti was the location of the village, which never strayed from its original site at the south end of the island. There is no archaeological evidence of another settlement anywhere on Meinarti. Finally, as no good building stone was available, every permanent structure from first to last was built of mud brick.

The Changing Settlement Pattern at Meinarti

The architectural history of Meinarti resolves itself into seven phases. each of which exhibits a distinct developmental trend. Each of the phases is represented, in the stratigraphic record, by two or three levels.[13] Most phases endured between one and two centuries.

[13] Since it was not always possible to estimate the extent or significance of individual levels when they were first encountered, the level numbers that were assigned in the field are not absolutely consistent. Some levels are differentiated only by "a" and "b" designations, and there is no Level 10. Level 1 is omitted from con-

Phase 1 (Levels 18-16; c. 300-450 A.D.)

The original plan of Meinarti village (Strat. Level 18) is of unusual interest, partly because it differs so markedly from anything that followed (Fig. 1). The settlement seems to have been "planned" from the outset, in that the first structures were not ordinary farmhouses but a complex of substantial public buildings, including, apparently, a small temple (Fig. 1, A), a public granary or market, (Fig. 1, B), and a community wine press (Fig. 1, C). The whole complex suggests the modern suburban development, in which the promoters lay out a central shopping plaza, church, and swimming pool, and advertise lots " . . . convenient to shops, churches, recreational facilities." The founding of Meinarti village may not have conformed exactly to these circumstances, but certainly the same collective needs were taken into consideration.

The central buildings were laid out with unusual regularity and were characterized by massive walls and vaulted brick roofs. All of them were apparently whitewashed inside and out. They were built on slightly elevated ground – the top and sides of a low sand dune – presumably for the sake of a commanding position and also to afford some protection from the high Niles. The highest elevation was occupied by the temple.

Ordinary farmhouses undoubtedly surrounded the "civic center" on the adjacent alluvial flats. Because of their vulnerable location they were largely destroyed by floods at an early date, and very little remained of them except in the vicinity of the central buildings, where the ground was higher. From the traces that survived, they appear to have been much less substantially and less regularly built than the public buildings (Fig. 1, D).

Fortunately there are fairly well-preserved Meroitic farmhouses on nearby islands, as well as in more distant localities, which help to suggest the original appearance of Meinarti village. The "houses" comprise rather irregular but solidly built clusters of from ten to thirty rooms, most of which look as if they had grown by gradual accretion from smaller original nuclei. The rooms very commonly occur in connected pairs: a larger room, entered from the outside, containing one or two small ovens, and beyond it a smaller room containing storage vessels. Each of these recurring units may well have been the residence of a single biological family; if so, the average building housed a number of families. The walls are usually 35 cm thick and often formed of "header" bricks only (bricks laid at right angles to the line of the wall). The size and shape of the rooms and the thickness of the walls suggest that the walls could have supported only flat roofs of poles and thatch.

At Meinarti the public buildings were deliberately separated from each other by streets and plazas, and it seems more than probable that they were

sideration, as this designation was given to the Anglo/Egyptian fortification of the 1890's. The levels are, of course, numbered in reverse chronological order, i.e., in the order of discovery and excavation. The field numbers have been retained here because they are published elsewhere (Adams, 1964; 1965b).

similarly set apart from the ordinary residences that surrounded them. This tradition of segregation of public buildings, a survival from Pharaonic times, was to reappear several times at Meinarti.

The original, "planned" village did not retain its initial form for long. Probably within a generation or two of its building there was a flood that largely destroyed the farmhouses and also one side of the public market. The latter was not immediately rebuilt, and for a time the settlement may have been semideserted. The wine press was abandoned and became a refuse dump (Strat. Level 17).

Toward the end of Phase 1 there was a general rebuilding (Strat. Level 16). The destroyed eastern half of the market was restored, and other damaged walls repaired. Over the filled-up remains of the old wine press a new public building, perhaps a wine magazine, was built. The new structures, though still substantial, were considerably less so than their predecessors, and the restoration of the market somewhat simplified its plan. At this time the temple was deliberately destroyed, first by burning and then by razing, so that nothing was left but the stone foundations. For a time the entire area surrounding it was left unoccupied.

From the scanty remains that were preserved, it appears that the ordinary farmhouses remained on the flats, and that they too were repaired in the latter part of Phase 1. As in the central buildings, there was some architectural deterioration: the older 35-cm walls, as they were destroyed, were replaced or overbuilt with very flimsy walls, less than 20 cm thick, formed of "stretcher" courses only (bricks laid parallel to the line of the wall). This type of architecture was to become general in the succeeding period.

To summarize Phase 1: the original plan of Meinarti village involved a "civic center" of massive public buildings erected on slightly elevated ground, and a surrounding cluster of less imposing ordinary dwellings. There was considerable architectural deterioration in the later years, when the settlement was badly damaged by a flood, but the original concept of a segregated cluster of communal buildings, characterized by heavy walls and vaulted roofs, was retained until the end of this period. The ordinary houses, however, had evolved into a very insubstantial form.

Phase 2 (Levels 15b-14; c. 450-600 A.D.)

The remains of this developmental phase are generally well preserved over a large part of the village, and from this time onward it is possible to reconstruct with confidence the character and distribution of ordinary houses as well as public buildings. The latter, however, rapidly went out of use during Phase 2.

The plan of Meinarti village at the outset of Phase 2 (Strat. Level 15b) exhibits a radical departure from the preceding period. The public buildings have abruptly been surrounded and virtually engulfed by a tight, seemingly formless cluster of more than one hundred irregular, thin-walled rooms

(Fig. 2). At first glance, this might be taken as evidence to support the old theory of barbarian invaders in the X-Group period. However, other indications do not bear out such an interpretation. In fact, the change from Meroitic to X-Group pottery styles had already taken place during Phase 1.

A much more probable explanation for the new plan of the village is that the farmers of Meinarti, after suffering repeated damage from the high Niles, had been forced to quit the low-lying floodplain and crowd in upon the higher ground surrounding the public buildings. This may have been in response to a gradual rise in the level of the river, foreshadowing the long battle against the floods that was to shape the pattern of settlement at Meinarti during the centuries that followed. As the accumulation of drifted sand in the vicinity of the central buildings had not yet reached major proportions, the mound area available for building was severly limited. It was presumably this "land shortage" that resulted in the extremely congested plan of the village during its second evolutionary phase.

Superficially, the layout of the village appears chaotic. There is, however, a pattern of sorts to it. The mass of irregular rooms is divided into "blocks" by a network of narrow streets and alleys, and each "block" resolves itself into clusters of two, three, or four interconnected rooms, each cluster usually having only one entrance from the outside. The general plan of the houses probably does not differ markedly from that of the earlier farmhouses, save that they are now much more closely crowded together, apparently as a result of the shortage of protected building sites.

The absence of permanent interior fixtures makes it difficult to determine the function of individual rooms in this period. There is the same pattern of paired long and short rooms as was common in Meroitic times, although it is now less consistent. There are few ovens or storage vessels within the houses, and it is apparent that a good deal of the cooking was done out of doors.

At the outset of Phase 2 one more public building was erected at Meinarti (Fig. 2, A). It was apparently designed as a replacement for the earlier wine magazine (?), for it was built immediately beside the older building, and was virtually identical in size and plan. This structure, like its predecessor, stood slightly apart from the surrounding houses. At the time it was built, the older building was repaired with much flimsier walls and was converted to an ordinary house (Fig. 2, B); the same fate befell that portion of the Meroitic market that still remained standing (Fig. 2, C).

The second wine magazine, if such it was, was the last heavy-walled, vaulted building erected at Meinarti for more than a century. All of the ordinary houses on the site were characterized by excessively thin, irregular walls that could have supported only very light roofs of poles and thatch. The longer walls were often reinforced by small buttresses, but to a large extent the structures of this period must have relied for support on sheer clustered mass, like a house of cards. Every house leaned partly on its neighbors, and probably could not have stood alone.

The persistent trend during Phase 2 was toward architectural impermanence. As the older, heavier buildings fell into decay, they were first repaired and later entirely overbuilt with irregular, thin-walled houses, until at the end of the period (Strat. Level 14) there was not a substantial, vaulted building left in the village. In this way the original "civic center" gradually disappeared, and there was no longer any "zoning" in the village plan. The whole mound was occupied by ordinary residences.

There were no important floods during the second phase of Meinarti's history. Instead, wind-blown sand accumulated steadily around the lower slopes of the mound, particularly at the windward (north and west) sides. The pressure of drifted sand resulted in sagging and buckling of many house walls, requiring frequent repairs and reinforcements. Sometimes the only defense against the accumulating dunes was to raise the floor levels within the houses as well, thus equalizing the pressure against the bases of the walls. This of course necessitated heightening the walls and raising the level of the ceilings. Many houses seem to have been abandoned altogether at times, when the accumulation of sand became too great, but the shortage of suitable building sites always drove the inhabitants to rebuild them in the end. Thus the average height of the Meinarti mound rose by more than one meter during Phase 2, without any significant alteration in the plan of the village. There were periodic rearrangements of interior partitions, presumably in response to the changing needs of individual families, but the overall layout remained remarkably static. However, by the end of the period (Strat. Level 14), a good many of the outermost and lowest structures had been engulfed in sand and abandoned.

Phase 3 (Levels 13-12; c. 600-800 A.D.)

This period in Meinarti's history is marked by a reversal of the preceding architectural trend, and a revival of massive walls and vaulted roofs (Fig. 3). The new trend may have been sparked, in the beginning, by the building of a church at the east side of the village, on a tract of ground that had earlier been used as a refuse dump. This event marks the emergence of Christianity as the established religion of Nubia, though there is evidence that it was espoused by at least some of the Meinarti villagers as much as a century earlier.

The Meinarti church, like other Nubian churches, was built according to a conventional "basilican" plan, and was characterized by heavy walls and vaulted roofs.[14] Like the public buildings of earlier times, it stood slightly apart from the mass of the houses, and had no adjoining secular structures

[14] The original Meinarti church had a grotesquely "skewed" plan; the corners deviated by more than 15° from a true right angle (*vide* Fig. 3, A). This feature is also encountered in some other very early Nubian churches, and was apparently adopted in the belief that it would impart additional strength to the very long vaults that spanned the nave and aisles. At Meinarti, it was corrected when the church was rebuilt at the beginning of the eighth century (Fig. 4, A).

(Fig. 3, A). The church was to be destroyed and rebuilt several times in the centuries that followed, but always on the same foundations. It remained in use, with minor interruptions, until the village of Meinarti was abandoned 800 years later. During most of the intervening time it was the only public building on the island.

Concurrent with the building of the church, a massive vaulted building was erected near the southeastern limit of the village (Fig. 3, B). Elsewhere there was no immediate change in the town plan, and most of the older, thin-walled houses remained in use for a time. The Nile, however, was beginning to rise, and early in Phase 3 Meinarti was struck by the first of a long succession of floods. As the flimsy house walls sagged and collapsed, they were doubled and doubled again for reinforcement. The first major damage seems to have resulted from capillary absorption rather than from direct flooding, but it is apparent that in later years the flood waters coursed freely through the village on many occasions.

The architectural history of Phase 3 seems to represent one long battle against the rising river. The earlier walls were at first reinforced, but later, as they inevitably crumbled, they were overbuilt with more massive walls. These in turn were damaged and repaired many times, the general effect being to make them always more substantial. During all this time the villagers apparently clung to the belief that the periodic inundations could be withstood by sufficiently heavy construction.

For obvious reasons, the remains of Phase 3 were preserved only on the upper parts of the Meinarti mound, and were so denuded as to make interpretation of the social order difficult. For example, the function of the large building in the southeastern part of the village is quite uncertain, for its floors and walls were largely destroyed long before excavation. It probably had some public function—perhaps as a tavern[15] for it was separated from most of the neighboring houses by a street.

Over a large part of the village, the heavy walls of Phase 3 were built directly on top of thinner walls from the preceding period; a good many of them incorporated the upper courses of the older walls in their foundations. At the summit of the mound there was even a small group of thin-walled rooms that survived nearly intact from the beginning of Phase 2 (Fig. 3, C), having been protected from the general flood damage by elevation. Thus the village of Meinarti (i.e., that portion of it that survived) at the end of Phase 3 (Strat. Level 12) still bore much the same aspect as it had at the beginning of Phase 2, in spite of the much more solid construction. There were still irregular streets and "blocks," and there is no reason to suspect any significant change in residence pattern.

[15] Such buildings are known from other early Christian sites, and are easily recognized by the enormous numbers of fragmentary wine amphorae found in and around them. A scattering of such sherds surrounded the building at Meinarti, but the whole surface was too scoured to offer conclusive evidence.

An innovation of Phase 3 was a central latrine (Fig. 3, D), which remained in use in the following period. It is the first recognizable example of such a facility at Meinarti, though latrines were to become common in later houses. As the original structure was apparently the only one on the island at the time, and occupied a central location adjoining a street, it must have been essentially a public convenience.

Phase 4 (Levels 11b-11a; c. 800-1000 A.D.)

This chapter in the architectural history of Meinarti corresponds to the climactic phase of the "era of high Niles." So denuded are its remains, and so limited in extent, that it would be fruitless to speculate on the size or social character of the village at this time. The one apparent fact is that during Phase 4 the inhabitants finally gave up the effort to withstand the recurring floods with ever more massive architecture, and resigned themselves to the prospect of periodic destruction and evacuation. The result was a reversion to the most insubstantial sort of construction (Fig. 4).

The structures that were built at this time exemplify a pattern that is repeated throughout the Second Cataract region during the "era of high Niles." They are tiny, flimsy huts with irregular and usually markedly curving walls. They were generally huddled together in clusters of from half a dozen to a dozen rooms. Wherever a more substantial wall remained standing it was utilized for "backing," much as cliffs and boulders were utilized on some of the rockier islands nearby. Many of the walls of Phase 4 are so thin and so irregular that they could hardly have stood as much as a meter high; they were, in all probability, mere footings for huts of brush or grass. In a word, the houses of this period were designed for economy rather than for endurance. The one exception was the Meinarti church (Fig. 4, A), which, by dint of frequent reinforcement, was kept in repair during most of Phase 4.

That the inhabitants chose to remain on the island of Meinarti at all during this time says a good deal about the prevailing socioeconomic conditions. With little difficulty, the inhabitants could have removed to high ground within half a kilometer of the Nile on either side, and so been safely out of reach of any flood. In fact, however, there are no remains of Christian houses on the river terraces opposite Meinarti, and few anywhere else in the region. Throughout Nubia, the farmers apparently chose to stay where they were and suffer periodic inundation.

The explanation undoubtedly lies partly in the fact that Nubians do not consider their houses to be of much value. Even today one buys a substantially built house in Nubia for the price of the woodwork and metal fittings; the mud is "thrown in." But there was probably a more positive and compelling reason for remaining on the island of Meinarti during the era of high Niles. There is evidence that the recurring floods carried away a good deal of alluvial soil – evidence, in fact, that much of the Nile floodplain was in effect redistributed at this time. Whole settlements were abandoned when their fields were swept away, and there must for a time have been a general and acute land shortage.[16] Those who were fortunate enough to retain their land intact probably were conscious of a need to guard it as closely as possible against seizure by the dispossessed portion of the population.

Notwithstanding this consideration, it seems that the floods finally did succeed in driving away the inhabitants of Meinarti at the conclusion of Phase 4 (Strat. Level 11a), and for a brief time the village lay in ruins.

Phase 5 (Levels 9–7; c. 1000–1150 A.D.).

This phase of Meinarti's history is marked at the outset by something of a mystery. After a short period of abandonment, the entire village was rebuilt within a matter of a few years, according to a plan that suggests no further expectation of flooding. How the inhabitants can have been certain that the era of high Niles had come to an end is not clear, but their expectation was justified by the event. The settlement never again suffered major damage from the Nile.

The architectural remains of Phase 5 were better preserved than any others in the site; many of the houses were buried up to and including the roofs, which remained in situ. We have, therefore, an unusually clear and complete picture of the character and organization of the village at this time.

The plan of Meinarti at Phase 5 is much more suggestive of Phase 2 than of either of the two intervening periods (Fig. 5). The prevailing method of construction was for all practical purposes the same: thin walls, composed of "stretcher" courses only, reinforced at intervals by buttresses, and supporting light, flat roofs of poles and thatch. The layout of the village is also much the same, comprising closely clustered dwellings partially subdivided into "blocks" by streets and alleys.

There is, however, a suggestion of spaciousness in the aspect of the village at the beginning of Phase 5 (Strat. Level 9) that is lacking in any earlier period. The houses and the rooms within them are notably large, the streets are fairly wide, and there is a large open plaza near the center of the village (Fig. 5, A). The church (Fig. 5, B) stands well apart from the neighboring houses and is adjoined by an extensive cemetery (Fig. 5, C).[17] Despite the contiguity of groups of houses, the architectural trend in Phase 5 seems to express a prevailing security both from natural dangers and from human enemies, and provides a notable contrast to the earlier congested conditions.

It is quite easy to recognize individual family houses within the larger

[16] It may have been this circumstance that led to the Nubian invasion and occupation of a considerable area in Upper Egypt in 962 A.D. (Shinnie, 1954, p. 6).

[17] The cemetery had probably occupied the same location since the original building of the church, but all trace of the earlier graves was destroyed by the intervening floods.

"blocks" of this period. They are, in nearly every case, regular rectangular units entered from the outside by a single door, and comprising from four to eight rooms. Each house included, at a minimum, a large "parlor" (usually the first room entered) and a smaller room beyond it; in the constant relationship of these two rooms may almost certainly be seen the survival of the paired rooms of Meroitic and X-Group times (Phases 1 and 2). Now, however, there was a distinct innovation: every house also included, beyond the smaller room, a narrow, right-angle passage ending in a latrine. A degree of central planning is implicit in the fact that groups of contiguous houses were always so oriented that their latrines were located adjacent to their common-corner—thus limiting the number of "contaminated" areas in the village.

The larger rooms clearly served in part for food storage and preparation, for most of them contained mud silos and bins for grain and dates, as well as numbers of milling stones. However, most of the cooking was done on open, walled terraces adjoining the houses. The smaller rooms rarely contained much furniture, and may have served primarily for sleeping. Some of the larger houses had more than one pair of the large and small rooms, and probably housed more than one biological family. Nearly every house also included a flight of steps leading to the roof.

The only substantial vaulted building on Meinarti during Phase 5 was the church, which was restored virtually to its original plan when the village was reoccupied. (It is this fact more than anything else which suggests the hiatus between Phases 4 and 5 was not a long one, and that the inhabitants who returned were the same ones who had left.) During and after Phase 5, the church was adjoined by the village cemetery, which extended east and south from the building as far as the limits of the mound.

There may have been one other "public," or at least specialized, structure at this time. This was a very large, L-shaped room whose flat roof was supported in part on interior columns (Fig. 5, D). It seems to have contained a large wooden table surrounded by a low bench of mud brick, and it was adjoined by a smaller room containing several ovens. In these features there is a suggestion of a public dining hall or refectory. There is nothing else to indicate the presence of a monastery at Meinarti at this time, but it is notable that the refectory of the later monastery was built upon this same site, and in fact continued to utilize the same east wall. There may, therefore, have been some sort of religious organization or confraternity during Phase 5, which evolved into the monastery of the succeeding period.

Floods caused only minor, peripheral damage to the village of Meinarti during Phase 5. A more active enemy was the unceasing Nubian wind and the inexorable piling up of drifted sand against the buildings. After the initial restoration of the village, virtually all of the building that took place was in the form of defenses against the dunes. Windward walls were buttressed and in some cases doubled, doors and windows were blocked up, and the height of walls and ceilings was raised, once in some houses and twice in others, by adding additional courses to the tops of the walls. The central plaza became one enormous sand dune, and around its margins "drift fences" of brick were built whose sole purpose was to restrain the further piling up of sand against the adjacent houses.

These precautions notwithstanding, the dunes seem to have triumphed in the end. The circumstances are obscure, but it is apparent that at the end of Phase 5 (Strat. Level 7) the village of Meinarti, or at least the part of it that was excavated, was once again briefly abandoned. Before leaving, the inhabitants blocked up nearly every door in the place with brick, but the strategem failed to prevent the complete sanding up of the houses during their absence: within a few years, they were buried to the rooftops.

Phase 6 (Levels 6–4; c. 1150–1300 A.D.)

During these later years there were in effect two villages on Meinarti, which followed more or less independent lines of development. The southern extremity of the mound was occupied by a small monastery, which to a large extent continued the architectural trend of the preceding period. To the north of it, an entirely new residence pattern had evolved in the secular village (Fig. 6).

The monastery of Meinarti[18] seems to have been founded at the beginning of Phase 6, though it may have had its origins in an older institution or association within the village. It consisted initially of an enormous communal dining room or refectory (Fig. 6, A), which was adjoined by a kitchen, a large, open courtyard, and a latrine at the end of a long passage (Strat. Level 6). From this original nucleus there gradually grew outward in all directions an irregular cluster of tiny rooms or cells, which were ranged around a series of small plazas. Later additions included an elaborately decorated vaulted building – probably the chapel (Fig. 6, B) – and a massive lookout tower (Fig. 6, C).

There was no real architectural continuity between Phases 5 and 6; the older houses had been partly destroyed and buried in sand before the site was reoccupied. Only one wall, along the east side of the refectory, remained standing to a sufficient height to be incorporated in the later buildings. Nevertheless, the monastery generally conformed to the same architectural standards as the houses that preceded it. The walls in the beginning were uniformly 20 cm thick, reinforced at intervals with buttresses, and the rooms were notably irregular in size and shape.

The monastery rooms were generally far smaller than those of earlier

[18]The presence of the monastery is attested by the medieval Armenian traveller Abu Salih, writing at the beginning of the thirteenth century (1895, pp. 261-62). The monastery was dedicated to Saints Michael and Cosmas. The place at that time was known as the Island of Michael (*geziret mikhail* in Arabic; *mikhailnarti* in Nubian), and this may be the source of the modern name.

times, and merit the designation "cells." They very commonly included built-in fireplaces and sleeping benches (*mastabas*)–features that were rare in the older houses. The whole complex of rooms, plazas, and built-in furniture was decorated with a uniform coat of salmon-pink plaster, which was renewed from time to time. In addition, the refectory was whitewashed and was adorned first with painted Greek inscriptions and later with frescoes.

An exception to the general architectural character of the monastery was a substantial building that stood at its eastern side. It was apparently the chapel, for every wall was adorned with polychrome frescoes, as in the Meinarti church. It was the only structure in the monastery complex that had heavy walls and a vaulted roof.

Unlike most monasteries, in Nubia and elsewhere, the Meinarti monastery never had an enclosing wall, and its outer limits seem to have been in a state of constant fluctuation. There was no sharply defined boundary between the monastery and the secular village–only a narrow, unoccupied space. The village continued to occupy the central and northern parts of the mound, and probably still numbered the great majority of the community's inhabitants.

At the outset of Phase 6, when Meinarti was first reoccupied, there was a brief resumption of the earlier system of construction in the village as well as in the monastery. New thin-walled houses were built upon the sanded-up roofs of the older houses, according to much the same plan (Strat. Level 6). They were soon deliberately dismantled, however, and a new type of detached "unit house" made its appearance (Fig. 6, D).

Unit houses are characteristic of the later Christian settlements throughout Nubia, and seem to have come into fashion over the whole region at about the same time. They are heavy, rectangular or square family dwellings of from four to eight rooms, with a single doorway to the outside. Their interior details recall the houses of the preceding period, and usually include a large "front room," a smaller "back room," and a right-angle passage ending in a latrine.

What distinguishes the unit houses from their predecessors is, first, their much heavier construction, and second, their architectural independence. Whenever space permitted, they stood apart from their neighbors, even if the gap between them was too small to admit a man. Where a shortage of space made it necessary to build them contiguously, they rarely if ever shared a common wall. Like the buildings in a modern city block, their walls stood face to face, but each supported its own roof and only its own roof. This development seems almost to express a rebellion against the "herding" of earlier times, and is perhaps a symptom of the decay of the central polity.

At Meinarti, about half a dozen unit houses were built early in Phase 6 (Strat. Levels 6 and 5), and their number rose to perhaps a dozen by the end of the period. They were not arranged in an orderly pattern, but were scattered rather unevenly over the mound – though, like Nubian houses of all times, they maintained a fairly consistent orientation parallel to the course of the Nile. The Meinarti mound had by now grown to such proportions that there was ample building space available for such inhabitants as remained in the village, and there was therefore no need for the houses to crowd closely together as they did in some other late Christian communities. The unit houses at Meinarti never directly adjoined each other, though some of them were adjoined by thin-walled "satellite structures."

The twelfth and thirteenth centuries were restless times in Nubia; the fabric of Christian society was beginning to disintegrate, and enemy peoples were making their appearance. These conditions are reflected in the settlement pattern of Meinarti village during the sixth phase of its history. There is no longer the sense of stability and order that manifested the preceding period; there are instead indications of continual change and modification, both in the monastery and in the village. Major population shifts were under way, and there were probably a good many comings and goings from the island, so that the size of the settlement fluctuated from year to year.

In the middle years of Phase 6 (Strat. Level 5) occurred another of the mysterious events in Meinarti's history. The monastery, and perhaps the village as well, was temporarily abandoned for no obvious reason. The inhabitants did not carry their valuables with them, but left them neatly stacked in a few store rooms, with no special precautions for their safety. No natural or manmade calamity followed the evacuation, and the abandoned goods were left unmolested as sand gradually piled up around them. When the villagers eventually returned, they made no attempt to recover the buried valuables, but simply laid in new floors on top of the sand that covered them, often within a few centimeters of the tops of the objects themselves. The result was, of course, an unexpected treasure trove for the archaeologist.

At about this time – perhaps immediately upon the return of the villagers – there were systematic modifications in the unit houses (Strat. Level 4). Their original timbered roofs were without exception removed and replaced by brick vaults. Many of the walls were strengthened at the same time, and in some houses the doorway to the "back room" was solidly blocked up, so that it could only be entered by a hatchway in the roof. There were comparable reinforcements in the monastery, where a line of stout rooms was built along the south side. One of these was certainly a lookout tower.

Beyond any doubt, these architectural mutations are indirect evidence of the appearance of nomadic raiders in Nubia. There was, and is, plenty of building timber available on the island of Meinarti, and the substitution of vaulted for timbered roofs is best explained by a desire to make them less vulnerable to fire. The reinforcing of walls and the closing off of interior rooms, making them accessible only from above, suggest the protection of food stores from marauders. The consistent trend during Phase 6 was toward increasingly sturdy architecture, as it was 500 years earlier in Phase 3. Now, however, the enemy was man, rather than nature.

Direct evidence of enemy activity appears for the first time at the close of Phase 6, when the religious frescoes both in the church and in the refectory were defaced by raiders.[19] This event probably drove the villagers once again from the island, and may have delivered the *coup de grace* to the monastery.

Phase 7 (Levels 3–2; c. 1300–1400 A.D.)

The defensive trend evident in the latter part of Phase 6 at Meinarti reached its culmination in the final phase of the community's history (Fig. 7). The one significant relic of this period was a huge square building (Fig. 7, A), the largest ever built on the island, which clearly represents the last effort of the Meinarti villagers to protect themselves and their stores from attack. Although built directly over the sanded-up walls of the refectory, it bore no functional resemblance to the older monastery; it was, in fact, a hypertrophied version of the unit house. Its outer walls were a meter thick, and access was severely limited. Two rooms formed a sort of crypt in the center of the building, which could be entered only by a highly circuitous route, and three others were entered only through hatchways in the roof. Access to the roof was provided by a long ladder in the heart of the building, whose base was guarded by a narrow passageway and two tiny doorways. The roof of the "blockhouse" was nearly five meters above its foundations, and it undoubtedly served the same function as the older lookout tower, which was dismantled when the later building was built (Strat. Level 3).

One room in the "blockhouse" had a whitewashed wall with a painted religious inscription. It was the only religious embellishment in the building, and there is nothing else to suggest that the monastic community still existed at this time. The blockhouse itself occupied a considerable part of the area that had formerly been the monastery, although a few of its outlying rooms (Fig. 7, B) had been partially cleared and restored to use–possibly by squatters. Some of the unit houses certainly also remained in use in Phase 7 (Fig. 7, C).

The blockhouse has counterparts in other late Christian communities, and suggests a communal undertaking by such inhabitants as remained on the island to protect themselves and their food stores from attack. Since one of the original buildings at Meinarti was apparently also a communal mag-

[19]Defacement of sculpture and paintings, in obedience to the strict Islamic injunction against graven images, is a recurring feature of Moslem raids upon Christian settlements throughout the Near East.

azine, it might be said that the settlement had come full circle since its founding 1,200 years earlier. In no intervening period was the community's effort centered upon its public buildings to the same extent as it was at the beginning and at end of its existence.

It is doubtful whether the blockhouse remained in use more than a generation or two, for there was very little accumulated refuse within it. Even before its abandonment, however, the central rooms and "keep" were broken into. The damage was never repaired, and it appears that from this time until their final departure the inhabitants of Meinarti were merely "camping" in their own ruins (Strat. Level 2).

Meinarti was one of the very few settlements in Lower Nubia that remained inhabited until the close of the Christian period.[20] Its final abandonment was part of the general depopulation that occurred in the fourteenth century, and was not the result of local conditions. How long the region as a whole remained uninhabited is uncertain, but Meinarti Island was not reoccupied until the latter part of the nineteenth century. The new settlers were linguistically and racially descended from the old, but their culture and society had been thoroughly "arabized" during the intervening centuries. The houses they built are made of coursed adobe rather than of brick, and neither their construction nor their distribution recalls the village of the past.

Determining Factors in the Settlement of Meinarti

Although it supported a small monastery for a time, Meinarti was from first to last primarily an ordinary farming community. During most of its history it was probably little different from scores of other villages scattered through this part of Nubia. There was nothing unusual about its situation or its character, save that the absence of other high ground kept the settlement confined to the same spot from beginning to end. It was this circumstance, of course, that presented an unparalleled stratigraphic record to the archaeologist.

Most of the architectural trends that have been noted at Meinarti conform to widespread general patterns; they can be observed in many villages of comparable age in this part of Nubia. This is specifically true of the substantial public buildings of Phase 1, the flimsy X-Group houses of Phase 2, the contiguous vaulted buildings of Phase 3, the rude huts of Phase 4, the unit houses of Phase 6, and even the blockhouse of Phase 7. Only the spacious houses of Phase 5 are not represented elsewhere, simply because Meinarti is the only settlement of this particular age that has so far been excavated.

[20] Only five Nubian towns were specifically named among the dominions of the Mameluke Sultan Bybars, who nominally annexed the region in 1275. The southernmost of the five was the Island of Michael (Moufazzal, 1919, p. 282).

In short, it is possible to explain the changing settlement pattern at Meinarti almost entirely in terms of cultural trends that were general throughout Nubia. At the same time, it is not necessary to refer to such general trends to account for the developments within the individual village. The trends themselves arose in response to changing conditions in the physical and social environment, which, insofar as they were constant throughout the region, are manifest in the specific environment of Meinarti. To this extent it is possible to analyze the architectural evolution within the village without reference to a wider sociocultural context, yet without implying that it was in any sense a special product of this one site and its microenvironment. Meinarti simply constitutes a representative microcosm of Nubia as a whole.

Obviously, not all of the developmental changes at Meinarti are subject to deterministic explanation. Some of them undoubtedly arose in response to conditions that are no longer apparent, and some may have been essentially capricious. It is possible, however, to recognize perhaps half a dozen variables in the natural and cultural environment that had a direct effect upon the size and character of the settlement. Of these, the most obvious and the most easily defined are the natural factors.

Natural Determinants Soil, water, wind, and sand were the variables in the physical environment of Meinarti. Of these, by far the most constant was soil. The island seems to have varied little in contour or overall productivity during the period of its occupation, in spite of the considerable redistribution of soil that took place in other parts of the Nile floodplain. In land-short Nubia, it was this constant availability of low-lying, easily irrigated alluvium that led to the original founding of the village, to its continued occupation in the face of repeated destruction by floods, and to its persistence after most of the neighboring settlements had been abandoned.

The level of the Nile was certainly the most variable and the most immediately influential factor in the environment of Meinarti. When the village was founded, the Nile had been low for a millennium, and the first settlers felt safe in building their houses directly on the floodplain. Within a few generations they were assailed by the first of many floods, and by the beginning of Phase 2 the rising river had driven the inhabitants off the flats and onto the higher ground surrounding the "civic center," until their houses literally engulfed the older public buildings. For the next 500 years the high Nile was the principal enemy the Meinarti villagers faced. Time and again it inundated and largely destroyed the settlement, provoking the villagers to build more and more massive walls in defense, until they finally yielded and accepted the prospect of periodic destruction as inevitable. For a time they took to building the rudest sort of huts, which could be easily and cheaply replaced. However, the high Niles ceased abruptly in the eleventh century, and the river never again played a major part in determining the aspect of the village.

The effects of wind and sand were generally in inverse proportion to those of the high Nile. In Nubia, the wind blows out of the north the year around, picking up loose sand both from the deserts flanking the river and from enormous sandbars that are exposed at the low Nile. Dunes pile up inexorably against any immovable object, and in a matter of a few years the average house is half buried along its north and west sides.

At Meinarti, the action of the wind was in part countered by the action of the Nile, in that accumulated sand was periodically swept away by floods. Thus it was chiefly during the eras of low water that wind-drifted sand was a menace to the settlement. Its effects are seen most clearly at Phase 2 and at Phase 5. In the former case it buckled many of the outer walls of the X-Group houses, necessitated frequent reinforcement and rebuilding, and finally swallowed up a good many outlying rooms. In Phase 5 the effects were even more severe, forcing the inhabitants to heighten walls and ceilings throughout the village, and finally to take active countermeasures in the form of restraining walls. Even so, the village was eventually buried to its rooftops.

The wind and sand have been blowing at Meinarti ever since, but after Phase 5 the mound had risen to such a height that its sheer elevation afforded some protection from the dunes, and the rate of sanding-up was never again as rapid in later years. However, the monastery of Phase 6 had largely filled with sand by the time it was overbuilt with the blockhouse of Phase 7. The latter had in turn filled to the roof when it was briefly converted to a gun emplacement during the Dervish Wars of the 1880's.

Cultural Determinants Fluctuations in the physical environment had an obvious, direct effect upon the settlement of Meinarti. The effects of a changing social environment were generally more diffuse, and are often difficult to define. There were not, as in many other parts of the world, any important technological improvements to alter dramatically the relationship between man and nature. The one such development during the whole of Nubian history was the introduction of the *saqia* (water wheel), which occurred two or three centuries before the founding of Meinarti village. It was, however, the factor that made possible the reoccupation of Lower Nubia as a whole, and to that extent was ultimately responsible for the colonization of Meinarti itself. Throughout its history, the village depended primarily on agriculture, and agriculture depended primarily on the *saqia*.

The most conspicuous variable in the social environment of Meinarti involved the community's external relations. During the Meroitic and X-Group periods, as well as in the earlier part of the Christian period, the Nubians seem to have lived largely at peace with their neighbors. There was a lively and prosperous trade with Egypt most of the time, and the Meinarti villagers obviously relied on it for a considerable portion of their household goods. This relationship was only briefly disturbed by the Moslem conquest of Egypt; trade continued to flourish under the early Caliphs, and serious religious strife did not break out until several centuries later. There seem to have been some Moslem settlers in Nubia itself between the ninth and eleventh centuries,[21] but they were obviously a small minority of the population and did not threaten the security of the majority.

The influence of human enemies is not perceptible at Meinarti until the last two centuries of its history. During that time, however, their effect upon the development of the community was decisive. Nearly all of the changes which took place after the beginning of Phase 6 were defensive in character, including the strengthening of walls, the replacement of thatch with vaulted roofs, the closing up of storerooms, and finally the building of the massive blockhouse. The pressure of enemies was certainly responsible in some measure for the final abandonment of the community.

One other category of social influence is reflected in the changing aspect of Meinarti village; it is the least tangible and least measurable of the variables that affected the growth of the community, yet its influence cannot be ignored. This was the degree of social and cultural integration that prevailed at different times within the community and throughout the surrounding region.

In its social history, as in its relation to its natural environment, Meinarti epitomizes the history of Nubia as a whole. The planned, centrally oriented village of Phase 1, with its complex of communal buildings, reflects the strong central polity of the Meroitic state. The helter-skelter growth of Phase 2, with the destruction of the temple and abandonment of the public buildings, symbolizes the disintegration and overthrow of the central power and the emergence of independent local communities. The reinforcements and reconstructions of Phase 3, together with the building of the church, suggest the reintegration of Nubian society and the re-emergence of ecclesiastical power during the early Christian period; and the spacious and well-planned village of Phase 5 corresponds in time to the heyday of power and prosperity of the medieval Nubian kingdoms. (The huts of Phase 4 must be regarded as a temporary anomaly resulting from exceptional physical conditions, for they were built at a time when Nubia was otherwise peaceful and prosperous.) The unit houses of Phase 6, with their deliberate structural independence and rather irregular distribution, probably represent a reaction against the tight social integration of the preceding period, paralleling the decay of the central polity of Christian Nubia. Finally, the defensive architecture of Phase 6, culminating in the blockhouse of Phase

[21]Several eleventh-century Arabic tombstones were found in the village of Meinarti; they had all been removed from their original settings and employed for various utilitarian purposes. This was not necessarily a mark of disrespect, for the same fate often befell Christian tombstones after the graves had been untended for a time. There was also a bilingual inscription, in Arabic and Old Nubian (the latter written in Greek-Coptic characters), in one of the houses dating from the latter part of Phase 5.

7, marks the arrival of the enemy peoples who finally brought to a close this 1,200-year chapter in Nubian history.[22]

The foregoing analogies are not intended to suggest a causal relationship between the history of Meinarti and the history of Nubia. They do, however, sustain the proposition that Meinarti is a faithful microcosm of Nubia as a whole, and that events and causes that might be deduced from a study of settlement pattern over the whole region can also be perceived through the changes that took place within the microcosm of a single community.

[22] In the late fourteenth century, the Arab historian Ibn Khaldun wrote of Nubia: "No trace of kingly authority remained in the country, and the people are now become bedouins, following the rains about as they do in Arabia." (Crowfoot, 1927, p. 148).

General Notes on the Site Plans (Figs. 1-7)

The area shown, measuring 100 meters north-south by 80 meters east-west, is the same on all seven plans. This area includes all of the surviving structural remains of the southern half of Meinarti village, at every period. The limits shown at the south, east, and west sides of the village are therefore the limits of preservation. Since the northern half of the mound remained unexcavated, the limit shown at the north in each case is the limit of excavation.

During the Christian period (Phases 3-7), the cemetery of Meinarti adjoined the village church along its southern and eastern sides. Graves which can be specifically associated with Phases 5 and 6 are shown on the plans of those periods. Graves with brick superstructures intact are indicated by solid rectangles representing the actual form of the tomb. Graves without superstructures are indicated by dotted outlines. At both Phases 5 and 6 the cemetery extended eastward at least 10 meters beyond the area covered by the plans.

Dashed contour lines indicate the approximate configuration of the mound at each period of occupation. Where no buildings are shown (i.e., on the slopes of the mound), contour lines represent destruction levels following abandonment, but before overbuilding at later periods. Zero contour, marking the base of the mound, represents the average level of the Nile floodplain surrounding the village. The contour interval is one meter.

In the northwest corner of each plan, the solid arrow indicates magnetic north. The wavy arrow indicates the direction of flow of the Nile ("local north"), which normally determines building orientation in Nubia.

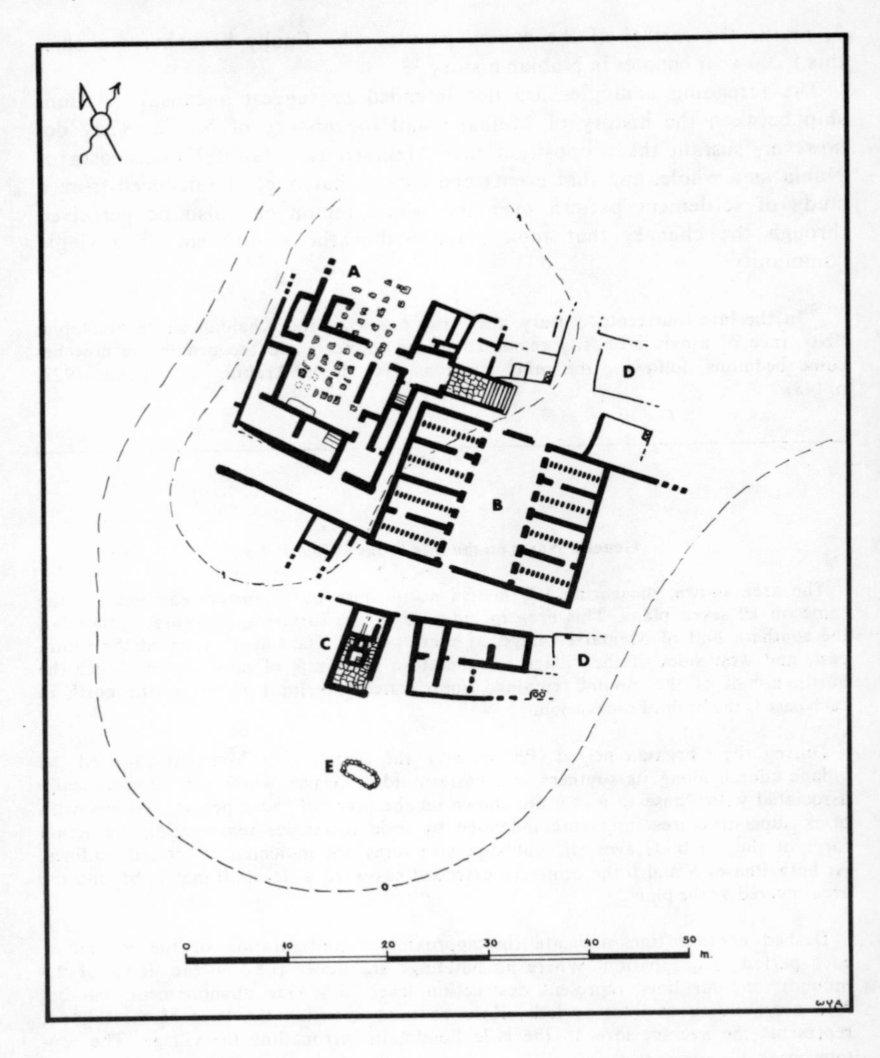

Fig. 1. Plan of Meinarti village at Phase 1 (Strat. Level 18).
A, temple; B, market or granary; C, wine press; D, farm houses; E, *saqia* well (possibly associated with wine press). For detailed explanation see *Notes* following text.

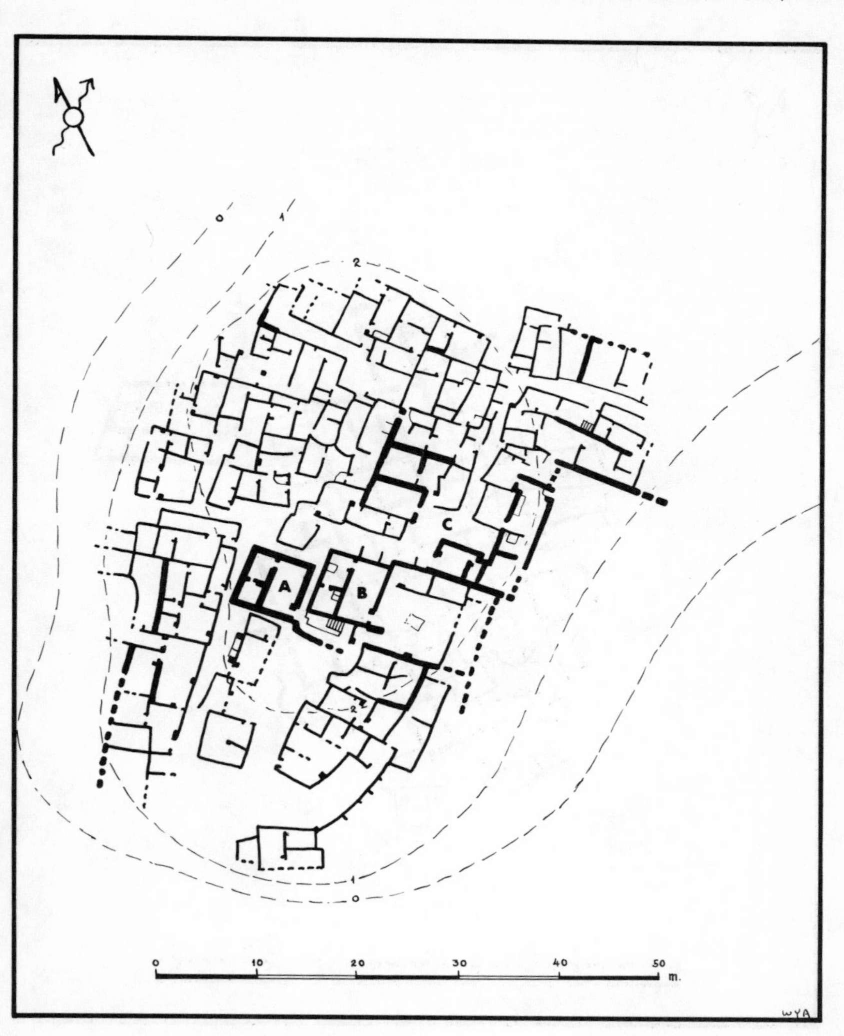

Fig. 2. Plan of Meinarti village at Phase 2 (Strat. Level 15b).
A, wine storage magazine (?); B, earlier wine magazine converted to dwellings; C, remains of Meroitic market. See *Notes*.

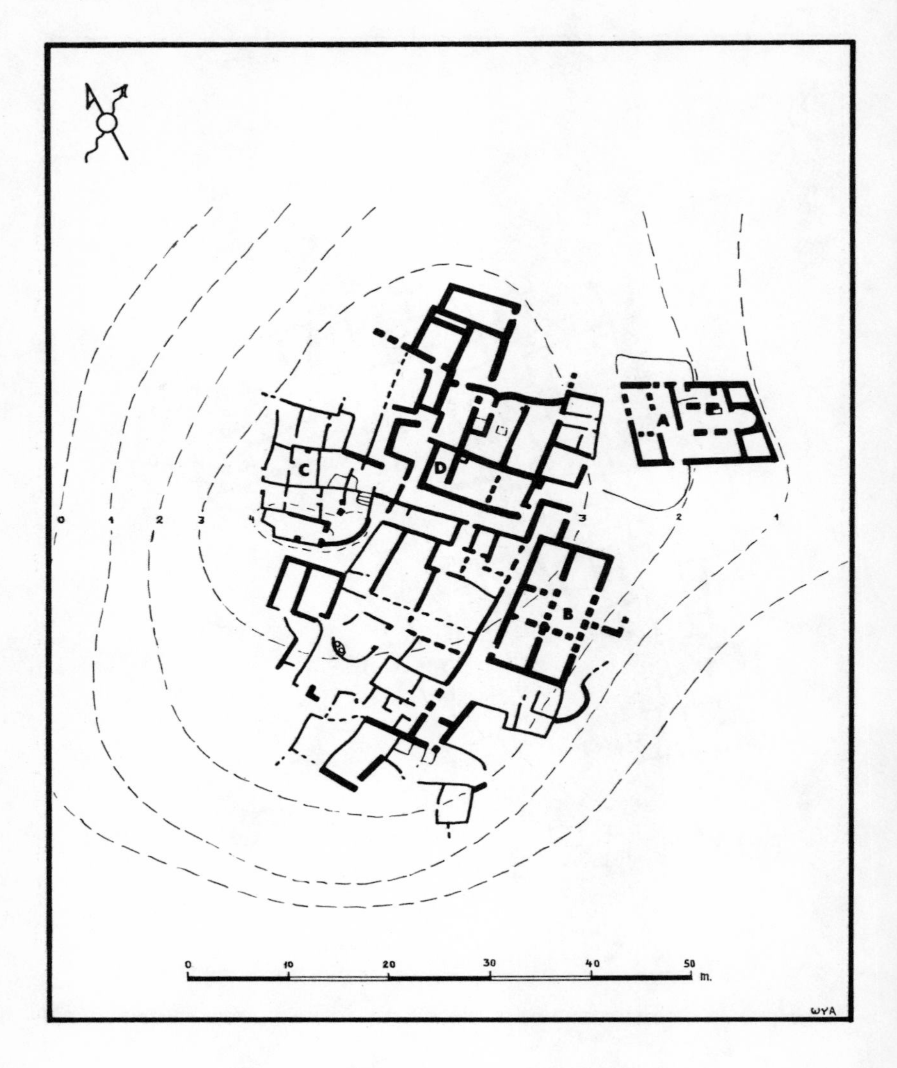

Fig. 3. Plan of Meinarti village at Phase 3 (Strat. Level 13). A, church; B, tavern (?); C, surviving X-Group buildings; D, latrine. See *Notes*.

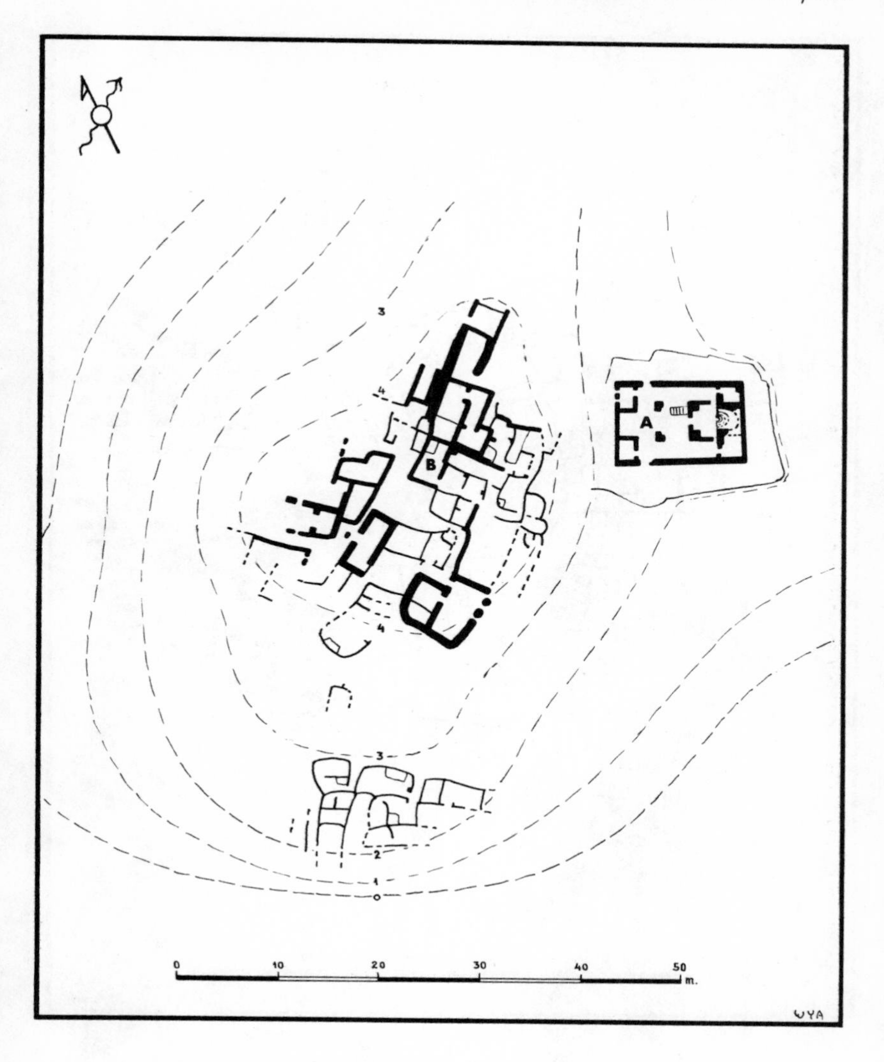

Fig. 4. Plan of Meinarti village at Phase 4 (Strat. Level 11b). A, church; B, latrine. See *Notes*.

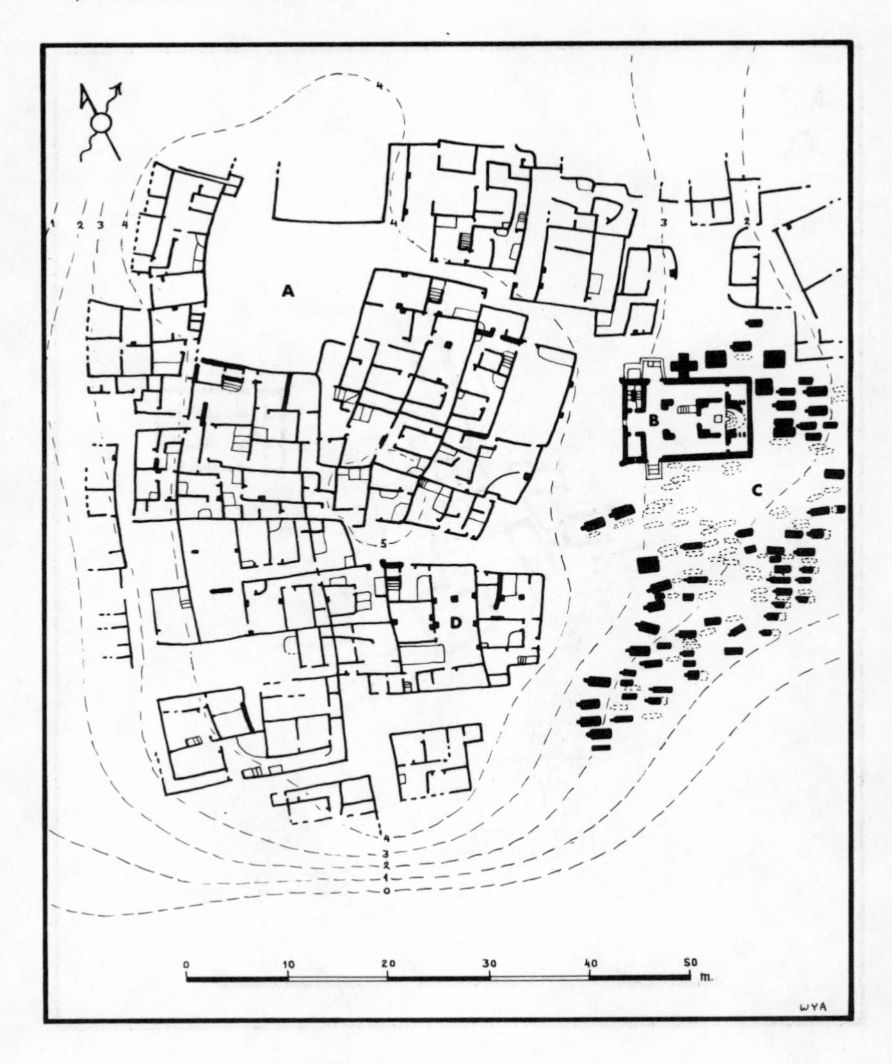

Fig. 5. Plan of Meinarti village at Phase 5 (Strat. Level 8). A, plaza; B, church; C, cemetery; D, refectory (?). See *Notes*.

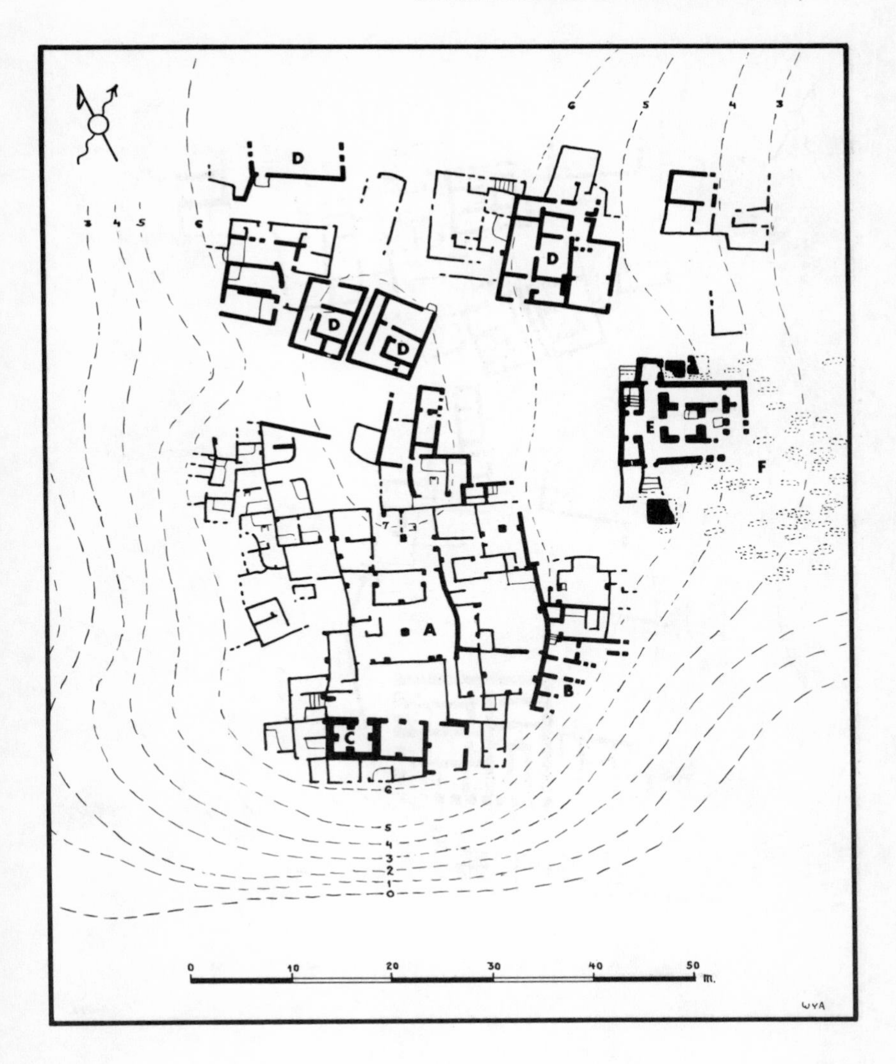

Fig. 6. Plan of Meinarti village at Phase 6 (Strat. Level 5). A, refectory; B, chapel; C, lookout tower; D, unit houses; E, church; F, cemetery. See *Notes*.

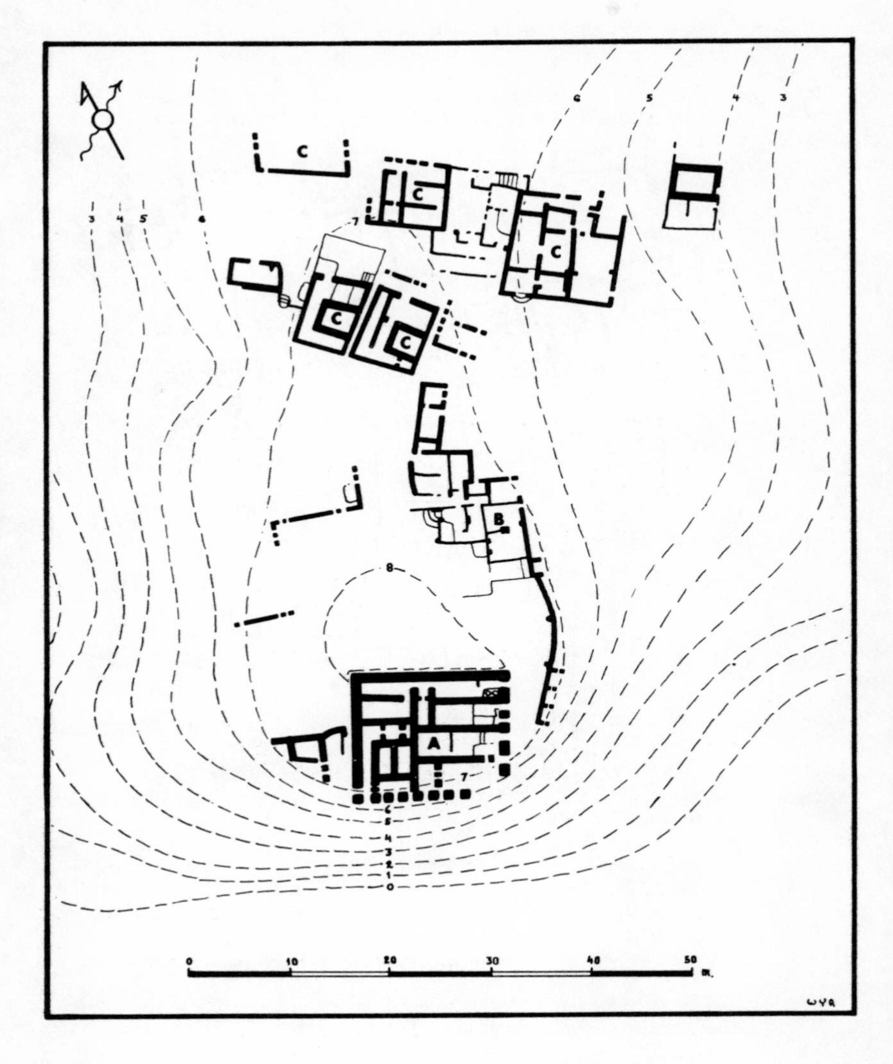

Fig. 7. Plan of Meinarti village at Phase 7 (Strat. Level 3). A, "Blockhouse"; B, monastery rooms remaining in use; C, unit houses. See *Notes*.

References

ABU SALIH
1895 *The churches and monasteries of Egypt and some neighbouring countries*, translated by B. T. A. Evetts (Oxford: Oxford University Press).
ADAMS, W. Y.
1964 "Sudan Antiquities Service excavations in Nubia: Fourth season, 1962-3," *Kush*, Vol. XII:222-41.
1965 "Sudan Antiquities Service excavations at Meinarti, 1963-4," *Kush*, Vol. XIII
ARKELL, A. J.
1955 *A History of the Sudan* (London: Athlone Press).
CROWFOOT, J. W.
1927 "Christian Nubia," *Journal of Egyptian Archaeology*, Vol. XIII:141-50.
EMERY, W. B.
1938 *The Royal Tombs of Ballana and Qustul* (Cairo: Government Press).
FIRTH, C. M.
1912 *The Archaeological Survey of Nubia: Report for 1908-1909* (Cairo: National Printing Dept.).
1927 *The Archaeological Survey of Nubia: Report for 1910-1911* (Cairo: National Printing Dept.).
GODLEY, A. D.
1946 *Herodotus, with an English Translation* (London: W. Heinemann).
KIRWAN, L. P.
1939 *The Oxford University Excavations at Firka* (Oxford: Oxford University Press).
MACMICHAEL, H. A.
1922 *A History of the Arabs in the Sudan* (Cambridge: Cambridge University Press).
MONNERET DE VILLARD, U.
1938 *Storia della Nubia cristiana* (Rome: Pontificium Institutum Orientalium Studiorum).
MOUFAZZAL, IBN ABIL-FAZIL
1919 "Histoire des sultans Mamelouks," *Patrologia Orientalis*, E. Blochet, editor, Vols. XII, XIV.
REISNER, G. A.
1910 *The Archaeological Survey of Nubia: Report for 1907-1908* (Cairo: National Printing Dept.).
1919 "Outline of the ancient history of the Sudan," Pt. 4, *Sudan Notes and Records*, Vol. II:35-67.
1922 "The pyramids of Meroe and the Candaces of Ethiopia," *Sudan Notes and Records*, Vol. V:173-96.
1923 "The Meroitic kingdom of Ethiopia: a chronological outline," *Journal of Egyptian Archaeology*, Vol. IX:34-77.
SÄVE-SÖDERBERGH, T.
1941 *Agypten und Nubien* (Lund: Hakan Ohlssous).
SHINNIE, P. L.
1954 "Medieval Nubia," *Sudan Antiquities Service Museum Pamphlets*, No. 2.
1935 *Aniba* (Hamburg: J. J. Augustin).
TRIGGER, B. G.
1965 "History and Settlement in Lower Nubia," *Yale University Publications in Anthropology*, No. 69.

XI

GORDON R. WILLEY

Settlement Archaeology: An Appraisal

This volume is a collection of essays on various substantive and reflective aspects of the settlement pattern in archaeology. The first two papers in the collection go directly to a controversy that has long been latent in our discipline – a debate that has been expressed, if at all, only occasionally or obliquely. The gist of the controversy may be stated as a question: is there a "settlement pattern approach" to archaeology or prehistory that may be said to constitute a "new archaeology," a radical break with the past of the discipline? A dozen or so years ago, when I organized a symposium on "Prehistoric Settlement Patterns in the New World," I had not considered such a question, and so was surprised at the reaction of some members of the symposium audience, in indicating that they believed such an issue to be at stake. These reactions prompted me to review my own thinking on the matter. In my only previous writing on the subject of prehistoric settlement patterns (Willey, 1953a), I had presented my research as part of a larger project or "team" effort on the archaeology of the Viru Valley of Peru. In this context, I relied to a great extent on other lines of archaeological investigation – site survey and stratigraphic excavation, ceramic analysis, horizontal seriation, and the formation of culture complexes, phases, and periods by these means. I was at pains to point this out (*op. cit.*, pp. xviii-xix, 9-12), but I also emphasized the nature of my own work as something of a new departure in the " . . . understanding of the structure and function of ancient societies." In considering this in retrospect, I concluded that the investigation of settlement patterns did not, and could not, in itself compose a self-contained approach to prehistory, that it was not a "new archaeology." At the same time, it was, to a very great extent, a "new" approach within archaeology, or at least one relatively little exploited by archaeologists. These views were stated in a brief introductory note to the published papers of the above-mentioned symposium on prehistoric settlement patterns (Willey, 1956a); I adhere to these views today, and have expressed them again in a recent monograph (Willey, Bullard, Glass, and Gifford, 1965, pp. 5-6, 581). The reader will, I trust, forgive this digression into personal history, for it has a bearing on the Chang-Rouse debate and on my own attitude toward that debate.

Chang and Rouse: A Question of Precedence and Emphasis

The differences of opinion between Chang and Rouse are largely procedural, and involve the sequence of steps in archaeological investigation. Chang argues that no part of archaeology or prehistory takes logical precedence over any other part, that the interpretation of artifacts is not on a more basic and more reliable level than, say, the interpretation of religion. Accordingly, the selection or acquisition of data is not a first step, because the very matter of choice in the selecting is conditioned by interpretive hypotheses. Rouse, on the other hand, takes the position that the first four logical steps of prehistory are: (1) recovery of the remains; (2) classification of the remains; (3) reconstruction from the remains; and (4) interpretation of the remains. It is his feeling that Chang, in his desire to proceed directly to the study of prehistoric society, omits the first of these steps.

It seems to me that Chang does not so much ignore this step as he does take it for granted. For procedurally it is impossible to define a meaningful prehistoric settlement pattern unless one begins with the unit of a cultural complex; and cultural complexes are defined by the clusterings or associations of artifacts and remains at given points in space and time. Once such complexes are known, through the procedures of recovery and classification, it is then possible to correlate settlement features into patterns that represent, or are the residues of, former social institutions. Before this is done, the individual settlement features are no more to us than bumps or marks upon the landscape – lacking in cultural identification, chronological position, or functional significance. Once these kinds of information are known, in any particular region or area, it may then be possible to evaluate a prehistoric settlement pattern on its formal settlement properties alone; but this is a secondary operation, underpinned by the primary procedures of culture complex definition.

It is in a procedural sense that tools or artifacts are on a lower or more basic level of archaeological interpretation than religion. This is quite different from claiming that " . . . the study of technology is both preconditional to and more reliable than theology." The question here is not one of cultural determinism, or of the determinative influences of one aspect of culture upon another, but of what must, of necessity, come first in field investigation. As archaeologists, we address ourselves first to the "hard goods" – sherds and flint and buildings, or whatever – because of the very nature of the discipline. Thus I would have to enter a disagreement, or strong qualification, to Chang's statement that: "Studies of artifacts and of religions belong to different fields of inquiry . . ." They must, I think, at the outset, represent no more than different aspects of a common inquiry, while the limits of form, space, and time are being staked out. After these formal-spatial-temporal systematics have been executed, a number of lines of inquiry will separate out.

Rouse is correct, then, I think, in holding that archaeologists have a sort of core discipline in common: the technical recovery, description, and classification of remains. He explains this further by stipulating that an archaeologist, so defined, must be more than simply a technician. He must be versed in theory–" . . . the theory of material culture, especially of artifacts and structures." I am not at all sure that I know what these "theories" are, or just what Rouse has in mind. In general, I should think, the methodological core of archaeological procedure is accommodated to the anthropological premises that culture, or cultures, change through time and that cultural and social behavior is in some way registered in material objects. As archaeologists we deal with this behavior through the surrogate of these objects, arriving at conclusions about time and place and change, and building these conclusions with the aid of concepts such as diffusion, evolution, and ecological adjustment drawn from anthropology and other disciplines. With this outlook the archaeologist has operated with certain rather well-defined techniques and with a growing battery of technical aids. Assuming that this follows Rouse's meaning, I concede it to be the common ground of archaeology and understand him when he remarks that to exceed this in interpretation carries us into the specialized realms of substantive knowledge: Egyptology, classics, or other culturally and regionally defined spheres of prehistory or art history. But I am not at all content with Rouse's further insistence that archaeology (methods and techniques, with a body of guiding theory) should as a discipline stand apart from, say, prehistory (the substantive results of archaeological recovery and their further interpretation).

Rouse develops this last idea at some length, and describes what he believes to be a trend in disciplinary organization. The archaeologist of the future, according to his view, will have been brought up in a different house from the prehistorian. He will be primarily the technician, the specialist in the retrieval of the data of the past, whatever that past. He and others like him will compose a sort of "service" cadre to those who are concerned with the substance of human history. The latter, the prehistorians, will be the thinkers, the formulators of ideas. Although acknowledging that we are in the age of the specialist, I look with dismay on the reduction of the archaeologist to such a fragmentary man, or on the sterilization of the prehistorian by removing him from the dirt, sweat, and tears of his methods and techniques. One of the great strengths of American archaeology is that it has grown up in the merging currents of anthropology and technical archaeology. As a result, the American archaeologist has been able to construct more sophisticated models of the past and to phrase a great range of new problems that would never have occurred to him if his outlook had been one of technical and mechanical proficiency alone. On the other hand, the technically trained archaeologist has been able to bring to anthropology a greater comprehension of the kinds of questions that may be asked of the data of prehistory with reasonable hope that answers will be forthcoming. Rather than to separate archaeology from prehistory – or method from substantive result – I should prefer to see them continue as yokefellows in a single discipline, and, whenever possible, and according to the dictates of personal taste, to continue as aspects of the same anthropologically trained personality. In all of this, I am closer to Chang's opinion, that archaeology, even as a field operation, cannot be separated fully from interpretation: there must be a coordinated problem direction to prehistory and to the archaeological methods devised to recover prehistory. This would certainly be true of methods devised to plot and reconstruct prehistoric settlement patterns – with overall problem direction in this case being, for example, the understanding of past social and political organization. My difference with Chang, as I have tried to make clear above, is not over the inevitability of a close relationship between archaeological field method and culture-historical interpretation, but over what I believe (along with Rouse) to be the necessity of taking certain basic methodological steps prior to the settlement pattern–prehistoric society interpretive step.

Procedural steps are, again, at the heart of the Chang–Rouse disagreement over the meaning and interpretation of such concepts as "settlement," "community," and "components." Chang says: "An archaeological settlement is the physical locale or cluster of locales where the members of a community lived, ensured their subsistence, and pursued their social functions in a delineable time period." Such is for him the basic unit of the science of prehistoric society. Rouse recognizes the value of such a unit in paleosocial interpretations but questions its suitability as the fundamental building block. He argues that the settlement can be recognized archaeologically only as "all those space/time components in which a particular community carried out its various activities," not as a single component. I must admit that, heretofore, I have always considered the "component" in archaeological culture classification to be the equivalent of the social category "community" and of the physical entity "settlement" (Willey and Phillips, 1958, p. 49). In other words, my thinking here has gone along with what Chang is suggesting. Rouse demurs, however, on procedural grounds, and asks: What is the primary unit perceived by the archaeologist? Is it (in West Indian prehistory) the village site *and* the ceremonial ball-court, when these are found some distance apart? Or are the village site and the ball-court each components at the level of basic archaeological classification? It can be, and has been, demonstrated, in this particular instance, that villages and ball-courts are remains left by the people of the same community. They represent two activities or aspects of the life of a community: domestic functions and ceremonial-recreational functions. Yet on initial investigation this may not be known. Should they, then, be classified apart? And is this sort of stricture what the device of the "component" has implied and should imply? I would agree that such physically isolated entities should be considered apart in the early stages of investigation, but I am hesitant to class them as separate "components." How, operationally, are we to draw consistent lines? Are ball-courts, burial mounds, temples, or sweat-baths always to be considered as components apart from domestic structures? Or only when found spatially apart from dwelling sites? And, if so, how far apart? It has not been general American archaeological practice to so proceed, either in those parts of the United States where the "component" concept has been formalized as an element of the Midwestern Taxonomic System or elsewhere; and I should think it a mistake to do so.

Thus, while recognizing the validity of Rouse's argument that the concept of archaeological settlement is not on a primary level of investigation, I think the concept important on the secondary level of investigation-interpretation. Chang's definition of the settlement as the locus of a community is apt and useful; and I should like to equate settlement and community with "component." I do not like the archaeological concepts of either "focus" or "phase" as the equivalent of settlement or community – as Rouse has suggested – for focus and phase have an established usage that carries them well beyond the usual geographical, chronological, and typological dimensions we are accustomed to associate with a community.

My understanding of Chang's "objective types" and "relative types" is that of a dichotomy between more or less universal traits or trait categories, on the one hand, and stylistically characterized traits or units, on the other. In this frame of reference, "objective types" are somewhat more than criteria of description from mineralogy or geometry. They are functional groupings. Thus, I would say that a chair is an "objective type" of furniture, but that a Louis XV chair is a "relative type." The first has meaning in the realm of general comparative inference and analogy; the second takes its meaning from stylistic identification within a specific historical tradition. The terminology ("objective," "relative") that Chang has chosen here seems somewhat abstruse. As I understand it, the qualities he is talking about are those of function and use, and a general comparative appreciation of these, and, set against these, style and historical uniqueness. The discussions of "function" and "style," by both Chang and Rouse, relate to this same question; and here I am in agreement with both and with Rouse's statement that style and function are best served separately in typology.

In "microstructure" and "macrostructure," Chang offers useful and systematic concepts for the intra-settlement or intra-community province, on the one hand, and the larger extra-settlement or extra-community domain, on the other. Rouse's reactions are largely favorable but, again, tempered by the reservation that the systematics of archaeological modes, types, and phase building be interposed as basic to settlement considerations. Here, at one point, I am uncertain what Rouse intends. With reference to the defining of macrostructures, he remarks that "settlements are unsuitable, because they are formed by inferring communities from the remains." But is not any archaeological type formed by making inferences from the remains? The pottery type – with its modes of shape, decoration, etc. – is arrived at with fewer inferences than the settlement pattern but inference is nonetheless involved. If we assume that a settlement pattern is a culture trait, and can, like other traits, be classified into types – in this case on the basis of modes of dwellings, other buildings, spatial arrangements, etc. – why cannot settlement serve as a device in the definition of a culture complex or culture phase, and in the building of macrostructural models of culture and society? Why cannot the "small ceremonial center-scattered hamlet" settlement pattern be a criterion of Phase X in the same way that the pottery type Rodriguez Black-on-White is a criterion of that phase? Perhaps Rouse would agree that it can be, but on condition that Phase X has first been plotted and defined by the presence of the Rodriguez Black-on-White pottery type, plus other suitable pottery and artifact types.

Throughout, I have the impression that Chang and Rouse are talking past rather than to each other. Rouse is convinced that the basic systematics of prehistoric archaeology – the plotting of cultural forms in time and space – will best be served by an initial study of artifacts. I, too, believe this. I believe that this condition obtains because small artifacts offer a greater vehicle for stylistic variation than such an entity as a settlement pattern. They present a greater range of what Chang has called "relative types." They give us the means of identifying and differentiating between the small, particular strands of human history. Also, by their very physical smallness and their occurrences in large numbers, most artifacts are amenable to techniques of chronological and associational control (stratigraphy, grave-lot association, architectural-fill associations, etc.). The settlement, on the other hand, offers only limited possibilities for "relative typology." The construction of large or special buildings for politico-religious purposes, the selection of cemeteries or special precincts for the disposal of the dead – these are efforts in response to universal human needs or desires, and the results are often appraised more readily as "objective types" than as "relative types." "Relative types" – stylistic variations – do, of course, occur in settlement pattern, as in all human activity; but they are usually more difficult to perceive, at least in the initial stages of archaeological investigation in any area The very fact that in the history of archaeological research the treatment of artifacts has had long precedence over an appreciation or even a mention of settlement patterns is testimony to this disparity. Chang has become impatient with this preoccupation with artifacts, and properly so, I think; we cannot have an adequate understanding of what went on in the past if we eschew the social dimension in prehistory. But I suspect that, in his impatience, Chang has been inclined to pass over those archaeological procedures that Rouse has spelled out in his criticisms. At least this is how I understand their argument and where I stand in it.

The remaining papers in the volume are addressed to various aspects of settlement patterns—as these are seen or inferred archaeologically, or as they are interpreted through ethnographic and ethnohistoric data.

DEETZ: ARTIFACT ARCHAEOLOGY AND CULTURE-CONTACT INFERENCES

The paper by Deetz has its central interests in "artifact archaeology"—to continue with the vocabulary and frame of reference of the Chang-Rouse discussions—but these interests are importantly, if indirectly, related to "settlement archaeology." According to Deetz's analysis, a series of opposite choices is crucial in the maker's selection of attributes during artifact manufacture. By viewing artifacts in this manner, Deetz sees them as indicators of nonmaterial culture change, as keys to the processes of culture contact, as the source of data for the reconstruction of technologies, and as more sensitive vehicles of seriation. In his own earlier work (Deetz, 1965), he has shown how fine-grained analysis of Arikara pottery can reveal kinship changes, and how both ceramic analysis and kinship data bear on residence and settlement. In his essay here, his formulations about prehistoric culture-contact situations also relate to settlement concerns. For example, earlier studies on prehistoric culture contacts (Willey, 1953b; Lathrap, ed., 1956) operated with a settlement concept called "site unit intrusion." This concept is quite similar to one of the four "attribute configurations" that Deetz describes here in his discussion of culture contacts viewed archaeologically. But what Deetz has provided is a careful analytic statement about artifacts under the conditions of "site unit intrusion." There is a clear implication throughout that "settlement archaeology" and "artifact archaeology" are equally integral elements of archaeology.

ASCHER: DISORGANIZATION AND DECAY IN THE SETTLEMENT

In his paper, Ascher asks the question: How does a living settlement become a part of the past? What are the processes of "disorganization" and decay whereby a community of the present is rendered an archaeological ruin? He examines a modern Seri Indian village in an attempt to suggest answers, and notes two such processes. One of these is the progressive "smearing or blending" of refuse and debris. Individual houses and garbage dumps recently abandoned show a pattern of concentration, or discontinuous distribution. In contrast, those portions of the village abandoned for a greater length of time reveal a steadily increasing obliteration of the refuse concentrations, tending toward a leveled, continuous distribution of remains. The other process is that of constant re-use and rearrangement of more durable and more favorable building materials or artifacts. These, in being rescued from refuse dumps or automobile graveyards, are thus carried forward or upward in time.

On the face of it, these would appear to be but slight findings, and they will probably prove to be applicable to archaeological situations only under certain cultural and natural environmental conditions. But so far as I know they are among the very few systematic observations on the processes whereby the physical present becomes the past.

TRIGGER: THE DETERMINANTS OF SETTLEMENT PATTERNS

To single out one paper from the collection for special praise is not, I think, to make invidious comparisons, for the various themes taken up are obviously quite different; but I was particularly pleased to see the theme "The Determinants of Settlement Patterns" treated in the book, and I am impressed with the thorough and imaginative way Trigger has dealt with the subject. For ten years now, archaeologists have had need of such a basic and definitive treatment.

Two cross-cutting approaches or classificatory devices have been employed, in one way or another, by nearly everyone who has written on the subject of archaeological–or ethnographic–settlement patterns. Trigger reviews some of these studies in his introductory statement. One of these approaches attempts to separate the natural environmental or ecological aspects of settlement from the sociocultural; the other focuses attention on the village, the community, the small locus of residence or the *microsettlement pattern,* as opposed to the zonal, regional, areal, widespread distribution of settlement over the landscape, the *macrosettlement pattern.* The two approaches can be, and frequently have been, used together, but there has been a tendency to view the macrosettlement pattern largely in the ecological context, and to reserve the sociocultural context for micropattern studies.

I would be opposed to any attempt to formalize an ecological vs. sociocultural dichotomy of settlement-pattern determinants, as presumably Trigger would also. To attempt to view settlements and their determinants in such a frame of reference would be to begin with an assumption or bias that we would do well to avoid. I do not mean to suggest that each new settlement situation should not be examined and analyzed with reference to both ecological or sociocultural conditionings; but a formal dichotomous classification not only loads the scales at the outset of the investigation but is otherwise limiting and disadvantageous. As Trigger has so well put it, the archaeologist is more concerned with making interpretations about cultures than in studying settlement patterns for their own sake, and as such would do well to adopt a flexible, noncommitted scheme.

Trigger has provided us with such a scheme for analyzing and synthesizing settlement-pattern determinants. He suggests three levels of primary observation: (1) the individual house or building; (2) the site or the community; and (3) the total landscape distribution. The first two would be subsumed under Chang's *microstructure* of settlement and the third under his *macrostructure.* (I take for granted, and I assume that Trigger has also, that the underpinning of archaeological systematics – modes, types, complexes, components, phase formations, and chronological control, all of which Rouse has insisted upon – has been properly attended to in arriving at levels 2 and 3). It should be noted that Trigger's three levels of primary observation become increasingly more difficult of definition as we proceed from small to large; that is, the individual dwelling or other structure is more readily isolated as a unit for observation than is an individual site. Indeed, there are many situations (such as the densely settled Viru Valley in Peru) where it becomes something of an arbitrary archaeological decision to determine just what is a site unit. In such cases, the archaeologist must proceed as best he can, leaving tentative site-unit definitions open to revision as analysis proceeds.[1] The total landscape distribution, or the macropattern, is the most difficult of all to comprehend. For one thing, it can be brought into focus only after considerable archaeological research has been carried out in a zone, region, or area, and after conclusions have been reached about the size and borders of the territorial unit under consideration.

But to return to Trigger's proposals, viewing the settlement data on these three levels of magnitude, he then submits each level to rigorous analysis. For the level of the individual house he asks such questions as: What are the conditioning factors of climate and local building resources? How does house construction reflect technological development? In what ways may house size and room arrangement be clues to family structure? What are the differentiations in size and quality among houses, and what do these signify? Is craft or manufacturing specialization indicated in individual houses? Have political institutions, such as the need for defense, affected house forms? Important to all of this is that the approach be in Taylor's (1948) term, "conjunctive"; or, more appropriately, that it takes cognizance of what Binford (1962, p. 218) has referred to as the " . . . different operational sub-systems of the total cultural system . . . ." A consideration of much more than sheer settlement data is needed to provide answers to most of these questions.

Trigger offers a good definition for the community, one that can be used as a measure in appraising archaeological settlement data. To paraphrase him, the community is either the maximal group in face-to-face association or any larger unit of stable, more or less continuous settlement representing

[1] I should emphasize that I do not mean or believe that archaeological sites have "no reality" or that "they exist only in the mind of the classifier." I think there is a good correspondence between site or settlement units and the social unit, the community. It is a task for archaeological research, however, to demonstrate the relationship by amplifying, modifying, or correcting its conclusions in order to increase the probabilities of such correspondences.

stable interaction patterns. At this level, again, factors of environment are to be considered as determinants, particularly as they bear upon subsistence technology. Family and kinship relations may be reflected in site patterns, as may wealth and status. The nature of government and religion are expressed in public buildings–temples, forts, palaces. Site patterns sometimes also replicate cosmological conceptions.

The determinants of zonal patterns, or macropatterns, also include natural-environmental and natural-resource conditions. What we are contemplating here is the phenomenon of the "culture area." Trade, particularly in raw materials, helps set limits to a zonal pattern. Political organization, warfare or the lack of it, the invasions of foreign peoples, and religious and ideational factors are all to be considered.

In settlement study on any of these three levels, or in a multilevel manner, integration of the data is achieved not only by an examination of the conjunctive effects of many determinants but by the observation of these through time. Thus, a community first established for defense or as a religious capital may take on other functions through time–those, for example, of governmental bureaucracy, of trade, of craft manufactures–until the community becomes an important and diversified center of population, functionally and formally a city. In a complementary sense, the data of settlement are integrated synchronously by a study and demonstration of the relationships between the cities, towns, and hamlets of a zonal pattern.

Cook and Heizer: Formulas for Population and Area in the Settlement

The Cook–Heizer essay is a "formula" attempt to arrive at population figures from settlement data, and it promises to be the best such effort in this direction to date. The particular approach is foreshadowed only by an earlier paper by Naroll (1962). [2] Data from California ethnography are used to fix a ratio of house floor space per person. This is computed first for individual dwellings, then for total settlement. The formula was found to be stable for aboriginal California; and one cannot help asking if we have here a functional correlation of wide, cross-cultural applicability. It is a question well worth exploring for other areas and other developmental ranges of culture. My immediate reaction–no more than a guess–is that it might hold for hunting-gathering societies and for farming societies up to a certain level of development; beyond this, at perhaps the threshold of urban life, other factors might operate to increase population beyond the ratio of one person per 20 square feet of floor space. But we do not know, and it may be that the ratio is one that is in some way grounded in basic human biological or psychological needs and limitations. More investigation along this line is to be awaited with interest.

[2] See also Cook and Heizer (1965).

WHITING AND AYRES: ARCHITECTURAL – CULTURAL CORRELATIONS

Whiting and Ayres are also concerned with microstructural or micro-settlement pattern problems and, like Cook and Heizer, their basic datum is the individual dwelling floor plan. They put the question: If shape and size of floor plan are known, what can be said about other features of culture? This is phrased promisingly for the archaeologist, of course, as floor plan data are frequently all that remain to him in site excavation. Whiting and Ayres select 136 cultures, on which there are historic or modern data, from the Ethnographic Atlas. Care was taken to select no two cultures that are in close genetic or diffusional relationship to each other. Attention was also given to seeing that nonagricultural, casual agricultural, and more intensive agricultural societies were all included in the sample. Six floor-plan forms were reduced to two: those essentially curvilinear and those essentially rectilinear. The following dwelling structural features were found to correlate with the two basic floor-plan types: (1) roof forms followed floor forms; (2) pliable materials were used for the walls of curvilinear houses, whereas rigid materials were used for those of rectilinear houses; (3) rectilinear houses tended to be larger than curvilinear ones; and (4) rectilinear houses tended to be multi-roomed more often than curvilinear ones.

Moving from the strictly architectural to architectural-cultural correlations, it was observed that large rectilinear, multi-roomed dwellings were correlated with large extended families, or with possible high position in a status hierarchy, or with both. Rectilinear floor plans were also found to be associated more frequently with permanence of settlement, whereas curvilinear plans were correlated with either permanent or nonpermanent settlement.

To this point, the correlations are what we might expect. In general, largeness, greater permanence, more demanding construction techniques, etc., relate to rectilinear floor plans, whereas the smaller dwelling, the flimsier structure, the simpler construction process, etc., tend to be associated with the curvilinear floor plan. Beyond this point, the causal factors of the observed correlations are more difficult to understand or appraise. For example, the statistical chances are three to one that curvilinear floor plans will be associated with polygynous families and that monogamous societies are more likely to dwell in rectilinear houses. Whiting and Ayres discuss this correlation at some length, and are inclined to accept an esthetic or esthetic-Freudian explanation deriving from child-rearing practices in polygynous societies. My competence to evaluate this discussion is extremely limited; I can note only that the high correlation between floor-plan curvilinearity and polygyny seems significant, and that it offers statistical support for archaeological inferences. The causality of the relationship remains, I think, to be explored further.

SEARS: THE STATE IN SETTLEMENT ARCHAEOLOGY

Sears tackles one of the most fascinating and most difficult problems for archaeology–the determination of the entity of the state in prehistory. Settlement data are important here in both the macrostructural dimension (the pattern of site distribution over a sizable territory) and the microstructural dimension (the differentiations between villages, towns, cities, "capitals," "provincial centers," etc.); but the approach outlined by Sears is, explicitly or implicitly, dependent on a good many other aspects of archaeology.

In Sears' paper the state is defined, with reference to Hoebel, as an organized association of men for whom a specialized suborganization functions to transmit state policy into action, or, in somewhat different terms, and with reference to Gearing, as a number of face-to-face communities drawn into a sovereign political unit in which there are mechanisms for exerting coercion over these member communities, over kin groups, and over individual members. How can such phenomena be inferred from the archaeological past? Sears begins with the definition of the territory to be considered, a definition based on the presence of highly similar ceramic complexes in a number of communities within this territory. The archaeological identification of the "sub-organization" (in Hoebel's terms) or the apparatus of state power is made by demonstrating settlement recognition of a major ceremonial center, city, or "capital," within the area of consideration, which in its size, form, and archaeological content is significantly different from the culturally related and contemporaneous lesser centers, towns, villages, or hamlets within the same area. Sears draws examples from the southeastern United States, an area lacking in good ethnohistoric or ethnographic models, and therein lies a weakness in his argument. His typology is cast in an evolutionary frame. At the base is the "village community" level. Here, the various sites or communities of the area share the common ceramic bonds, but the individual settlements are all essentially of the same pattern. Some may exhibit what appear to be ceremonial structures, but none are significantly larger or more elaborate than other sites of the area. On the second level we see the emergence of the "priest state." Now, for the first time, one site or settlement of the area has become distinctly larger and more specialized than the others. Within such a special or ceremonial center the suborganization or power structure of the state is identified through specialized regalia found with important burials. The third level is the "militaristic state." In the southeastern United States it is represented by what Sears has called the "replacement conquest state," to distinguish it from the more advanced "incorporating conquest state" as seen in the Aztec or Inca Empires. In such a political formation a warrior class is closely affiliated with leadership, and leadership presents a dual aspect of secular-militaristic and religious functions. Distinguishing settlement features of the "militaristic state" are a single great urban ceremonial center, in addition to other towns and ceremonial centers, and fortifications.

Although sympathetic to Sears' approach, I would enter a caveat about letting evolutionary schema be the overriding consideration in classifying state "types." I do not question the general trend Sears sets out; it seems to hold for the Southeastern United States and also for much of Mesoamerica. But, as an exception, I am not convinced that some of the great Hopewell ceremonial centers of the Ohio Valley were not major centers for political territories. Sears, however, assigns the Hopewellian horizon to his "village community" level. Does he hesitate here because he considers, a priori, that the evolutionary level is too low? Or because the total territory concerned is relatively small and among the big Hopewell centers there is no particular center that is obviously paramount over all the others? If so, one is reminded of the Maya Lowlands of the Petén and surrounding regions, where there are a great many ceremonial centers of impressive size and magnificence in a relatively small territory, and where it would be difficult to single one out as a certain "capital."

The kind of thing Sears is trying to do is exciting but extraordinarily difficult, and I think that archaeologists working with this sort of macropattern problem will operate in the realm of relatively low probability for some time to come. What is needed is more observations on settlement and other aspects of culture as these pertain to historically documented state formations – the Inca in Peru, the Aztec in Mesoamerica, and, at a step down in the evolutionary scale, the states or kingdoms of sixteenth-century Colombia and Ecuador. Such information would not only promote the study of prehistoric political units in these particular cultural traditions but would strengthen the corpus of a general comparative or functional typology of the prehistoric state.

VOGT: ZINACANTAN AND THE CLASSIC MAYA

The present-day Maya municipio of Zinacantan, in the Chiapas Highlands, comprises a ceremonial center, outlying *parajes* or villages with minor centers, hamlets or small clusters of households, and, at the lowest level of organization, the individual household itself. Vogt sees in this settlement and social structure a model for the old life of the Maya in Pre-Columbian times. To be sure, there are differences. The modern main ceremonial center or *cabecera* is organized around a Roman Catholic church and a municipal office representing the Federal Government of Mexico: it is the main religious and governmental center for the 10,000 people of the municipio. But it is a "vacant" or "semi-vacant" town – inhabited largely by those individuals, with their families, who are in rotative residence for ceremonial or "cargo" positions. It throngs with life only at times of ceremonies, when the sustaining populations from the outlying *parajes* converge there. Life in the *parajes*, the water-hole groups, the *snas*, and the individual households is a farming life, and probably goes on much as it did in the ancient past. The politico-religious organization binding the municipio together is complex and essentially aboriginal, despite an overlay of Catholic ritual and doctrine. The ceremonies that dramatize this organization appear to have a symbolic significance. Among these are processionals, which originate within households, are further carried out within hamlets, then move from these to the minor ceremonial centers or shrines of the *parajes*, and finally to a climax in the main ceremonial center or *cabecera*. In such processionals, the images of the patron saints of the *parajes* are carried into the main center; moreover, images from municipios outside of, but tracing a history back to, Zinacantan are brought to the center. Thus, it is easy to see in these rituals a depiction of social, political, and religious ties laid out, as it were, on a settlement-pattern map.

A prominent feature of the Zinacantan system is the "democracy" of its social structure. Perhaps a better way to put it is that there is an absence of aristocracy, and that leadership tends to rotate. Young men hold "cargo" positions for brief periods of time; they then return to their *parajes* to resume farming for several years; later they may be recalled to the ceremonial center to serve a term in a more senior position, etc.

If the settlement pattern Vogt observes at Zinacantan is like the settlement pattern found archaeologically in the Maya Lowlands, is it a reasonable working assumption that many elements of sociopolitical and religious organization seen at Zinacantan can be projected back into the Maya past? One of the most debatable projections or inferences concerns the "democratic" quality of old Maya leadership. There are a number of lines of archaeological – as well as ethnohistoric – evidence that oppose this view (Ruz, 1964); Vogt has discussed some of these. I would also cite the themes of representational art of the Maya Classic Period (A.D. 200–900), and what is known of the hieroglyphic texts of that time, both of which strongly suggest aristocratic and even royal lineages (Proskouriakoff, 1960, 1961). However, I have previously argued for the "democratic" view (Willey, 1956b), and there is some archaeological support for that interpretation. The question is a special one for Mayanists, not to be pursued further here. Recent evidence for urban patterns at the Mayan archaeological sites of Tikal and Dzibilchaltun will be germane to its solution, as will continued research in a good many other aspects of Maya archaeology. The significant thing here is that settlement investigations – both archaeological and ethnographical – have put us in a frame of mind to even ask such a question.

Finally, it should be noted that Vogt asks a general theoretical question that none of our other essays have considered: To what extent does settlement pattern influence or determine, rather than merely reflect, social organization? Though he does not attempt to answer the question, there is an implication in Vogt's discussions that settlement may indeed be a causal factor of social forms.

ADAMS: HISTORICAL CORRELATIONS IN A NUBIAN SETTLEMENT

Adams' article is devoted to the study of a microsettlement pattern in time depth–an examination, through excavation, of the small (1 by 1/2 km) Nubian island of Meinarti located below the Second Cataract of the Nile. He analyzes the natural environmental and cultural constants and determinants of settlement pattern in this setting. Seven levels, or architectural phases, are traced from bottom to top, or in the direction of "time's arrow." The time span involved is twelve centuries. The presentation is interpretive as well as descriptive, in that settlement patterning is explained as a register of the more general culture changes that swept over the whole of Nubia during this span of time. The tightly planned communal buildings and public structures of the first settlement are seen as a reflection of the stable Meroitic polity; the helter-skelter assemblages and the evidences of temple destruction of the second level are taken as a measure of troubled times and a breakdown of central authority; subsequent planned communities and alternating periods of disorganization are interpreted similarly; and a final defensive architectural phase bespeaks war and invasion.

One comment should be made about the interpretations. They are made in a well-controlled, well-documented framework of Nubian prehistory and history. Thus, when Adams pairs tight architectural planning on the little island of Meinarti with centralized political authority, he is making a historical correlation. Is it also a functional one? And, conversely, is irregularity of settlement and architecture and lack of centralized authority another functional correlation, or merely a historical one? I am inclined to believe there are functional correlates or causal interrelationships here. But this is one of the things we cannot be sure about yet in settlement interpretation.

ASPECTS OF SETTLEMENT PATTERNS–CONCLUSIONS IN RETROSPECT

In retrospect, and briefly, what are the main things these essays have to tell us?

The Chang–Rouse controversy is a kind of archaeological "jurisdictional" dispute. That these two able archaeologists felt strongly about it indicates, perhaps, that such a dispute needed airing. I consider it a "given" that certain archaeological procedures should precede settlement pattern study; and I would have thought Chang also assumed this, but Rouse has interpreted him otherwise. I believe Chang sought primarily to inject an awareness of settlement pattern into archaeological investigation at as early a point in the procedures as feasible.

Deetz has made more sophisticated our ways of thinking about artifacts and their determinants. This is a primary step to the use of artifact analysis as a means to answer questions about nonmaterial culture. Such analysis has been, and may be, coordinated with settlement study.

Ascher asks archaeologists to consider how living communities entered the realm of prehistory: What are the mechanical and chemical ways this transformation took place, and through what cultural and natural-environmental agencies? He describes two processes of "disorganization" and in so doing offers a method of observation.

Trigger presents us with the first thorough outline on the determinants of human settlement patterns, including a scheme of analysis and synthesis. Much of his thinking is of a logical-theoretical sort. That is, he asks, in effect: What kinds of factors would we reasonably expect to be operative on settlement under such-and-such conditions? Therefore, much of what he has offered has not been tested by archaeological field inquiry. Still, there was no other alternative; there have been too few archaeological investigations directed toward settlement findings. Trigger's paper will undoubtedly be modified or replaced in time, but for now it is a most serviceable base of departure for settlement-pattern research.

Cook and Heizer offer a formula for an aspect of micropattern analysis—a floor-space/population ratio based on ethnographic observations of Californian tribes. We need more such observations from other areas. Does 20 square feet of floor space per person correspond to some human biologically or psychologically determined mean?

Whiting and Ayres present correlations, from a large ethnographic sampling, that can be drawn among house floor plans, other architectural features, and some general sociocultural features. But perhaps the most interesting is a high correlation with a specific social organizational feature—between curvilinearity of house floor plan and polygyny. The authors see the causal factors here as esthetic, or esthetic conditioned by sociosexual circumstances. The correlation is highly significant, and they have taken precautions to assemble their ethnographic sample from cultures that are not likely to be related. Leaving aside the causal explanation of the correlation, they have given archaeologists a basis for useful inference that has high statistical probability.

Sears defines the existence of the state in prehistoric times by its macrosettlement pattern: site-to-site ceramic uniformity over the area and a single "capital" settlement of impressive size with obvious "public" functions. He makes a good exploratory run with this model, using archaeological data from the southeastern United States. The model needs further testing, particularly against archaeological-ethnohistorical reference points.

Vogt draws a model of sociopolitical and religious functions correlated with a macrosettlement pattern in the Highland Maya municipio of Zinacantan. He notes a parallel between this settlement pattern and that of the prehistoric Maya of the lowlands. The question is then posed: How much of Zinacantan social, political, and religious behavior can be projected back into the Maya past through the linkage of settlement-pattern form? Vogt feels that much of it can be; others are not so sure. He also asks a general question: Is settlement arrangement a causal force in the development of sociopolitical forms?

Adams studies a microsettlement in time depth. The site is a Nubian island in the Nile River, and he is able to relate his settlement findings on the island to the wider cultural history of the area. In so doing he draws correlations between settlement forms and sociopolitical activities. These correlations are buttressed by known history, but the question arises how far settlement-pattern form (architectural regularity or irregularity) may reflect types of social behavior (centralized political authority, lack of authority, etc.) in a functional or causal way.

THE PROSPECTS FOR SETTLEMENT-PATTERN ARCHAEOLOGY

In prospect, what can we say about the future of settlement-pattern archaeology or, more properly, the use of settlement-pattern data in archaeological reconstructions?

To begin with, it seems safe to say that an interest in, and an awareness of, the settlement dimension will continue and increase. In the past decade, archaeological articles on, and monographs taking account of, site, regional, or areal settlement patterns have appeared with regularity, and have drawn upon data from all parts of the Americas and some parts of the Old World. A variety of attitudes or approaches has been addressed to settlement-pattern study, and this many-sided interest in the subject is reflected in the present volume. Personally, I see several courses in which more and new inquiry is indicated.

First, I should think exploration of human biological and psychological determinants or limitations of settlement needs would be extremely worthwhile. The Cook–Heizer paper is one such attempt; the Whiting–Ayres paper is another.

Second, settlement–natural-environmental relationships should continue to receive attention, particularly from a cultural-ecological approach, in both micro- and macropattern dimensions.

Third, archaeological-artifact analysis, in microsettlement-pattern contexts, promises to be tremendously rewarding in information about social organization, politico-religious systems, and technologies, because these can be discerned in settings of social class divisions or such institutions as craft guilds. We have mentioned Deetz's (1965) work in this connection; we may add as other examples the research of Longacre (1963) and Cowgill (1965 Ms).

Fourth, macrosettlement pattern offers many clues to the forms of social and political institutions – such as the state. This kind of analysis has only just begun.

Finally, if we consider the features of settlement patterns, in themselves, as artifacts – using that term in its broadest sense – we see that these features are adaptations to natural-environmental, social, and ideological factors. A settlement is thus constituted of what Binford (1962) has described as the " . . . three general functional classes of artifacts: technomic, socio-technic, and ideo-technic." Accordingly, the study of settlement patterns provides an ideal meeting ground for observations on the interaction of the cultural subsystems represented by these three classes of artifacts.

To conclude, the study of prehistoric settlement patterns does not seem to me to constitute a "new archaeology." The central motivation of archaeology is an interest in the human past. This motivation must be almost as old as man. Archaeology, as a science, begins at that point where we follow this motivation in some purposeful and systematic way. I am not just sure when and where this first occurred, but the Italian Renaissance serves as a meaningful historical starting point for the western world. For a long time following the Renaissance, archaeologists were antiquarians – uncovering, pondering, and celebrating the creations of yesterday. Gradually – and not so long ago – systematics aided in ordering, describing, and placing in time and in context the artifacts of the past. Such a threshold, or series of thresholds, might be considered to have marked a "new archaeology." Still, the old motivation, the humanistic interest in antiquity, remains. Today, archaeology has become a part of anthropology, and we are ambitious enough to believe we may find the answers to the old and ever-fascinating questions of how and why man behaved as he did. Well and good. At the same time, we should not become too condescending about our primitive scientific forebears. For the spirit of antiquarianism, a sense of wonder, is the link of continuity between us; and archaeology is not altogether changed by the fact that we may generalize beyond the specific event, seek cause as a statement of process, or become less the collectors of *objets d'art* and more the systematic reconstructors of the whole human past. The prehistoric settlement form or pattern is one important part of this whole past. It is an artifact that has been difficult to recover, and, perhaps for this reason, one that has only recently been made a part of archaeological discourse. It is now, I think, "here to stay" in archaeology, whether we consider that archaeology "new" or "old."

References

BINFORD, L. R.
1962 "Archaeology as anthropology," *American Antiquity*, Vol. XXVIII, No. 2: 217-25.

COOK, S. F., and R. F. HEIZER

1965 "The quantitative approach to the relation between population and settlement size," *Reports of the University of California Archaeological Survey, No. 64* (Berkeley: University of California Press).

COWGILL, G. L.

1965 Ms. "Computers and prehistoric archaeology," Department of Anthropology, Brandeis University.

DEETZ, JAMES

1965 *The Dynamics of Stylistic Change in Arikara Ceramics,* Illinois Studies in Anthropology, No. 4 (Urbana: University of Illinois Press).

LATHRAP, D. W.

1956 (editor) "An archaeological classification of culture contact situations," *Seminars in Archaeology: 1955*, Robert Wauchope, editor, Memoir No. 11 (Salt Lake City: Society for American Archaeology).

LONGACRE, W. A.

1963 "Archaeology as anthropology: A case study," *Science,* Vol. CXLIV: 1454-55.

NAROLL, RAOUL

1962 "Floor area and settlement population," *American Antiquity,* Vol. XXVII, No. 4:587-89.

PROSKOURIAKOFF, TATIANA

1960 "Historical implications of a pattern of dates at Piedras Negras, Guatemala," *American Antiquity,* Vol. XXV, No. 4: 454-75.

1961 "Portraits of women in Maya art," *Essays in Precolumbian Art and Archaeology,* by S. K. Lothrop *et al.*, (Cambridge: Harvard University Press): 81-99.

RUZ LHUILLIER, ALBERTO

1964 "¿Aristocracia o democracia entre los antiguos Mayas?" *Anales* (Universidad Nacional Autońoma de Mexico, Mexico, D. F.) Vol. I: 63-76.

TAYLOR, W. W.

1948 "A study of archaeology," *American Anthropologist,* Vol. L, No. 3, Pt. 2.

WILLEY, G. R.

1953a *Prehistoric Settlement Patterns in the Viru Valley, Peru,* Bulletin 155, Bureau of American Ethnology, Smithsonian Institution, Washington, D. C.

1953b "A pattern of diffusion-acculturation," *Southwestern Journal of Anthropology,* Vol. IX:369-84.

1956a "Introduction," *Prehistoric Settlement Patterns in the New World,* Gordon R. Willey, editor, Viking Fund Publications in Anthropology, No. 23: 1-2.

1956b "The structure of ancient Maya society: Evidence from the southern lowlands," *American Anthropologist,* Vol. LVIII, No. 5:777-82.

WILLEY, G. R., W. R. BULLARD, JR., J. B. GLASS, and J. C. GIFFORD

1965 *Prehistoric Maya Settlements in the Belize Valley,* Peabody Museum Papers, Vol. LIV, Harvard University.

WILLEY, G. R., and PHILIP PHILLIPS

1958 *Method and Theory in American Archaeology* (Chicago: University of Chicago Press).

About the Authors

WILLIAM Y. ADAMS, Associate Professor of Anthropology, University of Kentucky.

Dr. Adams received his A.B. from the University of California (Berkeley) in 1948 and his Ph.D. from the University of Arizona in 1958. After two years as Director of Field Research for the Glen Canyon Salvage Program of the Museum of Northern Arizona, he served from 1959 to 1966 as Unesco Liaison Officer and Co-ordinator of Archaeological Research in the Aswan Reservoir area, Republic of the Sudan. His major publications concern the archaeology and ethnology of the Southwest and the archaeology of Egypt and Nubia.

ROBERT ASCHER, Professor of Anthropology and Archaeology, Cornell University.

Dr. Ascher received his Ph.D. from the University of California (Los Angeles) in 1960. He has conducted field work in North America and the Middle East. Currently an Associate Editor of *American Anthropologist*, he is specially interested in archaeological theory and the origin of man.

BARBARA AYRES, Research Fellow, Department of Social Relations, Harvard University.

Dr. Ayres, who received her Ph.D. from Harvard in 1956, has taught at Harvard, Boston University, and Columbia. Her major interests are in comparative socialization, psychological anthropology, and she is currently engaged in cross-cultural studies of art and music.

K. C. CHANG, Associate Professor of Anthropology, Yale University.

Dr. Chang received his B.A. from the National Taiwan University in 1954 and his Ph.D. from Harvard in 1960. His primary research interests are the archaeology of East Asia and the history of ancient China, and he is the author of *The Archaeology of Ancient China* (1963) and *Rethinking Archaeology* (1967).

SHERBURNE F. COOK, Professor Emeritus of Physiology, University of California (Berkeley).

Dr. Cook received his A.B., M.A., and Ph.D. degrees from Harvard in 1919, 1923, and 1925, respectively, and has been on the University of California faculty at Berkeley from 1928 until his retirement in 1964. He has published widely in physiology and anthropology, and is a frequent collaborator with Dr. Robert F. Heizer in archaeological research and writings.

JAMES DEETZ, Professor of Anthropology, Brown University.

A graduate of Harvard College, Dr. Deetz received his Ph.D. from Harvard in 1960, directed the Field School in Archaeology at Santa Barbara during the summers of 1961, 1962, and 1964, and has served as Archaeological Adviser to Plimoth Plantation in Plymouth, Massachusetts, since 1961. He is the author of *The Dynamics of Stylistic Change in Arikara Ceramics* (1965) and *Invitation to Archaeology* (1967).

ROBERT F. HEIZER, Professor of Anthropology, University of California (Berkeley).

Dr. Heizer received his B.A. at Berkeley in 1936 and his Ph.D. at the same institution in 1940. He has taught at the University of Oregon and the University of California at Los Angeles, conducted archaeological excavations in North America and Mexico, and he is the author of numerous articles and site reports. He is also the co-author of *A Guide to Field Methods in Archaeology* (1967), published by the National Press.

IRVING ROUSE, Professor of Anthropology, Yale University.

Dr. Rouse received his B.S. and Ph.D. degrees from Yale in 1934 and 1938, respectively, and has been on the Yale faculty ever since. He is a member of the National Academy of Sciences, a past President of the Society for American Archaeology (1952-53), President-elect of the American Anthropological Association, and a Viking Fund Medalist of 1960. He has carried out extensive archaeological field work in the West Indies, Venezuela, Florida, and the Northeast, and he is the author of *Prehistory in Haiti* (1939) and the co-author of *Venezuelan Archaeology* (1963).

WILLIAM SEARS, Professor and Chairman of the Department of Anthropology, Florida Atlantic University.

Dr. Sears received his Ph.D. degree at the University of Michigan in 1951. He has carried out his research principally in the Eastern United States.

BRUCE G. TRIGGER, Associate Professor, McGill University.

Dr. Trigger, who received his B.A. from the University of Toronto in 1959 and his Ph.D. from Yale in 1964, is a specialist in the archaeology and ethnohistory of Egypt and the Sudan and the Eastern Woodland Indians of North America. His publications include *History and Settlement in Lower Nubia* (1965) and *The Late Nubian Settlement at Arminna West* (1966).

EVON Z. VOGT, Professor of Social Anthropology, Harvard University.

Dr. Vogt received his A.B., M.A., and Ph.D. degrees at the University of Chicago in 1941, 1946, and 1948, respectively. He has been on the Harvard faculty since 1946, and he is a fellow of the American Academy of Arts and Sciences. He has carried out ethnological field work in the Southwest and in Mexico and, since 1957, has been Director of Harvard's Chiapas Project. He is co-editor of *Reader in Comparative Religion* (1958), *The Genetic Model and Maya Cultural Development* (1964), and *The People of Rimrock* (1966), editor of *Los Zinacantecos* (1966), and co-author of *Water Witching U.S.A.* (1959).

JOHN W. M. WHITING, Professor of Social Anthropology, Harvard University.

Dr. Whiting received a Ph.B. degree from Yale in 1931 and his Ph.D. from the same institution in 1938. He was on the faculty of Yale from 1938 until 1947, and he taught in the State University of Iowa before joining the Harvard faculty in 1949. He is the author of *Becoming a Kwoma* (1941) and co-author of *Child Training and Personality* (1953).

GORDON R. WILLEY, Bowditch Professor of Mexican and Central American Archaeology and Ethnology, Harvard University.

Dr. Willey received his B.A. and M.A. degrees from the University of Arizona in 1935 and 1936 and his Ph.D. from Columbia in 1942. He is a member of the National Academy of Sciences and the American Academy of Arts and Sciences, a past President of the American Anthropological Association, president-elect of the Society for American Archaeology, and a Viking Fund Medalist. His principal research interests have been the southeastern United States, Peru, Panama, and the Maya area in Central America, and he is the author of *An Introduction to American Archaeology* (Vol. 1, 1966) and co-author of *Method and Theory in American Archaeology* (1958).